RAYMOND CHANDLER AND FILM

Ungar Film Library

Stanley Hochman, GENERAL EDITOR

RAYMOND CHANDLER AND FILM

WILLIAM LUHR

With photographs

FREDERICK UNGAR PUBLISHING CO.
New York

Copyright © 1982 by Frederick Ungar Publishing Co.

Printed in the United States of America

Library of Congress Cataloging in Publication Data

Luhr, William.
    Raymond Chandler and film.

    Filmography: p.
    Bibliography: p.
    Includes index.
    1. Chandler, Raymond, 1888–1959—Moving-picture
plays.   2. Chandler, Raymond, 1888–1959—Film adaptations.   3. Detective and mystery films—History and criticism.   I. Title.
PS3505.H3224Z69   812′.52   81-70115
ISBN 0-8044-2556-6   AACR2
ISBN 0-8044-6447-2 (pbk.)

For Judy

CONTENTS

ACKNOWLEDGMENTS

First thanks go to Peter Lehman, who introduced Chandler's work to me and whose critical insights over the years have been enormously valuable. Without the encouragement and patience of Stanley Hochman, my editor, this book might not have been begun, or completed. Randy C. Baer has assisted me in numerous ways, from research to the acquisition of stills to the tracking down of a wearying variety of materials. This project would have been much more difficult, some parts of it impossible, without his help.

Frank MacShane gave me advice, kindly let me see some of his own work at a prepublication stage, and put me on the trail of valuable material. His own work is indispensable to anyone working on Chandler; it was certainly of fundamental importance to this book. Roy V. Huggins, who has a large collection of Chandler material, generously sent me a copy of the script Chandler based upon *The Lady in the Lake*. Chris Steinbrunner, of the Mystery Writers of America, not only helped me with his encyclopedic knowledge of mystery fiction and films but also unearthed important material. I should also, for their various kindnesses, like to thank Helga Greene, Kathrine Sorley Walker, George Haight, James Sandoe, David Bordwell, Russell Merritt, Carol Brenner (of the Murder Ink Bookstore), Roberta Wrigg Salomon, Herbert Ruhm, Matthew J. Bruccoli, and an unknown benefactor who sent me a first edition of *The Big Sleep*.

Grace Luhr typed the manuscript, under frequently trying and always rushed circumstances, with unflagging good spirits, and John F. McElroy, Marilyn Campbell and Helen Luhr were of great help in editing it.

Brooke Whiting and Hilda Bohem, of the Department of Special Collections at the library of UCLA, were kind in guiding me through the basic archive of Chandler material. I am also grateful to David Parker and Emily Sieger, of the Motion Picture, Broadcasting, and Recorded Sound Division of the Library of

Congress; Charles Silver, of the Museum of Modern Art Film
Library; Mary Corliss, of the Museum of Modern Art Stills
Archive; Susan Dalton and Maxine Fleckner, of the Center for
Film and Theater Research at the Wisconsin State Historical
Society; David Shepard, of the Director's Guild of America; Sam
Gill, of the Library of the Motion Picture Arts and Sciences; and
Mark Urman, of United Artists. A number of my colleagues at
Saint Peter's College have encouraged my work; they include
professors Loren Schmidtberger, Steven Rosen, and Victoria
Sullivan, as well as James Pegolotti (now Dean of Western
Connecticut State College), the Reverend Edward Brande, S.J.,
and Bill Knapp, of the Instructional Resources Center.

I would like to express formal thanks to the following com-
panies: Paramount, Warner Brothers, RKO-Radio, Twentieth
Century-Fox, Metro-Goldwyn-Mayer, Universal, United Artists,
and Avco Embassy Pictures. And formal thanks also to the
Cinemabilia Book Store.

I am eternally indebted to members of my family: my mother,
Eillien Luhr, and my grandmother, Irene Luhr—both of whom
died during the writing of this book—and my father, Walter
Luhr. In addition, I got a great deal of support from Bob and
Carole and Jim and Ellen and Bill. Judy Challop Luhr, my wife,
has been of indispensable help to me in all stages of this project
and has my gratitude and love.

CHRONOLOGY

1888   Born on July 23 in Chicago.

1895   Moved to London with his mother.

1904   Graduated from Dulwich College.

1905–
1906   Studied in France and Germany.

1907   Worked for six months as a clerk in the Admiralty, London.

1908–
1912   Worked in London as a free-lance journalist with literary ambitions. Contributed to the *Academy*, the *Westminster Gazette*, and the *Spectator*.

1912   Returned to the United States and settled in California.

1918   Served in France as corporal with British Columbia Regiment. Joined Royal Flying Corps.

1919   Demobilized. Returned to California and entered oil business.

1924   Married Cissy Pascal after the death of his mother.

1932   Fired from oil business for alcoholism.

1933   Publication of his first hard-boiled detective story, "Blackmailers Don't Shoot," in *Black Mask*.

1939   Publication of his first novel, *The Big Sleep*.

1940   Publication of *Farewell, My Lovely*.

1942   Publication of *The High Window*. Appearance of *The Falcon Takes Over* (RKO-Radio Pictures), the first film to be based upon a Chandler novel (*Farewell, My Lovely*). Appearance of *Time to Kill* (Twentieth Century-Fox), based upon *The High Window*.

1943   Publication of *The Lady in the Lake*. Worked on first screenwriting assignment (*Double Indemnity*), with Billy Wilder, for Paramount.

1944   Worked on screenplays for *And Now Tomorrow* and *The Unseen*, both for Paramount. Appearance of *Murder,*

My Sweet (RKO-Radio Pictures), based upon *Farewell, My Lovely*.

1945   Wrote original screenplay for *The Blue Dahlia* for Paramount and worked on screenplay for *Lady in the Lake* for Metro-Goldwyn-Mayer. Published "Writers in Hollywood" in the *Atlantic Monthly*.

1946   Worked on screenplay for *The Innocent Mrs. Duff* for Paramount. Moved from Los Angeles to La Jolla. Appearance of *The Big Sleep* (Warner Brothers).

1947   Wrote original screenplay *Playback* (never produced) for Universal-International. Appearance of *Lady in the Lake* (Metro-Goldwyn-Mayer) and of *The Brasher Doubloon* (Twentieth Century-Fox), based upon *The High Window*.

1948   Publication of "Oscar Night in Hollywood" in the *Atlantic Monthly*.

1949   Publication of *The Little Sister*.

1950   Worked on screenplay for *Strangers on a Train* (Warner Brothers).

1952   Publication of "Ten Per Cent of Your Life" in the *Atlantic Monthly*.

1953   Publication of *The Long Goodbye* in England (American Publication in 1954).

1954   Death of Cissy.

1958   Publication of *Playback*.

1959   Died on March 26 in La Jolla.

1969   Appearance of *Marlowe* (Metro-Goldwyn-Mayer), based upon *The Little Sister*.

1973   Appearance of *The Long Goodbye* (United Artists).

1975   Appearance of *Farewell, My Lovely* (Avco Embassy).

1978   Appearance of *The Big Sleep* (United Artists).

PREFACE

Billy Wilder recently noted that of all the people with whom he worked during his Hollywood career (which dates to the beginning of the sound era), the two about whom he is most frequently questioned are Marilyn Monroe and Raymond Chandler. The interest in Marilyn Monroe is understandable because, especially since her death, she has come to symbolize Hollywood glamour. But Raymond Chandler, a recessive writer who never appeared before a movie camera, who published only seven novels and received screen credit for only five films, at first seems an unlikely candidate for the sort of enduring interest about which Wilder speaks, considering the fact that he has worked with such Hollywood luminaries as Greta Garbo, Humphrey Bogart, John Barrymore, Ernst Lubitsch, James Cagney, Erich von Stroheim, Gary Cooper, Marlene Dietrich, and Charles Laughton.

Yet the interest in Chandler exists and is growing. All of his novels are in print, and at least three of the films on which he worked are continually being revived. A major biography of him appeared in 1976, the same year that saw the publication of the screenplay for *The Blue Dahlia*, the only screenplay for which he received sole credit (as well as his second Academy Award nomination). In addition, an important collection of his letters appeared in 1981.

Filmmakers have always demonstrated a remarkable interest in Chandler's novels as film sources. Between 1942 and 1947, six films appeared based upon the four novels he had completed up to that time; they included Edward Dmytryk's *Murder, My Sweet* (1944), Howard Hawks's *The Big Sleep* (1946), and Robert Montgomery's *Lady in the Lake* (1947). The most recent films based upon Chandler's fiction have included Robert Altman's *The Long Goodbye* (1973), Dick Richards's *Farewell, My Lovely* (1975), and Michael Winner's *The Big Sleep* (1978).

Hollywood success came quickly to Chandler: his first screenplay, for *Double Indemnity* (1944), was nominated for an Academy Award. He remained, however, insecure about his writing all of his life. In 1957, two years before his death, he wrote that "no

writer worth the powder to blow him through a barbed wire
fence into hell is ever in his own mind anything but starting
from scratch."[1] But part of the very peculiar nature of his
Hollywood career is that he did not start from scratch, that his
reputation quickly gathered remarkable momentum because his
novels, his screenplays, and the films based upon his novels
rapidly became associated with an emerging style. Because the
popular perception of that style draws from all three of those
areas, it is useful to begin a study of Chandler and film with an
overview of crosscurrents, which are subsequently more fully
detailed. This overview outlines Chandler's work in Hollywood,
his influence upon the style subsequently called *film noir*, and
the historical and cultural trends within the industry that made
the kinds of film with which he is associated first possible, then
popular, and finally a distinctive tradition.

   Once this larger context has been established, the second part
of this book deals with the specific nature of Chandler's work in
Hollywood. It chronicles his frequently turbulent relationship
with the studios and with individuals such as Billy Wilder, John
Houseman, and Alfred Hitchcock, as well as the tensions between
his personal image as an English public school intellectual—
tweeds, pipe, and all—and the hucksterish studio atmosphere
in which he found himself. It also establishes the ways in which
critical and popular interest during the early 1940s in "hard-
boiled" fiction encouraged the studios to challenge existing
censorship codes and to allow the development of a new type of
film, one with which Chandler became indelibly associated.

   The final section of this book examines the films based upon
Chandler's fiction, and at this point, some of the reasons for his
extraordinary popularity should become evident. It does not
derive solely from his film scripts, or his novels, or the films
based on his fiction, but rather from the incremental and
symbiotic relationship among all three. The bedrock of his
reputation is his fiction, which already had a substantial following
when he came to Hollywood. In 1944, both *Double Indemnity*,
Chandler's first screenplay, and *Murder, My Sweet*, the first film
to use Philip Marlowe, Chandler's detective, appeared, and
Chandler's name quickly became associated with a style that
encompassed both contemporary literature and film. Chandler
was early considered a prototype for work with which he

personally had nothing to do—and it is upon the blending of the three separate but bound aspects of his work, and upon the high quality of much of that work, that the extraordinary interest in him is based.

As a group, the films based upon Chandler's fiction exhibit a concern with stylistic elements of the novels that is unusual for Hollywood film. They not only attempt to appropriate the story lines of the novels but often use large chunks of prose taken directly from the novels and frequently focus upon Marlowe's subjective perception of his situation. A number of the films use a voice-over narration and—more significantly—employ unusual and frequently experimental devices to underline Marlowe's perceptual presence. *Murder, My Sweet* uses a subjective delirium sequence quite unusual for the time. *Lady in the Lake* attempts an extreme experiment with point of view, such that although we see what Marlowe sees, we seldom see him. In addition, Marlowe films that do not highlight point of view are often notable for other kinds of experimentation. Robert Altman's *The Long Goodbye* juxtaposes detective genre and cultural codes of the 1940s with genre and cultural codes of the 1960s in a bizarre and remarkable film. Even Howard Hawks, generally known for his narrative clarity and austerity, built into *The Big Sleep* a narrative confusion about which he himself jokingly complained. Finally, although Chandler felt the ideal screen Marlowe would be Cary Grant, who never played the role, his detective has been played on screen by actors as diverse in image as Dick Powell, Humphrey Bogart, Robert Montgomery, James Garner, Elliott Gould, and Robert Mitchum.

Part I

CROSSCURRENTS

1

OVERVIEW

When in 1943 Raymond Chandler walked into Billy Wilder's office for the first time, he knew very little about the film industry and virtually nothing about screenwriting. The two men agreed to collaborate on a script based upon James M. Cain's novella, *Double Indemnity*, but when Chandler submitted his first draft, Wilder found it laughably inept. He hurled it across the room at the novelist, saying, "This is shit, Mr. Chandler."[1] They began again.

A year and a half later, their script was nominated for an Academy Award. Two years after that, Chandler received his second Academy Award nomination: Best Original Screenplay for *The Blue Dahlia*. By early 1947, Chandler was beginning to look like a one-man film industry. He had screenwriting credits on four produced films—*Double Indemnity* (1944), *And Now Tomorrow* (1944), *The Unseen* (1945), and *The Blue Dahlia* (1946)—two of which had received Academy Award nominations. In addition, all four of his published novels either had been or were in the process of being adapted for major studio productions.

Two had previously been the basis for "B" films. By 1947, then, Chandler's name had appeared on ten films from four different studios. And during that year he signed the most lucrative screenwriting contract of his life with a fifth studio.

Unlike the film work of many other established novelists, such as William Faulkner and F. Scott Fitzgerald, Chandler's screenplays, his fiction, and the films based upon his fiction quickly became associated with a style. The popularity of a work in one area often generated interest in works in one, or both, of the other two. The *Double Indemnity* assignment, for example, was offered to Chandler not because of any screenwriting experience he might have had, but because Joseph Sistrom, the producer, knew his literary work and felt it had stylistic affinities with the film project. And Dilys Powell of the London *Times*, an early champion of Chandler's fiction, first learned of the hard-boiled American detective genre not from fiction, but from John Huston's film, *The Maltese Falcon* (1941).

In the late 1940s, French critics, seeing wartime Hollywood films for the first time, noticed in them a quality that had begun to emerge during the war and was becoming pervasive. Using Marcel Duhamel's *Série Noire* books as an analogue, they called this quality *film noir*. The term means "black film," and it points to the presence in the films of a darker view of life than previously common, of a concentration upon human depravity and despair. The term also implies a cinematic style—a way of lighting, of positioning and moving the camera, and a choice of setting— commonly, a seedy, urban landscape, a world gone bad. *Film noir* has stylistic antecedents in German expressionist films and thematic antecedents in the hard-boiled fiction of the 1930s.

Double Indemnity and *Murder, My Sweet* (both 1944) are prototypical *noir* films; and *The Blue Dahlia, The Big Sleep* (both 1946), and *Lady in the Lake* (1947) are commonly considered classics of the genre. Chandler was involved with all of them.

Noir films were frequently low-budget "B" films, but many of those associated with Chandler were "A" films with major stars. *The Big Sleep* teamed Humphrey Bogart and Lauren Bacall at the height of their popularity; *The Blue Dahlia* did the same with Alan Ladd and Veronica Lake; *Lady in the Lake* was Robert Montgomery's first film after his service in World War II; *Murder, My Sweet* changed Dick Powell's screen image from that of a musical comedy star to that of a tough guy and rejuvenated his career; *Double Indemnity* gave Fred MacMurray and Barbara Stanwyck breakthrough roles. Because these films presented a grimier side of life than touched upon in previous Hollywood films and used many of Hollywood's most glamorous stars and the resources of its largest studios to do so, Chandler had it both ways. On the one hand, the films associated with him were part of the fashionable deglamorizing trend, but on the other, they benefited from Hollywood's glamour industry.

Chandler did not form this cinematic style, but he contributed significantly to it and rode the crest of its popularity. He was in the right place at the right time with the right qualifications. Many things have been cited as important to the development of *film noir*. Some see its bleak perspectives as a reaction against the Yankee Doodle optimism of many wartime films; others point to the critical attention given *Citizen Kane* (1941) as generating interest among filmmakers in the murky sets, oblique camera angles, and chiaroscuro lighting of German expressionism. The hard-boiled 1930s fiction of writers such as Chandler, Dashiell Hammett, and James M. Cain (all of whom worked in Hollywood in the 1940s) was becoming increasingly popular and respectable, and the unexpected success of John Huston's *The Maltese Falcon* (1941) pointed to audience interest in "tough" films. The studios in the mid-1940s, aware of shifts in popular tastes, were willing to test censorship restrictions and allowed more leeway in such films for dealing with areas of sadism, psychosis, and sexual deviation.

Chandler started writing hard-boiled detective fiction in 1933 and, although he did not originate the form, he quickly became one of its masters. He also did not originate the *Double Indemnity* project, but was called in when Wilder could not get James M. Cain. Again, Chandler learned quickly and did well. As interest in tough films developed, his film career skyrocketed.

It plummeted nearly as quickly. A number of factors contributed. The most evident were a cluster of personality and professional problems, present from the very beginning of his Hollywood career.

Only a few weeks after he had begun working with Wilder and making more money than he had ever made in his life, he went to Joseph Sistrom and threatened to quit unless his working

conditions were drastically changed. He saw himself as a novelist—working alone at home and at his own pace. Collaboration
on a nine-to-five schedule in an office building profoundly
disoriented him. Story conferences upset him further. He later
wrote: "That which is born in loneliness and from the heart
cannot be defended against the judgment of a committee of
sycophants. The volatile essences which make literature cannot
survive the clichés of a long series of story conferences."[2]

Chandler's notion of writing had little in common with Hollywood's. Although born in Chicago, he had spent much of his
youth in turn-of-the-century London and had abandoned a
successful civil service career in order to become an essayist and
poet. He could not make a living at it, but when he returned to
America in 1912, he continued to travel in intellectual circles.
When his career as an oil company executive collapsed in 1932,
in what Natasha Spender has termed a debacle of alcoholism,
he, without a job and without American publications, listed his
occupation in the Los Angeles Directory as a writer.[3] Ten years
later, when he had, in fact, become an established writer, he
viewed writing as more than an occupation: it was a cherished
ideal, to be defended at all costs against the Hollywood vulgarians.

Nearly all phases of the Hollywood writing process upset him.
He not only resented the intrusions upon privacy that collaboration and an office schedule entailed, but was horrified at the
fact that when a writer produced something under these difficult
circumstances, a director or a producer might change or even
cut it while the film was being shot. He once claimed that no
publisher had ever changed a word in any of his novels. He
could never say anything comparable about his film work.

Chandler gradually came to realize that the Hollywood process
was fundamentally incompatible with his notion of authorship.
As a novelist, he had almost complete artistic control over the
effects of his fictions. He knew that his audience would receive
his work exactly as he presented it—words arranged on paper.
As a screenwriter, he was only one of many hands in a collaborative
effort. Even if the words he wrote remained unchanged, they
would reach the audience as spoken by Alan Ladd or Barbara
Stanwyck, and the personalities and intonations of the actors
would affect audience response. And while the audience was

hearing the words, it would also be hearing music and sound effects and responding to an image on the screen. In effect, the writer's words would be competing with physical beauty, action, spectacle, lighting, and camera movement for aesthetic effect.

Chandler was fascinated with Hollywood and with the possibilities of film, but the more he learned about it, the more inclined he became to detach himself from it.

He made a number of attempts to adapt to the Hollywood system, largely because he was making more money at screenwriting than he could hope for anywhere else. Unhappy with the constraints of adapting novels to the screen, he turned to writing original screenplays. Uncomfortable with collaborators on a nine-to-five schedule at the studio, in 1947 he was to sign an amazing deal with Universal-International that not only allowed him to write an original screenplay at home, on his own schedule, but also guaranteed no studio interference. The script, *Playback*, was never produced, and it marked the end, with one exception, of his Hollywood involvement. (*Playback* later provided the basis and the title for his final novel.)

During his short career, he also published a number of essays critical of Hollywood in the *Atlantic Monthly*. Along with unpublished material and letters, they provide a complex and often perceptive insight into the filmmaking process during the final days of major studio control. They also reveal Chandler's increasingly sophisticated perceptions of the nature of film as a form, of Hollywood as an industry and as a process, and of his own screenwriting abilities.

Chandler's problems in Hollywood did not emanate exclusively from his notions of a writer's prerogatives. An intensely private man, he was extremely difficult to get along with. Billy Wilder seems to hate him to this day, and his last Hollywood working relationship, with Alfred Hitchcock, ended with bad feelings and nearly a lawsuit.

Chandler's alcoholism did not help. Halfway through his first original screenplay, *The Blue Dahlia*, Chandler told his producer, John Houseman, that he would not be able to complete it unless he could write at home, while drunk. Because production had already begun on the film and a delay would have meant abandoning the entire project at a considerable loss, Houseman set up round-the-clock nurses, and Chandler drank until he finished the script. It was the only original screenplay of Chandler's ever to be produced.

During this time, major changes were under way in Hollywood. Hollywood's most successful year was 1946. Chandler recalled that this was "a time when the box-office take was automatically terrific, when the only way you could make an unprofitable picture was not to make it."[4] But 1946 also marked the end of an era. As Tino Balio has pointed out in his book on the American film industry: "Beginning in 1947, the winds of ill fortune blew incessantly for ten years, during which weekly attendance declined by about one half. . . . With the precipitous drop in attendance, annual box-office receipts declined from $1.692 billion in 1946 to $1.298 billion in 1956, or about 23 percent."[5]

Chandler's contract to write *Playback*, signed in the spring of 1947, was the most profitable of his career. By September of that year, he realized that the industry circumstances that had made the deal possible had disappeared. He wrote his friend, James Sandoe:

> My agent is scared to death I won't meet the deadline. The deal is so far out of line with anything that could be obtained now that he thinks U-I [Universal-International Pictures] are waiting at the mousehole for a chance to smash it. They say Hollywood is really a shambles. Paramount had around 35 writers working a year ago, of whom about 22 were contract writers. Today they have 2 contract writers and 7 all told. The writers building is so empty that one guy has a suite of 5 offices. The atmosphere is hysterical.[6]

Chandler subsequently cited industry retrenchment as the reason the script was never produced.

During this same time, Chandler's fiction began to receive the serious literary recognition he had always craved. In a *Harper's Magazine* article of May 1948, entitled "The Guilty Vicarage," W. H. Auden wrote: "I think Mr. Chandler is interested in writing, not detective stories, but serious studies of a criminal milieu, the Great Wrong Place, and his powerful but extremely depressing books should be read and judged, not as escape literature, but as works of art."[7] Jacques Barzun, Somerset Maugham, and J. B. Priestley, among others, would soon also write respectfully of Chandler's fiction.

This praise by respected men of letters contributed to Chandler's growing sense of the incompatibility between his role as a writer of fiction and his role as a writer of screenplays. He had made his priorities clear in 1945 when he wrote, "to any writer of books a Hollywood by-line is trivial" ("Writers in Hollywood," p. 52). Chandler had not published a novel since he began his film work, which he felt was sapping his creative juices. *The Lady in the Lake* appeared in 1943; his next novel, *The Little Sister*, did not appear until 1949. The latter novel, written during and after the main period of his Hollywood involvement, deals in a minor way with Hollywood, and it is the only one of his novels that Chandler claimed he actively disliked. After it was finished, and after he had severed all ties with Hollywood, he produced *The Long Goodbye*, his most ambitious work of fiction. It marked, for him, a return to his most cherished vocation.

Between *Playback* and *The Long Goodbye*, Chandler worked on his last film. The experience hammered the final nail into the coffin of his Hollywood career. In 1950 Alfred Hitchcock asked him to write the script for *Strangers on a Train*, based on a Patricia Highsmith novel. Chandler agreed. He spent a few weeks working on the script at home, with Hitchcock driving down to La Jolla for periodic story conferences. Relations between the two men gradually broke down. Chandler submitted a script that Hitchcok found unacceptable, and Hitchcock hired Czenzi Ormonde to rework it. Chandler felt that the final script had virtually nothing to do with his work and considered having his name removed from the film's credits (as he had done with *Lady in the Lake* in 1946). He wound up sharing screen credit with Ms. Ormonde and never worked in Hollywood again.

II

The seven-year period during which Chandler actively worked as a screenwriter marked neither the beginning nor the end of his involvement with film. In his fiction, Hollywood provides a continual metaphor for a tawdry world. His first detective story, "Blackmailers Don't Shoot," deals with the kidnapping of a film star for the purpose of generating publicity. Two of his novels had been sold to Hollywood before he began work on the *Double Indemnity* script. They were used as the basis for films that have few of the qualities now associated with Chandler, and for good reason. The plots of the novels were integrated into already existing series formats, each with its own style. *Farewell, My Lovely* became the basis for *The Falcon Takes Over* (1942), with George Sanders as the dashing detective-socialite known as the Falcon. *The High Window* provided the plot for *Time to Kill* (1942), a Mike Shayne mystery starring Lloyd Nolan.

But the first Philip Marlowe film, and the one that marks the real beginning of Chandler's impact on film, is *Murder, My Sweet*. This film attempted to appropriate much more than Chandler's plot, and in doing so, became a kind of model for subsequent films.

Marlowe's personality dominates the novels. Not only is he an ever-present character, but since he narrates the novels in the first person, the characters, events, and settings are all presented to the reader filtered through his point of view. Many of Chandler's fans respond most enthusiastically not to the plots, but to Philip Marlowe's unique and idiosyncratic perceptions, as embodied in Chandler's unique and idiosyncratic verbal style.

Edward Dmytryk, director of *Murder, My Sweet*, was sensitive to this aspect of Chandler's fiction and presented Marlowe not only as a character but also as a presence that determines our perception of events. Realizing that two of Chandler's greatest assets were his skill with dialogue and his first-person description, Dmytryk capitalized upon these by violating standard practice and presenting most of the story in flashback, with Marlowe's running narration (including much of Chandler's dialogue and description). Marlowe appears both as the central character and as the narrative voice, frequently describing on the sound track what we see him doing on the visual track (again in violation of contemporary practice).

Until the mid-1940s, first-person narration had seldom been used in Hollywood films for anything more than a kind of narrative shorthand. At significant points in films, a narrator would summarize a series of plot events or even comment briefly upon them, as in John Ford's *How Green Was My Valley* (1941) or in William Wyler's *Wuthering Heights* (1939), but seldom did such narrative interjections contain detailed descriptive passages and seldom, as frequently happens in the Marlowe films, did such passages contain elaborate similes.

Marlowe, played by Dick Powell, narrates *Murder, My Sweet* (1944) and appears in most scenes. At times, we see subjective camera shots not only of what he sees but also of what he thinks he sees as during an hallucinatory sequence in which he has been drugged. His perception of events is given equality with the events themselves. His personality rules all we see and hear. Furthermore, the film uses a voice-over narration that incorporates descriptive passages from the source novel, *Farewell, My Lovely*.

John Paxton, the screenwriter, has written that the narration served "not so much for the purpose of direct story-telling, [but] in a subjective way . . . [it was] what I choose to think of as syncopated narration, or narration that is not directly related to the images one is seeing on the screen at the time."[8] For example, as Marlowe revives after having been knocked out, his voice-over tells us, in a line close to one in the novel, that "I felt pretty good—like an amputated leg." When he meets Mrs. Florian, he comments: "She was a charming middle-aged lady with a face like a bucket of mud. I gave her a drink. She was a girl who'd take a drink—if she had to knock you down to get at the bottle."

These nondialogue verbal descriptions are not essential to the plot and were placed in the film, presumably, for their verbal pungency. The very term *syncopated narration* indicates a rationale for a running narrative line that neither parallels images nor summarizes story events.

The film presents Marlowe as tired, middle-aged, and down on his luck. His surroundings are shabby, mysterious, and often dangerous. He is frequently savagely beaten, encounters labyrynthine webs of betrayal, experiences hallucinatory drugs, and becomes aware of strange sexual goings-on. Little fazes him; he endures. And in the midst of all of this, he demonstrates an incorruptible integrity.

The lighting, sets, and camera work are all in full-blown *noir* style, which became a model for subsequent films. It is also very much a Chandler film in that it contains so many things—the crisp dialogue and first-person description, the Marlowe character, the Los Angeles–in–decline setting—that have come to be associated with Chandler's film image. It is the first film that attempted to deal with a Chandler work as much more than a plot; it attempted to deal with the cluster of things that constitute Chandler's style.

Double Indemnity added to the popular perception of Chandler. Billy Wilder recognized Chandler's gifts and capitalized upon them. He also recognized his weaknesses.

> I read two or three of his novels. . . . They have nothing to do with the Conan Doyle or Agatha Christie type of superb plotting. They weren't even as well plotted as Dashiell Hammett; but by God, a kind of lightning struck on every page. How often do you read a description of a character who says that he had hair growing out of his ear long enough to catch a moth? Not many people write like that; and the dialogue was good, and the dialogue was sharp. . . . Also, I must say that Chandler's great strength was a descriptive one.[9]

Like *Murder, My Sweet, Double Indemnity* is also told in flashback by a major male character, and Chandler's imprint is on the dialogue and the first-person description.

These two films, *Double Indemnity* and *Murder, My Sweet,* mark the beginning of Chandler's active involvement with Hollywood and of Hollywood's serious interest in Chandler. A number of films have subsequently been based upon Chandler's novels, drawing upon the different aspects of his writing for what the films' several creators felt to be the "real" Chandler. Over a forty-year period, these films form an implicit testament to what has variously been interpreted as Chandler's heritage.

In *The Big Sleep* (1946), Howard Hawks drew not upon the verbal texture of Chandler's descriptions but rather upon his perception of Los Angeles as a depraved place in which anything is possible and where very little makes sense. The film uses neither a flashback format nor a first-person narration; indeed, Hawks often bragged that he never used a flashback in his life. Many reviews of the film (as did reviews of *The Blue Dahlia,* the same year) considered it brutal; many also considered it incomprehensible. It is a Hollywood legend that during production, Hawks asked William Faulkner, one of the screenwriters, if he knew who killed the chauffeur, an early victim in the complicated plot. Faulkner replied that he didn't know. Hawks then wired the question to Chandler, who replied that he didn't know either. Hawks shrugged his shoulders and shot it anyway.

This anecdote has been used to support the contention that the film makes no sense. One might reply that the film is tightly controlled but that it deals with a world that makes little sense— something altogether different. It is also interesting to find this film in the middle of Howard Hawks's career. Hawks's films are generally known for their linear, often austere plot structures. In the one film he made based upon a Chandler novel, he used desire, deviation, and confusion in often remarkable ways to structure a perverse world. He placed a Hawksean hero, quite unlike the Marlowe of the novel, into the middle of it. The film nevertheless remains one of the most popular and studied of all of those based upon Chandler novels.

Robert Montgomery's *Lady in the Lake* is one of the most extreme experiments with point of view in the history of Hollywood cinema. Most often we see only what Marlowe sees. We seldom see the star, Robert Montgomery, unless he walks past a mirror. Characters address the camera directly; when Marlowe smokes, we see a hand with a cigarette move to just below screen level, and in a few seconds the screen is momentarily obscured by a puff of smoke; during fight scenes, characters throw punches at the camera. However, in the preface to the film, Marlowe directly addresses the audience: "You'll see it just as I saw it. You'll meet the people; you'll find the clues. And maybe you'll solve it quick and maybe you won't." After thus giving the rationale for the film, Marlowe speaks to, and is frontally seen by, the audience on three other occasions, filling us in on plot events and summing things up. With the combination of the subjective camera and the direct address to the audience, Marlowe's presence so dominates the film as to become almost oppressive.

It is significant that an experiment this extreme should occur with a Chandler novel; that, in other films based upon Chandler's novels, different directors should repeatedly devise ways to imprint the perceiving presence of the main character onto the film and repeatedly indicate that the way the film's events are perceived is as significant as what they are.

Lady in the Lake also marks a clear point of departure for Chandler from his own work and points to the ways in which it was developing a life of its own. Chandler worked on the script of the film in its early stages, then withdrew and refused screen credit. It was the only time he ever worked on a script based upon one of his novels, and he hated it, describing it as "just turning over dry bones" (*Selected Letters*, p. 53). In a letter to Sandoe (May 30, 1946), he commented: "Anyhow, one thing is sure. It is not my story at all. So the hell with it." Which is more easily said than done.

Quite clearly, the film went on without him. His work has continued to form the basis for other people's perceptions of his talent, and those perceptions have in turn formed the basis of works with which he had nothing to do and yet which are popularly perceived as "Chandler" works.

Nineteen forty-seven saw not only the virtual end of Chandler's active involvement with Hollywood but also *The Brasher Doubloon*, the last of his novels to be adapted during his lifetime. It received little attention, and twenty-two years were to pass before another Marlowe film would appear. Another 1947 film, *My Favorite Brunette*, indicates that the *noir* style associated with Chandler had become sufficiently pervasive to be parodied. The film is a Bob Hope vehicle, in which he plays a child photographer who assumes the role of a tough private detective, played in a cameo role by Alan Ladd, who had, only a year before, appeared in *The Blue Dahlia*. Parodying *noir* style, Hope tells the story in a running first-person narration that contains many of the film's jokes. Much of the film's humor depends upon the audience's prior knowledge of *noir* film style, and this assumption of such audience familiarity on the part of the filmmakers points to how pervasive a style that had been brand-new only three years before had become.

The next film to be based upon a Chandler novel was Paul Bogart's *Marlowe* in 1969, and it faced a problem with which all succeeding Marlowe films have had to deal. By the late 1960s, Chandler's writings had become widely associated with the 1940s, and the *noir* style with a world view now identified with a particular period in the past. Chandler's work was now considered dated material, and films that have used that work have chosen in some way to confront the time gap.

Paul Bogart chose to "update" the novel's material. The film's story is set, not in Hollywood of the 1940s as is *The Little Sister*, its source novel, but in Los Angeles of the late 1960s. It deals not with the film industry but with the television industry.

Marlowe, played by James Garner, is allowed a girlfriend with whom he sleeps. The film is the first Marlowe movie in color, and the shadow-drenched tonalities of the Marlowe films of the 1940s have been replaced by the glossy, plasticized colors of the 1960s. Like Chandler's character, Garner's Marlowe is a lonely man of integrity, isolated from a vulgar and corrupt society by that very integrity. The film is clearly an attempt to indicate that Marlowe, as presented by Paul Bogart, embodies the values of the 1940s but remains a man of interest to the 1960s.

Robert Altman's *The Long Goodbye* (1973) frontally assaults this notion. Altman constructed his film upon the notion that Marlowe is not, as Chandler conceived him, a kind of Byronic hero, but an out-and-out loser. On the set, Altman referred to his central character as "Rip Van Marlowe," a man who has been asleep for thirty years and who is now hopelessly out of touch with the times. Marlowe is played by a particularly scruffy Elliott Gould. The film makes no attempt to affectionately recuperate the Marlowe style and values of the 1940s; rather it takes an antinostalgic stance: it presents that style and those values as not only outmoded, but as never having been worthy of admiration. Chandler viewed Marlowe as having little but deserving much; Altman views him as having nothing and deserving it. Possibly because of this view, devotees of Chandler's fiction frequently consider this film with particular loathing. However, although the film was not commercially successful, it has a strong following among film students.

Richard T. Jameson has referred to the visual style of *The Long Goodbye* as "Son of Noir," a style of sharp colors and hard surfaces evident in recent color films that have a number of affinities—primarily generic and thematic—with *noir* films of the 1940s. Jameson includes Blake Edwards's *Gunn* (1967) and Roman Polanski's *Chinatown* (1974) in this category.[10] This visual style may be seen as another way of dealing with the time gap problem raised by recent Marlowe films.

Dick Richards's *Farewell, My Lovely* (1975) is unabashedly nostalgic, and in this quality differs radically from both *Marlowe* and *The Long Goodbye*. Whereas *Marlowe* is a snappy, contemporary film that draws upon certain old values associated with Chandler, and whereas *The Long Goodbye*, also set in contemporary Los Angeles, trashes those values, *Farewell, My Lovely* affectionately returns to the past as a lost, heroic time. The film is set in the Los Angeles of the early 1940s and shot with an attention to neon and pastels that tends to romanticize the seediness of the environment. Robert Mitchum, who plays Marlowe, began his Hollywood career in 1943, the same year Chandler did, and is himself an icon of the 1940s. He appeared in many of the most celebrated *noir* films—*Undercurrent* (1946), *Out of the Past* (1947), and *Crossfire* (1947), among others—and his presence in this film gives it an added nostalgic resonance. The central female character, played by Charlotte Rampling, is shot in such a way as to recall the Lauren Bacall of Hawks's *The Big Sleep*. Richards's *Farewell, My Lovely* also courts comparison with Dmytryk's *Murder, My Sweet*, based upon the same novel. It uses a similar first-person narration, similar dialogue, and many similar camera setups. Mitchum's Marlowe, however, is older, wearier, less successful, and more isolated, but also more Byronically noble than Dick Powell's. Powell's Marlowe ended up with the girl; Mitchum's ends up with nothing but his integrity, which the film presents as considerable.

The commercial and critical success of *Farewell, My Lovely* led to a sort of sequel, Michael Winner's *The Big Sleep* (1978). The film also presents Mitchum as Marlowe, but as a well-dressed, urbane Marlowe in contemporary England. Neither the critics nor the public liked the film, and critics could not decide whether its inferiority was demonstrated more by comparison to *Farewell, My Lovely* or to Hawks's *The Big Sleep*. Its strategy resembles that of Paul Bogart's *Marlowe;* it updates the plot with a contemporary milieu. Interestingly, it uses more plot events from the source novel than did the Hawks film, and also uses a running, first-person narration, which Hawks did not, but neither of these tactics has earned it any substantial reputation as a Chandler film.

Interest in Chandler's work remains strong, and more films based upon his fiction will undoubtedly appear. Although all of his novels except the last (*Playback*) have been used as film sources, it is curious that not one of his nearly two dozen short stories, many of novella length, has been touched.

Part II | RAYMOND CHANDLER IN HOLLYWOOD

2

DOUBLE INDEMNITY

When *Double Indemnity* opened in New York in September 1944, it was recognized not only as a superior film but as something brand-new in American films. In their search for analogues, reviewers went to foreign films and filmmakers. Howard Barnes of the *New York Herald Tribune* (September 7, 1944) wrote: "Alfred Hitchcock has achieved the curious cinematic power that resides in *Double Indemnity* on several occasions. A foreign picture called *M* had it. You will not find it often in Hollywood films." His praise of the film was delirious. He wrote that it "tells a tale of deliberate murder with such eloquence, fluency and suspense that it is something more than a fascinating thriller. On more than one occasion it reaches the level of high tragedy."

Bosley Crowther of the *New York Times* (September 7, 1944), while not quite so extravagant in his praise and clearly put off by the film's lack of sympathetic characters, also went outside of Hollywood for antecedents and located the film's unique quality in what he felt was its tone of sadistic brutality. He wrote: "Billy

Wilder has filmed the Cain story of the brassy couple who attempt a 'perfect crime' . . . with a realism reminiscent of the bite of past French films. He has detailed the stalking of their victim with the frigid thoroughness of a coroner's report, and he has pictured their psychological crackup as a sadist would pluck out a spider's legs. No objection to the temper of this picture; it is as hard and inflexible as steel."

Crowther's reference to French films of the time was paralleled by another reviewer's (John T. McManus's in *PM*) explicit comparison of *Double Indemnity* to Jean Renoir's 1938 *La Bête Humaine*. Leo Braudy, in his book on Renoir, has observed that "All of the images of *La Bête Humaine* are images of entrapment: by heredity, by the weakness of personal will, by uncontrollable emotion, by the mechanical forces of society. In the face of these pressures, Lantier's [the central character's] final act at the end of the film, when he jumps off the train . . . is an attempt to tear himself away from the nature that has in so many ways pressed him into an inescapable mold." Speaking of Renoir's use of mirrors in the film, Braudy comments that "in *La Bête Humaine* the mirrors reflect a constant turning inward and, conversely, an inability to get outside the self or to be free of the demon self revealed by the mirror."[1]

Such notions of deterministic entrapment, of self-involution, are central to the traditions that created a context for *Double Indemnity* and to the tradition that it helped create. These notions were relatively new to American films, but not to popular American fiction and, in fact, stood behind a central literary tradition of the 1930s.

James M. Cain has been linked with Chandler, Dashiell Hammett, Horace McCoy, and others as one of the hard-boiled or "tough-guy" writers of the 1930s. Their novels are often distinguished by the smell of doom about them, by the cloud of inevitable destruction under which the central characters exist. A major influence on most of these writers is Ernest Hemingway, the Hemingway of the stoical Jake Barnes of *The Sun Also Rises* (1926) or of the Frederick Henry of *A Farewell to Arms* (1929). The hard-boiled writers of the 1930s generally share with Frederick Henry the assumption that "the world breaks everyone and afterward many are strong at the broken places. But those that will not break it kills. It kills the very good and the very

Chandler (standing, second from left, with pipe) at a dinner for *Black Mask* writers (including Dashiell Hammett, standing far right) in 1936. The group consists of, left to right, (standing) R. J. Moffat (a guest), Chandler, Herbert Stinson, Dwight Babcock, Eric Taylor, Hammett; (seated) Arthur Barnes, John K. Butler, W. T. Ballard, Horace McCoy and Norbert Davis. *(Photo courtesy of the University of California Library Photographic Department.)*

gentle, and the very brave, impartially. If you are none of these you can be sure it will kill you too but there will be no special hurry."[2]

Edmund Wilson saw James M. Cain as a leader of the "tough" California-based, Hemingway-indebted writers he called "the boys in the back room," and observed: "All these writers are also preeminently the poets of the tabloid murder. Cain himself is particularly ingenious in tracing from their first beginnings the tangles that gradually tighten around the necks of the people involved in those bizarre and brutal crimes that figure in the American papers."[3]

The association of Cain's mode with that of tabloid murder coverage is important and goes beyond the fact that Cain himself had been a newspaper reporter and had based *Double Indemnity*

upon a particularly garish subject of tabloid journalism. The
novella was inspired by the 1927 Snyder-Gray case, in which
Ruth Snyder of Queens Village, New York, and her lover
murdered her husband with a window sash. The murderers were
executed, and the *New York Daily News* printed, on its front
page, a picture of Ruth Snyder at the moment of her electrocution.

Of Cain, Joyce Carol Oates has written:

> The fable of the man under sentence of death, writing to us from
> his prison cell or from the cell of his isolated self, is one of the
> great literary traditions. Stendhal's Julien Sorel does not write a
> journal, but he speaks most passionately and eloquently of the
> education that his imprisonment makes clear. . . . Cain's heroes
> have an aura of doom about them, suggested to us by the flatness
> of their narration, their evident hurry to get it said. They follow
> the same archetypal route, obeying without consciousness the
> urges that lead them (and their tragic ancestors) to disaster. . . .
> It is the fact such pessimistic works are entertainment that
> fascinates. No happy endings, no promise of religious salvation,
> not even the supposition that society has been purged of evil—
> society is always worse than Cain's victims! Nothing is handed
> out to the reader; no obvious wish is fulfilled. A course of action
> is begun with terrifying abruptness; once begun it cannot be
> stopped, and it comes to its inevitable conclusion with the same
> efficiency criminals are usually brought to "justice," with their
> photographs appearing at once in the tabloid press.[4]

Ms. Oates is perceptive in all that she says here, except when
she indicates that "Nothing is handed out to the reader; no
obvious wish is fulfilled." The urge that is satisfied is what the
tabloids still satisfy: a ghoulish fascination with the mechanics
and with the details of doom. One has only to remember the
New York Post's close-up photos in recent years of the corpses
of Steve McQueen and John Lennon. The appeal of tabloid
journalism lies not only in *what* happened but in *how* it
happened—in the details. The reader knows what happened
from the headline; the rest of the article must live up to the
shock of the headline, must serve forth the titillating details the
headline promises. Suspense is not a major attraction, because
the headline has already diffused it; the attraction is rather the
specificity of doom.

Cain wrote *Double Indemnity* from the point of view of a
murderer who knows that he is about to die. The novella was
first published in 1936, one year after the appearance of Cain's

first novel, *The Postman Always Rings Twice*. The narrator of that first novel, also a murderer, is writing his story just before he is to be executed. Neither work explicitly states the narrator's imminent death at the beginning, but both quickly establish an atmosphere of inevitable doom. Cain's *Double Indemnity* refers to tabloid journalism in its first paragraph:

> I drove out to Glendale to put three new truck drivers on a brewery company bond, and then I remembered this renewal over in Hollywoodland. I decided to run over there. That was how I came to this House of Death, that you've been reading about in the papers. It didn't look like a House of Death when I saw it. It was just a Spanish house, like all the rest of them in California, with white walls, red tile roof, and a patio out to one side.[5]

The reader knows from the beginning, then, that the narrator, and the house, will eventually become involved in some form of death garish enough to be exploited by the tabloids. Because of this, the reader cannot help but place everything that happens in the novel into the perspective of its sinister outcome.

In their screenplay based upon Cain's novella, Billy Wilder and Chandler were much more explicit in immediately establishing the fate of their narrator, in immediately throwing the specter of failure and death over the entire film. They open not with the beginning of the story but with the end. Walter Neff sluggishly enters his office building at night and speaks into a dictaphone. He calls his story an "office memorandum" to Barton Keyes, claims manager, and says Keyes was correct in suspecting that the Dietrichson life-insurance claim for double indemnity was a cover-up for a murder. He admits: "Yes, I killed him, killed him for money and for a woman. I didn't get the money, and I didn't get the woman." He returns to "last May" to tell the story from the beginning, and his story, told in flashback, is punctuated with voice-over comments, reminding viewers that what they are watching is doomed to end in failure.

The film, then, even more explicitly than the novel, adopts a narrative structure that simulates a tabloid headline; one can almost envision it: "NEFF KILLED DIETRICHSON—LOSES DAME AND DOUGH." Clearly, there is no attempt to develop viewer interest in "whodunit"; that is already known. All the viewer can look forward to are the specifics.

Such a strategy abandons a traditional linear narrative, and Hollywood was beginning to experiment with this in the early 1940s. Films of the early sound era deviated very little from clearly chronological, linear narrative structures. Even when using well-known literary sources with diverse and often complex narrative organization, Hollywood would commonly reorder the plot events into a chronological narrative progression. Rouben Mamoulian's *Dr. Jekyll and Mr. Hyde* (1931) is one example; John Ford's *The Grapes of Wrath* (1940) is another. But in the 1940s, experimentation with linear narrative became widespread. *Citizen Kane* (1941) is a milestone, beginning with the death of its central character and then presenting a number of flashback narratives from different points of view, with a great deal of temporal overlap. Michael Curtiz's *Passage to Marseilles* (1944) is another example, using flashbacks within flashbacks, but what has since come to be known as the *noir* tradition takes nonlinear, often retrospective and non-"suspenseful," narrative almost for granted. In Robert Siodmak's *The Killers* (1946), based upon the Hemingway short story, the central character is murdered at the very beginning, and the rest of the film involves an exploration of the man's past by an insurance investigator. An early draft for Chandler's unproduced screenplay, *Playback*, opened with a shot of the central character dead in an alley. The rest of the film would have shown what brought her there.

A strategy in which the outcome is known at the beginning clearly raises the issue of determinism. The audience watches such films knowing that the characters' fates are already decided. A central metaphor of the film *Double Indemnity* recalls the train in *La Bête Humaine*. It is that of a trolley car on which one is trapped; it goes in only one direction and the only way off is death. When Neff and Phyllis plan to murder her husband, he tells her, "It's gotta be perfect, you understand—straight down the line," and she replies, "Straight down the line." The film immediately switches into the voice-over of the doomed Neff, who says, "That was it, Keyes. The machinery had started to move and nothing could stop it." Later, when Neff realizes he must commit the murder that night, his voice-over comments: "Yes, Keyes, those Fates I was talking about had only been stalling me off. Now they'd thrown the switch. The gears had meshed. The time for thinking had all run out."

The machine analogy expands when Neff realizes that events are taking unexpected turns, that he is caught up in a mechanism larger than he had foreseen. Right after the murder, his voice-over tells us: "That was all there was to it. Nothing had slipped. Nothing had been overlooked. There was nothing to give us away. And yet, Keyes, as I was walking down the street to the drug store, suddenly it came over me that everything would go wrong. It sounds crazy, Keyes, but it's true, so help me. I couldn't hear my own footsteps. It was the walk of a dead man."

Long before Keyes hears Walter's confession, he too describes reality as functioning like an independent mechanism; he describes the evidence as pieces fitting into a machine, and says, "I tell you it all fits together like a watch." Then he parallels Neff's "straight down the line" perception: "They've committed a murder, and it's not like taking a trolley ride together where they can get off at different stops. They're stuck with each other, and they've got to ride all the way to the end of the line, and it's a one-way trip, and the last stop is the cemetery."

The implications—of the narrative structure, of the characters' awareness—are that mankind is controlled by unknown and omnipresent forces. This awareness pervades *film noir,* and it appears in the careful attention given to environment, creating the sense that the "Fates" affect not only man but the physical world as well, that everything is slowly decaying, and that the process is irreversible. Human despair is displaced onto the environment itself, onto the rain-soaked, urban back streets at night, onto the deep and disorienting shadows that darken and seem to threaten everything. About all one can do is search the past to see how one's particular demise came about. In much of *film noir,* there is no future, and films like Jacques Tourneur's *Out of the Past* (1947) show the present as absolutely determined by the past; one can not get off the trolley car, or even change direction.

This notion has parallels in classical tragedy. For example, Sophocles' Antigone says, "It is the dead, / Not the living, who make the longest demands: / We die for ever." Prior to her suicide, she clearly, as happens in many *noir* films, places responsibility for the present on the past, "O Oedipus, father and brother! / Your marriage strikes from the grave to murder mine."

Braudy's comments about *La Bête Humaine* apply to *Double Indemnity* and to most of *film noir*. The characters are entrapped by forces that determine their fate. Although there is no major mirror motif in *Double Indemnity*, it does have the "constant turning inward and, conversely, an inability to get outside the self or to be free of the demon self revealed by the mirror." In *Double Indemnity*, in *Out of the Past*, and in many other *noir* films, this pervasive, oppressive interiority is developed by means of the voice-over narration, which presents and interprets all that the audience sees and hears within the perspective of a single, doomed point of view.

The events of *Double Indemnity* appear in the form of a confession, and confessions have enormous tabloid appeal, because they purport to "tell all," to reveal what has not previously been revealed; to reveal, by implication, what has previously been concealed. This film lays bare socially reprehensible behavior, and such behavior, sprung loose from the social codes that repress it and its revelation, has a good deal to do with much of *film noir*. And the social codes have a good deal to do with censorship.

Cain's first novel, *The Postman Always Rings Twice*, was banned in Boston, and much of the hard-boiled fiction in the 1930s was considered morally depraved. Many early reviews of Chandler's *The Big Sleep* share a similar attitude. By the early 1940s, some hard-boiled fiction, especially that of Cain, was beginning to gain critical respectability, but the social acceptability of similar content had yet to be tested in films, where censorship codes had traditionally been more strict. *Double Indemnity* was the first of Cain's novels to serve as the basis for an American film, and Wilder knew he was playing with fire. The characters in Cain's fiction are often unredeemed felons— petty, ruthless, and driven by savage compulsions they barely understand. Love is sex, tied to violence and death. Shortly after Frank sees Cora in *The Postman Always Rings Twice*, he tells us, "I wanted that woman so bad I couldn't even keep anything on my stomach." Soon he tells us:

> I took her in my arms and mashed my mouth up against hers. . . . "Bite me! Bite me!"

> I bit her. I sunk my teeth into her lips so deep I could feel the blood spurt into my mouth. It was running down her neck when I carried her upstairs."[6]

In *Double Indemnity*, Cain links sexual excitement with murder. As soon as Walter and Phyllis determine to murder her husband, there is the following exchange:

> "Walter—I'm so excited. It does terrible things to me."
> "I too."
> "Kiss me."
>
> (Cain's *Double Indemnity*, p 29)

Both of these novels have at their center the black widow motif: a female who seduces and then kills her sexual partners.

Wilder made this motif thematically central to his film, a central image of which is that of a man on crutches. The credits appear over a silhouette of such a man hobbling ominously toward the camera. Phyllis's husband is murdered when he has a broken leg, and Walter Neff impersonates him by walking on crutches onto a train and making it appear that the crippled man died as the result of an accidental fall from the train.

Near the end of the film, Walter Neff learns that Nino Zachette is suspected of being the man who impersonated Phyllis's husband, because Zachette, who had been dating Lola, Phyllis's stepdaughter, is now secretly involved with Phyllis. When Walter confronts Phyllis with the information, she tells him that she was attempting to get Zachette to kill Lola, and thus eliminate a potentially harmful witness against Walter and her. Walter tells her: "You got me to take care of your husband for you, and then you get Zachette to take care of Lola and maybe take care of me too, and then somebody would've come along to take care of Zachette for you. That's the way you operate, isn't it, baby?"

The image of the crippled man on crutches applies to three men—all, it is implied, sexual partners of Phyllis, and all marked for doom by her. The broken leg, the crutches, all, within this context, symbolically point to a phallic injury, an emasculation suffered by men who become involved with this black widow. Her husband literally has a broken leg and needs the crutches; Walter, who kills the husband, impersonates him at the time of his death by faking the broken leg and using the crutches—he also takes over the husband's sexual role with Phyllis; and Nino, because he has very possibly taken over Walter's sexual role with Phyllis, is perceived by Keyes to have been the man on the train with the crutches. In all cases, the film links this image of debilitation, deformity, and death to sexual association with Phyllis.

Phyllis also destroys the family unit at the most basic levels—
the physical and the cultural. She entered the family by murdering her husband's first wife, eventually murders her husband,
and plots to murder his daughter, actions that would once more
leave her alone, without a family. But even if Phyllis did not set
out to physically obliterate the family unit with which she has
become involved, she clearly destroys its cultural function as a
unit of interpersonal cohesion, sexual containment and trust, and
intergenerational support. Lola sums up her home situation even
before her father is murdered: "I'm having a very tough time at
home. My father doesn't understand me and Phyllis hates me."
Once more, sex and death are linked. Not only does Phyllis
murder her husband, but she is also unfaithful to him, and it is
implied that part of her plan to murder Lola involves her
seduction of Lola's boyfriend, Nino, in a kind of almost incestuous
sexual betrayal. She is neither a faithful wife to her husband nor
a mother to her stepdaughter; in fact, she is her stepdaughter's
sexual rival. And she wants to murder both her husband and
stepdaughter.

This is a pretty sordid state of affairs, and one can easily see
that those connected with the project might have justifiably been
concerned with possible censorship problems. Even when what
might be termed "redeeming" qualities appear in the major
characters they appear within a hopelessly irrelevant context,
consonant with Wilder's famed cynicism. Phyllis's first flash of
compassion appears near the film's end when she has just shot
Walter, who had been preparing to shoot her. She suddenly
realizes that she does not want to fire the second shot, that she
does not want to finish him off, that she loves him. She embraces
him, and, as soon as she declares her need for him, he fires two
shots into her. Her one act of compassion literally dooms her.
Walter, who might have extricated himself by blaming all on
Zachette, performs a similarly compassionate act by confessing
his crimes and sending Zachette back to Lola, thus sealing his
own doom.

Because of its controversial content, Wilder had a good deal
of trouble casting the film, and his difficulties point to contemporary fears about the outrageousness of that content. Barbara
Stanwyck volunteered, but no major star at Paramount wanted
to play Walter. Wilder recalls:

I remember I went one day, in my despair, and told the story of the film to George Raft. And he was sitting there looking bewildered and he kind of interrupted me once in a while and then he said, "When do we have the lapel?" And I said, "What?" And he said, "Well, go on." And I went on, and then he asked again, "Where's the lapel?" And he would not explain to me what this meant until I came to the end, and he said, "Oh, no lapel." I said, "What is the lapel?" He said, "You know, at a certain moment you turn the hero's lapel and it turns out that he's an FBI man or a policeman or someone who works for the govern- ment—a good guy really." (Wilder interview, p. 48)

Eventually, Wilder talked a reluctant Fred MacMurray into the role, which proved a major one in MacMurray's career and showed that he could play more than happy-go-lucky saxaphone players. But Wilder's difficulty in casting the role because of its downbeat nature indicates the relative newness of what he was attempting. The film's success points not only to its quality, but to the fact that the time was right for the types of things it was presenting. They were new at the time, and now have become part of a tradition.

II

And what did Raymond Chandler have to do with all of this? Wilder, who has always liked to work with collaborators, could not get Charles Brackett, his writing partner on the two previous films he had directed, to work on *Double Indemnity* with him, because, reportedly, Brackett found Cain's novel disgusting. Wilder also could not get James M. Cain, who was then working at Twentieth Century Fox on *Western Union* for Fritz Lang. Joseph Sistrom, who had drawn Cain's novel to Wilder's attention, suggested Raymond Chandler. It seemed like a good choice. Chandler also wrote hard-boiled novels of life in southern California and was considered one of Cain's peers. In actuality, as often happens with writers who are popularly classified as "of the same school," Chandler felt that he had little in common with Cain: "It has always irritated me to be compared with Cain. My publisher thought it was a smart idea because he had a great success with *The Postman Always Rings Twice*, but whatever I have or lack as a writer I'm not in the least like Cain. Cain is a writer of the faux naif type, which I particularly dislike." (*Selected Letters*, p. 26)

His particular point of difference appears to have been a moral
one. The *faux naïf*, or that in which the author assumes a
narrative voice less intelligent, more naive than his own, and in
which he expects the reader to understand more about the
significance of the narrated events than the narrator does (Mark
Twain's *The Adventures of Huckleberry Finn* and Henry James's
What Maisie Knew are examples), exists in an altogether different
mode from that of Chandler's Philip Marlowe novels. Chandler
assumed Marlowe to be at least as intelligent as himself, and
probably more moral. Chandler's Marlowe provides a moral

Chandler and Billy Wilder during the time they worked on *Double
Indemnity*. (*Photo courtesy of the University of California Library
Photographic Department.*)

strength and perception that counter the environmental depravity presented in the novels. In a world gone bad, at least the central character remains good. Chandler seems to have felt that Cain's novels lacked that countering moral voice.

But regardless of his sense of the differences between his work and Cain's, he appeared at Wilder's office quite willing to give screenwriting a try. Wilder has described his first encounters with Chandler:

He had never been inside a studio; he had never worked on a picture; he had no idea what the hell the whole thing was about. Sistrom asked him to read the story, which he did, and he came back and said yes, he would like to do it, could he see what a screenplay looked like? So we gave him a screenplay. He had that idiotic idea, you know, that if you know about "fade in" and "dissolve" and "close-up" and "the camera moves into the keyhole" and so on, that you have mastered the art of writing pictures. He had no idea how these things were done. I remember well what he said: "I would be interested if you think I am the right man; but this is already Tuesday; I cannot promise you the script until next Monday." And we looked at him as though he was a maniac. He didn't know that he was going to work with me. Then he said: "I want a thousand dollars." We just looked at each other.

Chandler returned on Monday with some eighty pages of "technical drivel" obviously stemming from the script he had been given and was told that henceforth he would be collaborating with Wilder, "who is a writer too."

He was sort of taken aback. It wasn't the thing for a man who was a novelist to have a collaborator. Then he repeated that he wanted a thousand dollars. We said, "None of that thousand dollar shit. You are going to get 750." And he said, "750, I will not work for 750." We said, "No, relax, 750 a week. . . ." And he said, "Oh, really? Then it only goes two or three weeks?" And we said, "No, fourteen weeks. You don't know how scripts are written." (Wilder interview, p. 45)

And he didn't. But he soon learned. He got an agent, H. N. Swanson (a Hollywood literary agent who also represented F. Scott Fitzgerald, William Faulkner, and John O'Hara), became friendly with Sistrom, and quickly learned the Hollywood ropes. He and Wilder seem to have disliked one another from the beginning. Wilder attributes much of Chandler's dislike of him to envy: Wilder, at 37, was much younger than Chandler (who was then 55), knew his way around Hollywood, and was used to living well. He was also involved with a number of young women and frequently spoke to them over the telephone while Chandler was present. He feels that Chandler, who was shy, who had lived in genteel poverty for the previous decade, and who was married to a woman in her seventies, felt that his own youth had passed him by and resented Wilder's. Wilder, on the other hand, has at times been called dictatorial and brutally critical of others. He may have flaunted his youth and his film experience before the older man. He may also have struck the reserved Chandler as crass and vulgar.

After roughly three weeks, Chandler failed to appear for work. Instead, he sent a letter to Sistrom complaining of Wilder's behavior and demanding instant redress. Wilder has described it:

> It was a letter of complaint against me: he couldn't work with me any more because I was rude; I was drinking; I was fucking; I was on the phone with broads, with one I was on the phone— he clocked me—for twelve and a half minutes; I had asked him to pull down the Venetian blinds—the sun was beating into the office—without saying, "please." (Wilder interview, p. 46)

The letter represented Chandler's first ultimatum to Hollywood, and it worked. Wilder apologized.

Although they were never to like each other, they developed respect for one another's talent. Wilder has called Chandler a perfectly miserable man but has said that he far preferred Chandler to a charming partner without talent: "Give me a collaborator like Chandler any day" (Wilder interview, p. 48). Of Wilder, Chandler wrote: "Working with Billy Wilder on *Double Indemnity* was an agonizing experience and has probably shortened my life, but I learned from it about as much about screen writing as I am capable of learning, which is not very much" (*Selected Letters*, p. 237). In 1953, after Chandler's Hollywood career had ended, he was asked which of the films with which he had been associated was his favorite. He replied: "Without question, *Double Indemnity*, which I wrote for an odd little director with a touch of genius, Billy Wilder."[7]

Chandler's specific contribution to the film is difficult to isolate and can only be discussed tentatively because of the collaborative nature of the project. Wilder has unqualified praise for Chandler's skill at description and dialogue, and it has been suggested that the decision to present the film in first-person, narrated flashback was made to give free rein to Chandler's descriptive skills.

Most of the film's dialogue is original. Wilder had wanted to use dialogue from Cain's novel, but Chandler objected, saying that it was written to be seen on a page, not heard by the ear. He said that naturalness was only apparent, the result of careful typographical arrangement on the page. Wilder still disagreed, and to convince Chandler of its usability, even brought actors in to read the dialogue from the book. Chandler was not convinced, and the two men finally consulted with Cain himself, who agreed with Chandler. Wilder gave in.

It is interesting that Chandler's ultimatum to Sistrom was accepted. Given the setup in Hollywood, one would assume that a novice who so immediately and aggressively confronts an experienced filmmaker would simply be dropped from the picture. But Chandler was not. One can only suspect that Sistrom and Wilder put up with Chandler's demands because his talent, even at this early stage in his apprenticeship, was evident. The Academy Award nomination proved this.

Within this context, it is interesting to see what Chandler wrote that was not used in the picture, to see an early blind alley he went up. There is a twenty-page "Test Scene for *Double Indemnity*" in the Chandler archive at UCLA. Written in Chandler's hand in pencil on unlined yellow paper, it is the pivotal scene in which Walter realizes that Phyllis will accept his sexual advances and that she wants him to help her murder her husband. Surprisingly, much of the dialogue comes from the novel. Walter is also called Walter Huff, as in the novel, not Walter Neff as in the completed film. In the scene, they engage in veiled sexual banter and gradually agree to murder her husband. It closes as they embrace.

On the last page of Cain's novel, just as she had done before the murder of her husband, Phyllis prepares for death by making herself up as a grim, grotesque specter of death. "She looks like what came aboard the ship to shoot dice for souls in 'The Rime of the Ancient Mariner' " (Cain, *Double Indemnity*, p. 125). The passage referred to is in Part III of Coleridge's poem:

> *Her* lips were red, *her* looks were free,
> Her locks were yellow as gold:
> Her skin was as white as leprosy,
> The Nightmare Life-in-Death was she,
> Who thicks man's blood with cold.

Chandler's test scene uses these allegorical associations and gives Phyllis a long speech, just before she fully agrees to kill her husband; it goes, in part:

> There's something in me that loves Death. I think of myself as Death sometimes. Am I crazy? I'm not beautiful, but I'm beautiful then. I'm beautiful as Death. I'm beautiful and sad and hungry to make the whole world happy by taking them with me, away from all trouble, all happiness. This is the terrible part, Walter, but it doesn't seem terrible to me. It seems I'm doing something that's really best for all of them, if they only knew it. Do you understand me, Walter?

There is nothing in the film comparable to this, and one can assume that the deletion of this rather overloaded symbolic material and the development of a much more psychologically complex notion of Phyllis were part of Chandler's learning process.

Chandler's dialogue has most often been singled out for praise in his film work, and the justly famous initial encounters between

Phyllis Dietrichson (Barbara Stanwyck) and Walter Neff (Fred Mac-Murray), the doomed, homicidal lovers of *Double Indemnity* (Paramount Pictures). *(Photo courtesy of Cinemabilia Book Store.)*

Walter and Phyllis contain the type of dialogue associated with his work. Walter stops by the Dietrichson house to see the husband about an auto insurance renewal and finds the scantily clad wife. His smug sexual aggression is immediately evident. He tells her that her husband's policy has recently expired and, eyeing her attire, says that he'd "hate to think of your having a smashed fender or something while you're not . . . fully covered." She replies, "Perhaps I know what you mean, Mr. Neff. I've just been taking a sunbath." He retorts, "No pigeons around, I hope." This kind of tawdry, self-satisfied double entendre and implied sexual aggression continue when they move into the living room. He punctuates his insurance pitch with compliments about her ankle bracelet and then asks what is engraved on it. She says her name. The scene continues as he replies:

WALTER: "Phyllis." I think I like that.

PHYLLIS: But you're not sure?

WALTER: I could drive it around the block a couple of times.

PHYLLIS: Mr. Neff, why don't you drop by tomorrow evening around 8:30. He'll be in then.

WALTER: Who?

PHYLLIS: My husband. You were anxious to talk to him, weren't you.

WALTER: Yeah, I was, but I'm sort of getting over the idea, if you know what I mean?

PHYLLIS: There's a speed limit in this state, Mr. Neff. 45 miles per hour.

WALTER: How fast was I going, officer?

PHYLLIS: I'd say around 90.

WALTER: Suppose you get down off your motorcycle and give me a ticket?

PHYLLIS: Suppose I let you off with a warning this time?

WALTER: Suppose it doesn't take?

PHYLLIS: Suppose I have to whack you over the knuckles?

WALTER: Suppose I bust out crying and put my head on your shoulder?

PHYLLIS: Suppose you try putting it on my husband's shoulder?

WALTER: That tears it! [pause] 8:30 tomorrow evening then?

PHYLLIS: That's what I suggested.

WALTER: Will you be here too?
PHYLLIS: I guess so. I usually am.
WALTER: Same chair, same perfume, same anklet?
PHYLLIS: I wonder if I know what you mean?
WALTER: I wonder if you wonder.

The dialogue is sufficiently crass, sufficiently subtle, sufficiently direct, sufficiently tentative, and sufficiently witty to establish the basis for the relationship, and for the film. Chandler once described good writing as resembling an iceberg: it has to carry a great deal more weight than what is visible. After *Double Indemnity*, he was signed by Paramount to a long-term contract at $1,000 a week, and most of his early reputation in Hollywood came from his immediately recognized ability to write first-rate dialogue. After *Double Indemnity*, his apprenticeship was over.

3

UNDER CONTRACT: *AND NOW TOMORROW* and *THE UNSEEN*

Although Chandler had originally planned to return to novel writing after he completed *Double Indemnity*, he remained at Paramount for a number of reasons. The studio offered him a contract, and the money was good. He also seems to have become interested in learning about film, and he enjoyed the access that his position on the studio staff gave him to most stages of film production. For the next few years, he demonstrated an interest in Hollywood processes: the nuts and bolts of filmmaking, the aesthetics of the form, and the cultural and economic nature of the industry.

In addition, he found the social aspects of the Writers' Building a welcome change in his life. For more than a decade after leaving the oil industry, his life had been the reclusive one of a writer. He seems to have been a naturally recessive man, and as a reformed alcoholic, may have cut down on social activity to avoid the temptation to drink. His wife, Cissy, was eighteen years his senior, and Billy Wilder has said that the couple felt awkward in public, since Cissy was sometimes taken for Chandler's mother. As she grew older and infirm, they were less inclined to go out. Furthermore, he was reluctant to become involved in the Hollywood social whirl, partly from a distaste for what he considered its hucksterish and culturally primitive atmosphere, and partly because of the expense. He had just emerged from over a decade of genteel poverty, found much about Hollywood social life absurdly expensive, and did not know how long his success would last. He admitted that he was "a bit of a stinker in Hollywood. I kept the money. No swimming pool, no stone marten coats for a floozie in an apartment, no charge accounts at Romanoff's, no parties, no ranch with riding horses, none of the trimmings at all. As a result of which I have fewer friends but a lot more money" (*Selected Letters*, p. 191). However, although he often complained about the life-style and about the nine-to-five schedule at Paramount, it introduced into his life a social component that had long been absent, and he found himself genuinely enjoying the interactions at the writers' table at lunch in the studio commissary.

He cut a strange figure. In his mid-fifties, he was much older than most of the other writers at the studio. A sharp contrast to the slap-on-the-back, flashily dressed Hollywood types, Chandler, with his pipe, British tweeds, and quiet manner, struck many as academic, almost professorial. Those who expected him to be Philip Marlowe—two-fisted, arrogant, and brawny—were particularly jolted. Billy Wilder has described him as looking like an accountant and resembling Porter Hall, who played Mr. Jackson (from Medford, Oregon) in *Double Indemnity*. One of Chandler's secretaries has described him as looking like a Caspar Milquetoast. John Houseman recalls that "the first impression Ray gave was one of extreme frailty; it was not until later that you discovered the peculiar strength that lay behind his ashy, burnt-out look and his querulous hypochondria."[1]

When he was comfortable in his surroundings and not feeling threatened, Chandler could be witty and charming. He seems to have gotten along well with other writers, and to have become a presiding figure at the writers' table. It was his first regular contact for a long time with people with intellectual predispositions and wit, and he later wrote warmly of the experience:

> I've only worked at three studios and Paramount was the only one I liked. They do somehow maintain the country club atmos-

phere there to an extent. At the writers' table at Paramount I
heard some of the best wit I've ever heard in my life. . . . I
remember Harry Tugend's wonderful crack about ———, when
Tugend was trying to be a producer and hating it. He said, "You
know this is a lousy job. You got to sit and talk to that birdbrain
seriously about whether or not this part is going to be good for
her———career and at the same time you got to keep from being
raped." Whereat a rather innocent young man piped up, "You
mean to say she's a nymphomaniac?" Harry frowned off into
distance and sighed and said slowly, "Well, I guess she would
be, if they could get her quieted down a little." (*Selected Letters*,
p. 138)

There was a darker side. The conviviality at the studio led to
drinking, and the drinking led to women. After the collapse of
his career as an oil executive, Chandler had stopped drinking
and, by and large, remained sober during the time he had
established himself as a mystery writer. He seems to have done
his best work while living a quiet, rigidly structured life at home
with Cissy. But after joining Paramount, his drinking and his
involvement with other women eroded the security of his quiet
home life; his gradual loss of control over himself threatened his
coherence as a person and as an artist.

His contract ran until September 1944, and since the quality
of his dialogue was already well known, his job was mainly
dialogue polishing, or working on scripts that had already been
started. During this time, he received screen credit for two
films, *And Now Tomorrow* (1944) and *The Unseen* (1945). Neither
of them is well known today, even among Chandler's enthusiasts,
and they do little for his reputation. Chandler was known as a
"tough" writer, and that toughness seems to have been what the
studio felt he could add to its films. But because no one quite
knew at the time what direction his particular style of writing
would take, he was first assigned to a romantic melodrama and
then to a terror film.

And Now Tomorrow is based upon the novel of the same title
by Rachel Field, who also wrote the melodramatically romantic
novel *All This, and Heaven Too*, which had been the source for
a successful film in 1940. The film tells the story of Emily Blair
(Loretta Young)—beautiful, rich, independent, and deaf. She
has gone to the best doctors for help, but receives no hope until
the young and brilliant Dr. Merek Vance (Alan Ladd) arrives on
the scene. Raised in the town (which is called Blairstown, after

Emily's family), on the wrong side of the tracks, he is contemptuous of Emily and of her family. However, he eventually cures
her deafness and her snobbishness. They have every hope, at
the film's end, of having a happy life together and contributing
to medical science.

The screenplay by "Frank Partos and Raymond Chandler"
bears little of what might be termed Chandler's mark. Dr.
Vance's first scene, however, does seem to have Chandler written
all over it. Vance enters a Boston coffee shop and, without being
aware of her, sits next to Emily Blair. He is described as having
"a pleasantly hard-boiled expression and a rather gruff voice
when he speaks." The dialogue sounds like Philip Marlowe, and
the establishment of male comradery by means of tough dialogue
is also quite reminiscent of Chandler's fiction:

> VANCE: Coffee. Hot, strong, and made this year.
> COUNTER MAN: You won't like ours.
> VANCE: [as both grin at one another]: Got a match?[2]

When he recognizes Emily, he blows out the match. Not only
does the dialogue here sound like Chandler but the business of
the lighting of the match as a sign of comradery recalls the use
of matches as a sign of affection between Neff and Keyes in
Double Indemnity.

In a later section of the screenplay, marked "Raymond Chandler, January 18, 1944," a camera direction recalls the offhanded
dismissiveness of some of Chandler's descriptive prose: "Emily
is still watching intently in the foreground, and the guests are
watching with whatever expressions guests have when they watch
this sort of foolishness" (*And Now Tomorrow*, p. 105).

The film received little critical attention, and most of it
unfavorable. Bosley Crowther wrote in the *New York Times*
(November 23, 1944):

> it indulges all the clichés of emotion peculiar to such yarns. . . .
> Miss Young gives a performance which may best and most
> graphically be compared to a Fanny Brice imitation of a glamorous
> movie queen. Whatever it was that this actress never had, she
> still hasn't got. Alan Ladd, just returned from the Army, plays
> the doctor with a haughty air that must be tough on his patients—
> and is likely to be equally tough on yours. . . . As you may guess,
> this is a very stupid film.

Dr. Merek Vance (Alan Ladd) and Emily Blair (Loretta Young) in their first scene together in *And Now Tomorrow* (Paramount Pictures). Vance orders "Coffee. Hot, strong, and made this year." *(Photo courtesy of Cinemabilia.)*

It is interesting that Crowther points to Ladd's abrasiveness as a jarring note, because that may precisely be Chandler's contribution. It appears as little more than an aberration, something out of its milieu, since that milieu, the brutal world of *film noir*, was only just emerging. The Ladd character seems almost too tough, too bitter for the context this film creates. A year later, Ladd would appear in a classic *noir* film, *The Blue Dahlia*, this time entirely written by Chandler and destined to become a major film in both of their careers.

The next project for which Chandler was to receive screen credit was *The Unseen*, a film less important for Chandler's work on it, which seems to have been minimal, than for the curious cross-connections it marks in his career.

After the writing team of Billy Wilder and Charles Brackett broke up, providing Chandler with the opportunity to work on *Double Indemnity*, Brackett produced *The Uninvited* (1944), an English ghost tale that was unexpectedly successful. Hoping to capitalize upon that success, the studio took a story that it already owned, based upon the novel *Her Heart in Her Throat* by Ethel Lina White, renamed it *The Unseen,* and assigned both the director (Lewis Allen) and the female lead (Gail Russell) of *The Uninvited* to the project. John Houseman, who had just come to Paramount as a producer, took it as his first assignment.

The library of the Academy of Motion Picture Arts and Sciences has in its possession seven scripts for the film. The first, *Her Heart in Her Throat,* lists Ken Englund as the author and is dated July 6, 1943. The next four, all entitled *Fear* by Hagar Wilde, are dated November 10, 1943, February 11, 1944, February 17, 1944, and April 24, 1944. A censorship dialogue script, called *The Unseen,* is dated November 21, 1944, and the writing credits read "Screenplay by Hagar Wilde and Raymond Chandler; Adaptation by Hagar Wilde and Ken Englund; Based on Novel by Ethel Lina White." A release dialogue script, dated December 19, 1944, has the same credits. Chandler's work, then, came late in the process.

Most of the final script was done by Hagar Wilde, who fell ill before a suitable ending could be devised. Houseman hired Chandler to polish the script, but recalls that it "was not a good idea, and except for a friendship that lasted until his death fifteen years later, little came of Ray's three weeks' work" (Houseman, p. 115).

The film introduces Elizabeth Howard (Gail Russell) into the strange home of David Fielding (Joel McCrea). The governess of his two motherless children, she spends most of the film being puzzled, terrified, and eventually threatened by Fielding's strangely guilty behavior and by the ominous goings-on in the gloomy, boarded-up house next door.

The Unseen received respectable reviews as a genre suspense film, and the marketing of it and critical response to it give an indication of Chandler's increasing visibility.

When *And Now Tomorrow* opened in New York in November 1944, little attention was paid to Chandler's role in it. Much of the advertising concentrated upon the film as the first Alan Ladd vehicle since his return from the army—"Ladd's back—in his first picture in nearly two years."[3] *The Unseen* opened in New York in May 1945, after Chandler had received his Academy Award nomination for *Double Indemnity.* Although the main focus of the advertisements is on its relationship to *The Uninvited* ("Gail Russell as a girl fascinated by a love she fears . . . faces a menace even more deadly than *The Uninvited*"), it is also called "the successor to *Double Indemnity*."[4] The *New York Times* review (May 14, 1945), which called the film "genuinely gripping and generally devoid of the clutch of clichés to which such offerings are heir," makes the following assumptions about its authorship: "Credit, no doubt, is due Raymond Chandler, Hagar Wilde and Ken Englund, no newcomers to this field, who have adapted the Ethel Lina White novel to the screen. They, as well as the director, have told their story subtly and by indirection."

It is significant that Chandler here is given first mention in the credits, a position he does not hold in the actual film's credits. The fact that a project with which he had very little to do, that worked out well, could be viewed largely as "his" picture indicates that his star in Hollywood was rising. In addition, *Murder, My Sweet,* based upon Chandler's *Farewell, My Lovely,* had opened to generally favorable reviews two months earlier. Although Chandler had nothing to do with the film, reviewers frequently cited respectfully both the novel on which the film was based and *Double Indemnity.* Success was beginning to cling to Chandler.

4

THE BLUE DAHLIA

Chandler's Paramount contract expired in September 1944, and, while his agent was negotiating a new one for him, he worked at home. Part of what he did seems to have formed the basis for *The Blue Dahlia,* which marked the peak, and in many ways the end, of his Hollywood career. During this time, Warner Brothers bought the rights to *The Big Sleep* from Knopf for $10,000 (Chandler got $7,000 of this) and started work on what was to become the most acclaimed of the films based upon Chandler's fiction. Chandler was unable to work on the screenplay because of a prior commitment to Paramount.

By year's end, H. N. Swanson had gotten Chandler a three-year contract requiring twenty-six weeks of work per year, with an escalating salary scale starting at $1,000 a week. He was to work on an original screenplay and had the right to make the screenplay into a novel.

His film career was doing well, but his artistic priorities remained constant. The day before he began work under his new contract, he wrote: "Hollywood is just a way-station. If it

teaches me to turn out books a little faster—and I think it will—
it certainly won't do me any harm."[1]

The studio was in a state of panic when Chandler arrived.
Alan Ladd, its top star, was to be reinducted into the army in
roughly three months' time, and there was no Ladd film to be
released in his absence. Henry Ginsberg, head of production,
told the studio's producers that a prime priority was a Ladd
vehicle that could go into production within a month. John
Houseman has written:

> That same day, at lunch in one of Lucey's sinister little alcoves,
> Ray complained of being stuck on a book he was writing and
> muttered that he was seriously thinking of turning it into a
> screenplay for sale to the movies. After lunch, we went to his
> house . . . and I read the first 120 typed pages of his book. Forty-
> eight hours later Paramount had bought *The Blue Dahlia* for a
> substantial sum and Ray Chandler was at work on a screenplay
> for Alan Ladd. I was to produce it, with Joseph Sistrom as my
> executive producer. (Houseman, p. 137)

On February 10, 1945, Chandler ebulliently wrote Sandoe,
on "Paramount Pictures Incorporated" stationery (unusual for
him), that "I am very busy doing an original screenplay which
is much more fun than anything I have done in pictures so far,
because instead of fighting the difficulties of translating a fiction
story into the medium of screen, I can write directly for the
screen and use all its advantages." But three weeks earlier, he
had written: "I'm afraid I am going to be in trouble for some
time to come. I did a quick treatment on a story for Paramount
(an original in a purely technical sense only) and they are already
casting it, without a line of screenplay written. Why do I get
myself in these jams?" (MacShane, *The Life of Raymond Chandler*, p. 115).

At first, things went marvelously well. In three weeks, Chandler delivered the first half of the script. Soon a filming date was
set only a month away, and when shooting began, that went
well. Problems arose during the fourth week of production, when
it became evident that Chandler was having difficulty and that
the director was using up all the available script. The first part
of the script had come easily, since it had been blocked out in
the novel fragment, but once that material was used up, Chandler
began to wind down and his initial exhiliration was turning into
terror.

The studio executives began to worry as less and less script became available. Chandler did not help matters by teasing them about it, slapping them on the backs at lunch, and asking, "What do you think ought to happen next?" (MacShane, *The Life of Raymond Chandler*, p. 115).

Things came to a head on April 14, 1945, when Chandler announced that he was withdrawing from the film. He told the stunned Houseman that he had just come from Henry Ginsberg's office, where he had been offered a $5,000 bonus to finish the script. Rather than spurring him on, the offer had stopped him cold. It had demonstrated to him how much doubt the studio executives had about his ability to finish the script, and consequently shattered what little self-confidence he had left. Furthermore, he took the offer as a personal insult, since it was made to guarantee the completion of an assignment for which he had already contracted. And finally, he felt that he had been invited to betray a fellow English public school man, namely, Houseman, who had not known about the offer. Chandler felt he had no alternative but to withdraw from the project.

The next day, he reappeared in Houseman's office, this time with an amazing proposition. Citing his personal loyalty to Houseman and his awareness of the trouble Houseman, as producer, would be in if the film, already in production, were abandoned, he offered to complete the film if certain conditions were met. Foremost among these was that Chandler be allowed to write the script at home, while drunk.

Explaining that he was a reformed alcoholic, he said that only if he were drunk would he have the necessary self-confidence to complete the script. He told Houseman that completing the script would be done at great risk to his own life, but that he felt honor-bound to help out his friend. Then he presented Houseman, on the same kind of yellow foolscap paper on which he had presented his ultimatum concerning Billy Wilder, his list of "basic requirements." They were

A. Two Cadillac limousines, to stand day and night outside the house with drivers available for:
   1. Fetching the doctor (Ray's or Cissie's or both).
   2. Taking script pages to and from the studio.
   3. Driving the maid to market.
   4. Contingencies and emergencies.

   B. Six secretaries—in three relays of two—to be in constant
      attendance and readiness, available at all times for dictation,
      typing, and other possible emergencies.
   C. A direct line open at all times to my office by day and the
      studio switchboard at night.

Houseman recalls that his "first reaction was one of pure panic.
Such is my own insecurity that contact with a human brain that
is even slightly out of control frightens, repels, and finally enrages
me" (Houseman, pp. 143–44). Yet Houseman also has a remarkable track record in dealing with artistic prima donnas: during
the 1930s he was Orson Welles's main partner and helped him
produce much of his best work; nearly a decade after his
experience with Chandler he would produce *Julius Caesar* for
M-G-M, with Marlon Brando in the only Shakespearean role of
his career.

    In reality, Houseman had little choice in the matter. The film
was already in production, Ladd had less than ten days left
before vanishing into the army, and, as Joseph Sistrom pointed
out to Houseman, they would all be fired anyway if the film
were not completed. So Houseman gave the go-ahead, and
Chandler drank until he finished the film. The shooting script
(not the film) ends with the line, "Did somebody say something
about a drink of bourbon?"[2]

    Maurice Zolotow, one of Billy Wilder's biographers, sees the
incident differently from Houseman. His perspective is evident
from the title of an article he wrote about Chandler: "Through
a Shot Glass Darkly: How Raymond Chandler Screwed Hollywood." He does not see Chandler and Houseman as having been
betrayed by Henry Ginsberg; rather, he suspects that Chandler
orchestrated the entire situation to his own advantage. He
believes Chandler purposely slowed the pace of the final script
pages, knowing the bind the studio was in and that it would
have to accept his demands. He also believes that the Ginsberg
$5,000 offer was never made but that Chandler fabricated it to
precipitate his final demands. Zolotow sees such behavior as
pervading Chandler's career and calls him "the Willie Sutton of
screenwriters."[3]

    Whichever perspective is correct, and Zolotow's does seem a
bit too schematically satanic, it is clear that Chandler was losing
control over himself. He never productively worked at a studio

again, although the film was an enormous success and enabled him to set his terms for screenwriting contracts during the next few years. Houseman has remarked that, when he first met Chandler, "his creative days were almost over, but his great success was just beginning" (Houseman, p. 134). *The Blue Dahlia* is Chandler's only original screenplay ever to be produced, and although, as will be seen, he was not happy with it, much of his reputation as a screenwriter must rest on it.

The film deals with the return of Johnny Morrison (Alan Ladd) and two of his crewmates from military service in World War II. He discovers that his wife, Helen (Doris Dowling) has been unfaithful with Eddie Harwood (Howard DaSilva), a racketeer who owns the Blue Dahlia nightclub. He also learns that his wife's drunkenness was responsible for his son's death. He has a bitter argument with her and leaves. Soon she is murdered with his gun, and Johnny must apprehend the killer before the police catch him. He is assisted by Joyce Harwood (Veronica Lake), Eddie's estranged wife, and both quickly fall in love. Suspicion for the killing is alternately focused on Eddie Harwood; Buzz (William Bendix), Johnny's sometimes mentally disturbed friend; and Dad Newell (Will Wright), a crooked house detective. Homicide Captain Hendrickson finally establishes that Newell is the guilty one, and Johnny and Joyce, although both recently bereft of spouses, appear prepared to live happily ever after.

The script is suffused with a sense of loss, and of loss of control. This is evident as Johnny, Buzz, and George (Hugh Beaumont), after having formed a close bond during the war, are about to part. In his first line, Buzz suggests a "goodbye drink." When he and George toast Johnny, Buzz calls Johnny a "lucky stiff" because he has "a wife and a kid to come home to,"[4] and George, who presumably already knows that Johnny's son is dead, nudges Buzz to silence him. Johnny is quiet and says little. When George suggests that Johnny call his wife before returning home, Johnny refuses. It becomes evident that Johnny is uneasy about returning home. It is also established that Buzz has a metal plate in his head as the result of a war wound and is subject to forgetfulness, disorientation, and outbursts of violence. Johnny and George obviously tolerate Buzz's frequently bizarre behavior only because of what he once was, and George has assumed the role of his protector and guide.

"Well, here's to what was." The melancholy return to civilian life of the three service buddies: Buzz (William Bendix), George (Hugh Beaumont) and Johnny (Alan Ladd) in *The Blue Dahlia* (Paramount Pictures). *(Photo courtesy of Cinemabilia.)*

Johnny's unease about returning to civilian life is established not only by means of his restrained, distanced behavior but visually by means of the dark, somber naval officer's overcoat he wears over his civilian clothes. He states a central motif of the film when he toasts his friends before leaving the bar: "Well, here's to what was."

Johnny's sense of loss becomes even more intense when he returns home to find a loud, drunken party going on in his apartment in the middle of the day. He soon learns that his wife has been having an affair with Eddie Harwood, and that his son had not died naturally but in an automobile accident in which his drunken wife was involved. His wife, who has been living extravagantly with the help of Harwood's money, has no intention of giving up either her heavy drinking or her new life-style. Consequently, Johnny realizes that he has come home to nothing, that there is no longer a place for him in what he had thought was his own home. He leaves. When his wife is murdered, he is forced to track down someone who has done what he secretly wanted done. What appears to be retribution for his family honor is, in fact, an attempt to avoid the ultimate implications of the collapse of his home. His wife's behavior in his wartime absence has set things in motion that have robbed him of his son and of his marriage. Unless he can track down the killer, he himself will be arrested for the murder, and consequently his loss of his own life will be the final result of his wife's infidelity. She threatens him even from the grave.

The sense of loss permeates everything. For example, Johnny and his friends have not come home because the war is over. When his wife wonders why Johnny is not in uniform, he says: "They decided I had enough for a while, so they've put me on the inactive list. Buzz and George are out too. Buzz was wounded and George's eyes went back on him." The film never establishes what it was that caused Johnny to be put on the inactive list, but it is clear that, even before he learns of his wrecked home, something else is wrong.

When Johnny meets Joyce Harwood, she is also aimlessly adrift after having removed herself from a marriage in which her husband is involved with another woman. She says she is driving to Malibu, and when asked why, says, "I flipped a coin. Heads I go to Malibu—tails I go to Laguna." Their meeting has a psychological logic to it, since both are similarly trying to distance themselves from a collapsed life in which "all blows up in your face sometimes." However, there is absolutely no narrative logic to their meeting, since it is only by the wildest coincidence that she happens to pick him up by the roadside in the rain.

Even Eddie Harwood is a haunted man. He has lost interest in Johnny's wife and would very much like to have his own wife back, but she no longer cares for him. He is also threatened with exposure. As a youth in New Jersey, he committed a murder. He changed his name and wound up in Hollywood, but, like all of the other characters, his past corrodes his present. Eventually it contributes to his death.

World War II is a central but subdued presence in the film. Although Johnny and his two friends have just returned from the war, they never wear their uniforms. Johnny wears his officer's raincoat at the beginning, but discards it when he hears on the radio that the police are looking to identify him by means of it. Like the overcoat, wartime service seems to be more of a stigma than anything else for the three men. The film shows little civilian reward for war service; there are no parades, no honors, just a disrupted life to return to. In the first bar scene, we see a marine in uniform playing music and dancing by himself. The only advantages of service seem to be the brief flurry of attention given to Johnny when he returns to his apartment and the fact that George's landlord has saved his shabby apartment for him. In contrast, Eddie Harwood, who has not been in service, has profited in the absence of those who have served. Not only has he become rich but he has also enjoyed the sexual favors of a serviceman's wife.

The war, then, appears as a disruption without compensation in the lives of those who return from it. Whatever they may previously have had is likely to be destroyed, and they are neither as young nor as whole as they were before they left. The life they return to is more licentious, more corrupt, and has less of a place for them than the one they had left. Like Johnny, all they can do is toast "what was."

The film deals not only with loss, but with loss of control. Buzz, with his head injury, is the most obvious example. He forgets where he is and what he has done, is excessively pugnacious, and goes mad when he hears "monkey music" on the radio. He may even have murdered Johnny's wife as the result of a violent, uncontrollable outburst, and then have lost memory of the event. Until the film's end, he honestly does not know whether or not he killed Helen Morrison.

Johnny has seen his life collapse around him without being able to do much of anything about it. His wife drifted away and his son died when he was in the Pacific, and when his wife is murdered he is unable to track down her killer. It is the stolid, overworked homicide captain who eventually tracks down his wife's killer. All Johnny can do is, by proving that Buzz is an expert marksman, demonstrate that it was unlikely that Buzz would shoot Helen at close range, as was done. He does not have the opportunity to avenge himself on either his wife's killer or his wife's lover; rather, both are killed by relatively peripheral characters as Johnny stands helplessly by. (Dad Newell is killed by the police; Eddie is accidentally shot by one of his own men after his past has caught up with him and his marriage has broken up.) Neither Buzz nor George is able to help Johnny in any significant way, nor can Joyce Harwood.

Although the film contains a good deal of violent, purposeful action, very little of it has much effect. The protagonists have little control over their fates, marriages seem doomed, and when Johnny and Joyce do appear to find mutual solace in a romantic relationship, this wildly improbable outcome takes place, almost literally, over the dead bodies of their former spouses.

Johnny and Joyce seem to maintain the integrity the film gives them by continual processes of denial and rejection. Both leave their unfaithful spouses. When Eddie offers Johnny a drink upon his return home, Johnny declines; later, when Eddie offers Joyce a drink at his apartment, she also declines. Soon after she picks Johnny up for the first time, he offers her a cigarette and she declines. When it becomes evident that she has forgotten about her original destination and is prepared to spend the night drifting with him, he leaves her, saying, "It's goodbye, and it's tough to say goodbye." He even walks out on Buzz and George when he realizes that they believe he killed Helen. In all cases, each person exhibits moral integrity by backing away from compromising or potentially compromising situations. Johnny explicitly reminds Joyce of "Last night, when I made myself walk out on you," at the film's end, and this continual rejection— of spouses, of friends—seems to bring both together as people out of place and unwilling to compromise in a world gone bad.

In the film, just after this reminder, Johnny and Joyce remain together. However, in the published screenplay, Joyce leaves for the last time. Johnny returns to his friends and they watch the lights go out at the Blue Dahlia, and then go off to drink. The film's ending corresponds to an established Hollywood pattern of leaving the hero and heroine together and at a new beginning. The screenplay's ending is much more consonant with the patterns established in the narrative: the three friends have gone through another horror together, and one has lost a good deal. There's little left to do but ask, when nobody has, "Did somebody say something about a drink of bourbon?"

Although Chandler enjoyed the idea of writing an original screenplay, a number of things about the finished film displeased him, and, after its release, he wrote Sandoe (May 30, 1946):

> When you write directly for the screen it may not be topnotch, but there is a feeling of fluidity and improvisation that I like. The Blue Dahlia would have been a much better show if the Navy Department hadn't butted into it and if Miss Moronica Lake

could somehow be made to act. The only time she's any good is when she keeps her mouth shut and looks mysterious. The moment she tries to behave as if she had a brain she falls flat on her face. The scenes we had to cut out because she loused them up! And there are three godawful close shots of her looking perturbed that make me want to throw my lunch over the fence.

Nearly three weeks later (June 17, 1946), presumably in response to a return letter, he again wrote Sandoe and explained more about his initial story concept:

I'm through with the Blue Dahlia—Anyway, it dates even now. What the Navy Department did to the story was a little thing like making me change the murderer and hence make a routine whodunit out of a fairly original idea. What I wrote was a story of a man who killed (executed would be a better word) his pal's wife under the stress of a great and legitimate anger, then blanked out and forgot all about it; then with perfect honesty did his best to help the pal get out of a jam, then found himself in a set of circumstances which brought about partial recall. The poor guy remembered enough to make it clear who the murderer was to others, but never realized it himself. He just did and said things he couldn't have done or said unless he was the killer; but he never knew why he did or said them and never interpreted them.

Buzz, then, was Chandler's original choice for the killer, and this would have darkened the implications of the film even further: one cannot trust others; one cannot even trust oneself. The loss-of-control motif would have become the dominating one. Furthermore, the discovery of Buzz's guilt would have necessitated his removal from the tightly knit group of three friends that provides the only enduring relationship in either the film or the published screenplay. Had Chandler had his way, even this would have been lost.

Possibly for autobiographical reasons, Chandler found the notion of memory loss, which threatens the coherence of identity itself, particularly fascinating. In his fiction, it adds an unusual dimension to criminal investigation, because the detective must move beyond traditional notions of whether suspects are clearly innocent or clearly guilty or cleverly covering up their guilt. Characters may think they have or have not done something and, as in Buzz's case, be unaware of their guilt; or as with Merle Davis in *The High Window* (published in 1942, before Chandler came to Hollywood), characters may attempt to cover up for a murder they think they have done, but in reality have not.

A similar situation occurs in *The Long Goodbye* (1953), published after Chandler had left Hollywood. His repeated return to the same type of perceptual confusion, here not only used but backed up by two additional examples, indicates its importance to his work. In *The Long Goodbye*, Roger Wade thinks that he murdered Sylvia Lennox while drunk, and tries to cover up. In actuality, he did not kill her, but he dies without learning the truth. When Marlowe is asked whether or not it is possible to kill someone without retaining an awareness of the act, he replies:

> I know of two well established instances. One was a blackout drunk who killed a woman he picked up in a bar. He strangled her with a scarf she was wearing fastened with a fancy clasp. She went home with him and what went on then is not known except that she got dead and when the law caught up with him he was wearing the fancy clasp on his own tie and he didn't have the faintest idea where he got it. . . . The other case was a head wound. He was living with a rich pervert, the kind that collects first editions and does fancy cooking and has a very expensive secret library behind a panel in the wall. The two of them had a fight. They fought all over the house, from room to room, the place was a shambles and the rich guy eventually got the low score. The killer, when they caught him, had dozens of bruises on him and a broken finger. All he knew for sure was that he had a headache and he couldn't find his way back to Pasadena. He kept circling around and stopping to ask directions at the same service station. The guy at the service station decided he was nuts and called the cops. Next time around, they were waiting for him.[5]

In all of these cases, we have loss of control at a fundamental level. A frequent terror in postwar films is a fear of being taken over by uncontrollable urges, often presented with a strong Freudian overlay. Even more insidious is the fear of losing a clear perception of reality: the hallucination scenes in *Murder, My Sweet* and in Hitchcock's *Spellbound* (1945) provide two examples of this; *The Blue Dahlia* provides another. This terror has devastating significance when placed within the context of the central use of point of view in much of *film noir*. When one is given access only to a particular point of view, few things are more fundamentally chaotic and terrifying than the breakdown of the integrity of that point of view. Such a breakdown denies one access to reality itself.

The Blue Dahlia was generally well received by the critics and was an enormous box-office success. It earned Chandler his second Academy Award nomination, and the "Edgar" of the Mystery Writers of America. It also seemed to indicate a kind of continuity for him at Paramount, since people involved with his three previous films kept popping up in this one. *The Blue Dahlia*, aside from being generally overseen by Joseph Sistrom and William Dozier, was Chandler's second picture with Alan Ladd and his second with John Houseman. In addition, Tom Powers, who had played Barbara Stanwyck's doomed husband in *Double Indemnity*, appeared in *The Blue Dahlia* as Captain Hendrickson.

The Unseen had been Houseman's first picture with Chandler and with Paramount; *The Blue Dahlia* was to be his last. He soon left the studio. And although Chandler's star seemed to be on the rise, although he appeared to be successfully digging in at the studio, *The Blue Dahlia* was also his last film there.

Curiously enough, just when Chandler's personal momentum was winding down, the momentum behind his reputation was building. Many reviews of *The Blue Dahlia* called it a Raymond Chandler film, and his name was becoming a salable commodity associated with a style. What would later be termed *film noir* was recognized even by American critics as a significant trend. Metro-Goldwyn-Mayer's *The Postman Always Rings Twice*, the first film to be based upon a Cain novel after *Double Indemnity*, opened in New York six days before *The Blue Dahlia*, and the opening of Warner Brothers' *The Big Sleep*, for which enthusiasm was already building, was only three months away.

Bosley Crowther, in his *New York Times* review of *The Blue Dahlia* (May 9, 1946), situated it within this trend, which he characterized by its brutality, sensuality, and mysteriousness:

> To the present expanding cycle of hard-boiled and cynical films, Paramount has contributed a honey of a rough-'em-up romance. . . . it has starred its leading tough guy, Alan Ladd, and its equally dangerous and dynamic lady V-bomb, Veronica Lake. What with that combination in this Raymond Chandler tale, it won't be simply blasting that you will hear in Times Square for weeks to come.
>
> For bones are being crushed with cold abandon, teeth are being callously kicked in, and shocks are being blandly detonated at close and regular intervals. . . . Also an air of deepening mystery overhangs this tempestuous tale which shall render it none the less intriguing to those lovers of the brutal and bizarre.

Crowther closes the review with a genially cautionary note, indicating that the issue of the moral suitability of such hardboiled material was still dubious: "The tact of all this may be severely questioned, but it does make a brisk, exciting show."

After *The Blue Dahlia,* Chandler started edging away from his Hollywood career. He did not do so at once, but slowly and in different ways. He worked on a variety of projects in Hollywood after this, and he published the articles outlining his perception of the industry and of the art. In essence, the next five years marked Chandler's slow detachment from Hollywood, but his involvement was still sufficiently strong, and his interest sufficiently substantial, to have produced a good deal of interesting work and commentary.

The reasons for this slow detachment involved more than his distaste for aspects of the industry and its working conditions, combined with the strain it placed on his personal life. They included an overall depression in the industry itself, Chandler's steadily improving financial condition, new alternatives available to him in radio and television, and a serious return to novel writing. His long goodbye to Hollywood after *The Blue Dahlia* was not, as has at times been suggested, simply a long collapse.

None of his later projects quite worked out as Chandler wanted them to, but they are well worth looking at.

5 | DETACHMENT: "WRITERS IN HOLLYWOOD," *PLAYBACK*, "OSCAR NIGHT IN HOLLYWOOD," *STRANGERS ON A TRAIN*, and "A QUALIFIED FAREWELL"

On September 21, 1944, two weeks after *Double Indemnity* opened in New York, Chandler wrote Charles W. Morton, managing editor of the *Atlantic Monthly*, saying that he would like to do a "devastating" article dealing with writers in Hollywood. The following March 5, while he was working on *The Blue Dahlia*, he again wrote Morton, promising to write the article in April. "Writers in Hollywood" appeared in the November *Atlantic Monthly*, and, later that same month, Chandler wrote that he had "been blackballed at all the best bistros and call houses for my remarks in November Atlantic" (postcard to Sandoe, November 28, 1945).

The article certainly ruffled feathers; many people felt that Chandler was bad-mouthing the industry while profiting from it. When Charles Brackett commented that Chandler's books were not good enough, nor his pictures bad enough, to justify the article, Chandler noted, in a letter of December 12, 1945, to Morton, that had his books been any worse, he should not have been invited to Hollywood, and had they been any better, he should not have come (*Selected Letters*, p. 56). But industry response to the article had little effect on the momentum of Chandler's career, which at this time was considerable, and still gathering.

"Writers in Hollywood" dramatizes Chandler's discomfort in Hollywood, even at this early stage, when times were good. It points to the basic antagonism between his notion of his role as a writer and his perception of the Hollywood system. This antagonism eventually led to his withdrawal from Hollywood altogether.

His thesis is that "the motion picture is a great industry as well as a defeated art" ("Writers in Hollywood," p. 52). He felt it is a defeated art because of the failure on the part of those in power to realize that "the basic art of motion pictures is the screenplay; it is fundamental; without it there is nothing. Everything derives from the screenplay" ("Writers in Hollywood," p. 50). He called Hollywood a "showman's paradise," interested not in nurturing art but in exploiting talent. He felt that its writers have no real creative autonomy and are mere employees of uncreative producers who decide what is to be written and then alter it at their whim. He regretted that the producers consider a good film not a medium for creative expression, but a "vehicle for some glamorpuss with two expressions and eighteen changes of costume, or for some male idol of the muddled millions, with a permanent hangover, six worn-out acting tricks, the build of a lifeguard, and the mentality of a chicken-strangler" ("Writers in Hollywood," p. 52).

Chandler noted that although screenwriters are paid well, they have little prestige within the industry, and their names are seldom used in marketing a film. He closed the article by noting that the nicest thing Hollywood can say to a writer is that he is too good to be only a writer.

"Writers in Hollywood" dramatizes the tug-of-war between literature and film that occupied Chandler throughout the late 1940s. His notion of a writer was a literary one: a private creator, such as a novelist or a poet. He could never reconcile that notion with the essentially collaborative role a writer has in film, and his indignation at story conferences and studio work schedules bears this out. For him, the final insult lay in the fact that the writer could not even claim creative ownership of the finished product. Producers might rewrite it, or directors might change it on the set. Chandler believed that the place writers held in the Hollywood system almost necessarily turned them into well-paid hacks, and that those with talent either accepted this or left.

"Writers in Hollywood" points to Chandler's long-standing fascination with the Hollywood system itself. In a letter of January 12, 1946, to Alfred A. Knopf, he called it "a great subject for a novel—probably the greatest still untouched. . . . It is like one of these South American palace revolutions conducted by officers in comic opera uniforms—only when the thing is over the ragged dead men lie in rows against the walls and you suddenly know that this is not funny, this is the Roman circus, and damn near the end of a civilization."[1]

A year later, in the *Atlantic Monthly* of January 1947, Chandler wrote that although the Hollywood system would make a wonderful topic for a novel, a successful Hollywood novel had not yet been written. The only one to come even close to succeeding was F. Scott Fitzgerald's unfinished *The Last Tycoon.*

Chandler felt that previous Hollywood novels had failed because the writers had tried to depict the system in terms of the people in it, when it is the system itself that is most interesting:

> The story that is Hollywood will some day be written and it will not primarily be about people at all, but about a process, a very living and terrible and lovely process, the making of a single picture, almost any hard-fought and ambitious picture, but preferably a heartbreaker to almost everyone concerned. In that process will be all the agony and heroism of human affairs, and it will be all in focus, because the process will be the story. Everything that matters in Hollywood goes into this process. The rest is waste. Above all the vice is the waste, and the vicious people, of whom there are many and always will be, because Hollywood is starved for talent, for a single facet of a single talent, and will pay the price in disgust because it has to. Why should it not? The theater always has, and the theater is a pygmy compared with Hollywood.[2]

On the one hand, then, Chandler felt Hollywood treated writers dismally, but on the other, he felt it provided a magnificent topic for writers. In addition, he felt that film had virtually unlimited potential as an art form. Granted, he felt that the few films he admired had been made in spite of the system, but they *had* been made, and the system that had destroyed so much had also made them possible. Throughout his Hollywood career he would continue to address himself in print to the workings of the industry he found so oppressive and so fascinating.

His choice of a forum is significant. The *Atlantic Monthly* is a prestigious literary journal. It offered Chandler little financial recompense, especially when compared with what Hollywood was giving him, but it did give him a toehold in the palace of high art. The fact that Chandler took the time and risked Hollywood censure in the articles he wrote for the *Atlantic Monthly* indicated, at least to himself, that he had not abandoned the world of literature for Hollywood, that he was still a writer in his sense of the term. He saw himself with one foot in two separate camps, each having much to offer, but each antagonistic to the other.

During this time, he was actively involved in studio work. After the completion of *The Blue Dahlia* in the spring of 1945, and a period of needed rest, he contracted with Metro-Goldwyn-Mayer in July 1945 to write a screenplay based upon his own *The Lady in the Lake.* Chandler originally took the job to protect his story from being ruined by a studio hack. A producer he respected, George Haight, was assigned to the project, but Chandler quickly lost interest in it. Once more he found himself writing in an office—this time on the fourth floor of the Thalberg Building on the Culver City lot. He left and, defying studio policy, worked at home. He soon became bored with what he had originally sought to protect: his own story. On August 18, 1945, he wrote Sandoe: "Am working on a screen treatment of *The Lady in the Lake* for M-G-M. It bores me stiff. The last time I'll ever do a screenplay of a book I wrote myself. Just turning over dry bones" (*Selected Letters,* p. 53).

Possibly as a way of dealing with this boredom, Chandler became what George Haight has described to me as "doubly creative": he began rewriting his own story line, moving it in new directions. Haight feels that this virtually negated the reason the studio purchased the novel in the first place and tried to get Chandler to follow more closely the novel's narrative line, but Chandler refused.

Chandler was not pleased with the work he produced; he

described it as full of loose ends and tired attitudes. He was also annoyed because the studio wanted to put the film into production by November. What he was viewing as a preliminary draft would actually be something very close to a final shooting script. At the end of the contracted thirteen weeks, he left this preliminary script behind and refused to have anything more to do with the project.

The script of *The Lady in the Lake* marks the only time Chandler worked on a film based upon one of his own novels. It is unwieldy (at 195 pages, it would probably run over three hours if filmed) and, as Chandler said, full of loose ends. Although it is unfair to consider it a Chandler work since he abandoned it, it does point to a number of his assumptions about screenwriting.

On April 20, 1947, he wrote Jean Bethel that although *The Maltese Falcon* came closest, "the really good mystery picture has not yet been made":

> The reason is that the detective in the picture always has to fall for some girl, whereas the real distinction of the detective's personality is that, as a detective, he falls for nobody. He is the avenging justice, the bringer of order out of chaos, and to make his doing this part of a trite boy-meets-girl story is to make it silly. But in Hollywood you cannot make a picture which is not essentially a love story, that is to say, a story in which sex is paramount. (*Selected Letters*, p. 90)

Chandler was not happy about this situation, but he does not seem to have fought it. His most basic plot alteration in basing a script upon his own novel was to take the relatively minor character of Adrienne Fromsett from the novel and make her a central character in the script. Much of the script involves romantic interactions between her and Marlowe that are virtually without parallel in the novel. The novel ended somberly with the virtual suicide of the main villain; the script ends with a cheery romantic scene between Marlowe and Fromsett. This shift in emphasis points to Chandler's acceptance of what he considered the realities of work in Hollywood.

In the novel, Marlowe is requested by Derace Kingsley, an executive in a perfume firm, to search for his missing wife. In the script, Marlowe is asked by Fromsett, Kingsley's executive assistant, to find the wife, whom Fromsett hopes to incriminate and replace. She and Kingsley work not for a perfume firm, but for Kingsley Publications. The script introduces the firm's product, and Miss Fromsett, with a close-up

> of two beautifully manicured feminine hands holding artist's sketch for the cover of a very lurid pulp magazine. The sketch on heavy cardboard shows a beautiful young girl, pressed back against the wall in an attitude of conventional terror, her mouth open to scream, etc. Her dress is partly torn off and on her arm ugly red scratches drip blood. On her, advances a savage-looking individual holding a blood-stained cheese grater.

Over this shot we hear Fromsett's cool, cultivated voice saying, "Not enough gore, Dick. Not nearly enough gore" (Chandler's script, p. 11).

Marlowe, dissatisfied with being a detective, hopes to sell her a story entitled "He Woke Up Bleeding." Fromsett has exploited his literary ambitions in order to get him to hunt secretly for Kingsley's wife. Much of the script has Marlowe and Fromsett going over the evidence together—she approaches murder from a literary standpoint, perceiving the evidence as a fictional detective might, and Marlowe gives the "real-life" approach. Their collaboration recalls the one between Marlowe and Anne Riordan in the novel *Farewell, My Lovely*. Chandler seems to have felt that one way to introduce a credible sympathetic female character was to make her a kind of a codetective.

Like Fromsett, Marlowe is introduced in a kind of misleadingly lurid way without parallel in the novel. We first see him in jail as a murderer is being dragged off by guards for sentencing. As Marlowe is being brought into the booking room, a sergeant asks Lieutenant Degarmo (who turns out to be the major villain) why he arrested Marlowe. Degarmo says, "He beat up on a female impersonator," and the sergeant retorts, "Is that bad?" (Chandler's script, p. 3).

This particular incident is barely developed, but the fact of female impersonation foreshadows a major plot device in the script. The dead lady found in the lake is not who she is originally thought to be, but her body is used to impersonate that of another woman, who wishes to be thought dead. That other woman is later murdered by Degarmo in a savage, mutilating way wholly appropriate for the cover of one of Kingsley's magazines.

It is interesting that Chandler presented Marlowe as fed up with detective work because, at this point in his own career, he was tiring of Marlowe. While he was working on this script, he was also writing *The Little Sister*, the Marlowe novel most loaded with self-loathing and despair, the only one of his novels Chandler said he actively disliked. It is not unlikely that many of the feelings of artistic stagnation and prostitution that informed *The Little Sister* were also beginning to erupt in the script for *The Lady in the Lake*.

When Chandler left the project, Metro-Goldwyn-Mayer brought in Steve Fisher to re-do the script; Chandler refused screen credit. Curiously, although Haight's main objection to Chandler's work seems to have been that he deviated too much from the plotline of the novel, Fisher does not seem to have returned to the novel, but rather used Chandler's script as the basis for the final shooting script. Even more curiously, the final film retains most of Chandler's deviations from the novel's plotline and in fact bears less resemblance to the novel than does Chandler's script.

Given these basic alterations, Chandler's script follows the narrative line of his novel reasonably closely. Fisher developed a new thematic structure; eliminated all scenes at Puma Lake (where the "lady" is found); and eliminated major characters found in the novel and in Chandler's script, including Sheriff Jim Patton, Dr. Almore and his murdered wife, Bill Chess, and Detective Talley's wife. Fisher used many of Chandler's scenes and much of his dialogue, but built them into a dominating point-of-view structure for the film, with a major Christmas motif. He also, in developing close parallels between Marlowe's relationship with Fromsett and Degarmo's relationship with Mildred Haviland, established a rigidly oppositional, partially sadomasochistic structure of sexual interactions. These draw little from Chandler's script and are discussed in chapter 7.

Fisher also dropped a very interesting scene without parallel in the novel, in which, to provoke a police investigation into corruption within their ranks, Marlowe himself confesses to a murder he is investigating.

Chandler seems to have detached himself completely from the project. Everything about its progress seems to have annoyed him, from the final script to Robert Montgomery's point-of-view technique for shooting the film, and especially the fact that, after he had walked away from it, the film was successful with many critics and at the box office. Haight doubts that Chandler ever even saw the finished film, and says he certainly never saw it at the studio.

Chandler did no significant film work for the remainder of 1945. In the fall, he and Cissy went on a vacation, and, in November, "Writers in Hollywood" appeared. His Paramount contract required that he return to work in January 1946, but he refused, desiring to renegotiate his contract and using Cissy's illness as the ostensible reason he could not report to the studio. Paramount placed him on technical suspension.

Paramount does not seem to have known what to do with him. After *The Blue Dahlia* chaos, the studio wanted to figure out a way it could keep Chandler working without his suffering a breakdown. Chandler's agent proposed that Chandler be paid a flat fee for a film script and be free of the pressure of deadlines. Paramount suggested instead that Chandler become a writer-director, like Billy Wilder, or even produce his own films. Chandler declined on the grounds that it would involve investing too much of his time in Hollywood. The situation was not resolved by January, and Chandler would not return to work until it was.[3]

By April, he had reached a truce with the studio, and it began sending him novels for possible screen adaptation. By May, when *The Blue Dahlia* opened in New York, he had begun work on *The Innocent Mrs. Duff*, a novel he had talked the studio into purchasing.

Chandler held the novel and its author, Elisabeth Sanxay Holding, in particularly high regard. Four years later, he would write of her: "For my money she's the top suspense writer of them all" (*Raymond Chandler Speaking*, p. 60). One of the reasons that he felt so strongly about this novel may be that it provides almost a textbook example of his ideal for mystery fiction.

Chandler was always aware that his success as a novelist was of a limited kind. He knew that he was often classified as a mystery novelist, not a novelist, and that that designation implied inferiority. This fact began to obsess him as his fame grew, and he dealt with it in various ways. In the early 1940s, partially through the efforts of James Sandoe (who later reviewed mystery fiction for the *New York Herald Tribune*), many newspapers and magazines began to review his novels as fiction and not as "mysteries." This pleased Chandler, and, as Philip Durham has observed in his book on Chandler, he never gave his novels titles that explicitly designated mysteries, such as *The Mystery of . . .* or *The Strange Case of . . . .* But, much as this would seem to point to a gradual estrangement of Chandler from mystery writing, he never jumped the track. He wrote only Philip Marlowe detective novels until his death.

This fact may have moved him in an apparently contradictory direction, and he spent a great deal of time not sidestepping, but defending, the mystery form. His first *Atlantic Monthly* essay, "The Simple Art of Murder" (1944), was his earliest, highly visible attempt. However, he continually felt himself in a double bind and, referring to the literary critic J. B. Priestley, capsulized his plight:

> He likes my books. . . . then he wishes I would write something without murders in it. Now isn't that a typical attitude? You slam murder mysteries à la Edmund Wilson, because they are usually written, you say, by people who can't write well. And the moment you find someone who you are willing to admit can write well, you tell him he should not be writing murder mysteries. (*Selected Letters*, p. 262)

He realized there was an enormous amount of prejudice against the genre in which he worked, and at the same time, felt a good deal of pride in having increased, by means of his work, critical respect for the genre. He wrote a good deal on the art of mystery writing, presenting as his ideal a novel that "ostensibly a mystery and keeping the spice of mystery, will actually be a novel of character and atmosphere with an overtone of violence and fear" (*Selected Letters*, p. 170). The definition suits *The Innocent Mrs. Duff* perfectly.

Jacob Duff is a wealthy executive whose life is collapsing. In the novel's first sentence, we learn that he is upset because he is gaining weight. We then learn that he is unhappy with his attractive second wife of one year, Reggie, whom he compares unfavorably with his first wife, now four years dead. As the novel progresses, it becomes apparent that his unhappiness is pervasive and profound. He is enraged at trifling annoyances and, when none appear, manufactures incidents, or interprets events so as to arouse his anger. He begins to drink secretly and heavily, even placing gin in water glasses in the morning to make it appear that he is drinking water; eventually, when in public, he will mix gin with whiskey to make it appear as if he is drinking a weak highball.

With no real reason, he begins to suspect that his wife is having an affair with his chauffeur, Nolan, and, after failing to entrap them into a compromising situation, fires Nolan anyway. When a friend of Nolan's objects, a fight ensues; Duff accidentally kills the man and then deliberately conceals the body. He eventually rehires Nolan, who produces evidence that Mrs. Duff may really be having an affair with a Captain Ferris. The two plot to kill Ferris, and eventually Nolan does kill him. After implicating Duff, Nolan escapes. There had never been any affair, and Mrs. Duff stands stalwartly by her husband. When Duff is placed in a police car at the end for arrest on probable manslaughter charges, he commits suicide, more from terror at not being able to drink in jail than from any remorse.

The novel is primarily a psychological one, chronicling the collapse of a depraved man. It is particularly interesting because it toys with our expectations of mystery fiction: Mrs. Duff seems much too good to be true, for example, and the experienced reader of mystery fiction would naturally view this as an indication of concealed and sinister behavior. Mr. Duff's very repellent nature leads us to feel that he deserves all he gets, but that his fears and resentments may not all be paranoia. Ultimately, the murder actually committed becomes largely irrelevant to the focus of the novel, which is Duff's collapse. To a careful reader, that collapse has been clearly inevitable from the beginning.

Duff's paranoia dovetails perfectly with the mystery aura of the novel. He suspects plots, sees clues everywhere, some of which can be pursued with possible result. But it is not at base a mystery novel, in what Chandler would see as the derogatory sense of the term. It is not an elaborate puzzle to be deciphered by a calculating reader able to assess the clues and put everything in place; it is a description of a man whose pathology is to see and to manufacture sinister clues everywhere. Ironically, he becomes involved in a real murder, but the reader following that murder mystery to its conclusion never gets there. The murderer gets away, and his motives are never fully known. The real path of the novel has been clear from the beginning; it will be, in Chandler's definition, "ostensibly a mystery and keeping the spice of a mystery," but actually a "novel of character and atmosphere with an overtone of violence and fear." The novel represented an ideal Chandler never felt he attained in his own fiction.

But however much Chandler admired the novel, his attempt to write a screenplay from it quickly deteriorated. By May 30, he wrote: "I'm bored with it already. I don't think I'll do any more pictures unless I write the story myself. The business of adapting things for the screen is more work than it is worth. When you write directly for the screen it may not be topnotch, but there is a feeling of fluidity and improvisation that I like" (Letter to Sandoe, May 30, 1946). Later he would blame the producers for the collapse of the project, claiming that they would deflate his interest in the story simply by referring to the main characters as "Ladd and Caulfield" (the actors they planned to star in the film) rather than by their fictional names. At another point, he wrote that Alexander Knox had agreed to play the lead. Such a change in lead actors would obviously mean reshaping the role. He worked with a collaborator for a while, but by the end of the summer, after having put in the contracted number of weeks on the script, he left Paramount with the screenplay unfinished. His main complaint was that the pressure of having to work with a studio producer—whom he felt was continually looking over his shoulder and trying to impose his own personality on the project—drained all his interest in and ability to function creatively on the project.

Now that Chandler's Paramount contract had run out, Swanson arranged a meeting with M-G-M executives, but Chandler said he had no intention of working for dominating personalities like David O. Selznick or Samuel Goldwyn. He still desired working conditions he had not yet achieved—a freedom from deadlines and what he considered the unnatural pressures of studio supervision—and he was willing to hold out until he got them.

Although he had not completed a project since *The Blue Dahlia* over a year and a half before and had been involved in two uncompleted projects, his star was still rising in Hollywood. *The Blue Dahlia* had not been released until the spring of 1946 (Chandler would soon receive an Academy Award nomination for the screenplay), and *The Big Sleep* had finally opened in August and was enjoying great success. *Lady in the Lake* was nearly ready for what would be another successful release, and Twentieth Century-Fox was preparing a film based upon Chandler's novel *The High Window*. All of these things increased his bargaining power in Hollywood, but, in a characteristic action, he left town. He and Cissy moved down the coast from Los Angeles to La Jolla, where he would spend most of the rest of his life. His success did not increase his involvement in the industry but enabled him to be more independent in his dealings with it. The physical move out of Los Angeles was only one of a series of actions that increasingly placed greater distance between Chandler and the film world.

The next film project in which Chandler became involved was a brief story idea that never seems to have gotten beyond the outline stage. It exists in a seven-page summary at the Chandler archive at UCLA, is entitled "Backfire (Story for the Screen)," and is dated December 1946. It is worth looking at in some detail not only because it is not generally available, but because it is apparently the first original screen project he worked on since *The Blue Dahlia*. There would only be one more.

The story concerns George, a returned serviceman who learns that his wife had been killed in an automobile accident while he was overseas. He moves to his wife's hometown and is introduced by Mary, a friend of his late wife, to Joe, who is also a returned serviceman. The two men decide to room together. Unknown to anyone, Joe had had an affair with George's wife and, when she became too possessive, had murdered her and made it appear to be an accident. He fears that George has come to town to trap him. Strange, suspicious accidents begin to happen to George, who confides to Joe his fear that someone is out to get him. Things become further complicated because both men are in love with Mary.

George receives a letter implicating Joe in his wife's murder. He reveals it to Joe, who tries to kill George. Joe's gun, the barrel of which had been plugged by George, backfires and kills Joe. George is also able to prove that his wife had been murdered.

Although the story at times relies on bizarre coincidences and esoteric information (George establishes that his wife was murdered when he discovers that her hyoid bone was broken, somehow proving that she died not from automobile injuries but because a man had swung her around by her ankles and smashed her head on a rock), it is interesting for its many relationships to the story line of *The Blue Dahlia*. Both stories involve a returning serviceman who learns his marriage has been destroyed while he was away. In each case, he learns his wife had been unfaithful with a man much flashier than himself. In addition, in both cases, the flashier man had discarded the hero's wife, increasing the hero's humiliation. Furthermore, the two men compete for the same woman: here it is Mary; in *The Blue Dahlia*, it is Eddie Harwood's wife. And finally, in both cases, the adulterer dies not at the hands of the hero but as the direct result of his own villainy.

There is an added similarity in "Backfire" to Chandler's original idea for *The Blue Dahlia:* a man is unknowingly involved in events having the most overwhelming implications for himself and those close to him. Since he hasn't the faintest idea of these implications, he acts in such a way as to bring them closer and closer to home. In "Backfire," George's growing friendship for Joe and gradual involvement with Mary only increase Joe's fears and George's own danger. In the original idea for *The Blue Dahlia*, Buzz's attempts to help Johnny implicate him more and more directly; the fact that he was to have killed Johnny's wife in her apartment after having been invited there by her also parallels the sexual involvement of Joe with George's wife.

Interestingly, both stories may have had their source in an undated entry in Chandler's notebooks called "Story Idea: Revenge":

> A man, greatly wronged, hunts down another man (who does not know him), makes friends with him, gets his confidence, then starts dropping idle hints which get the hunted man suspicious (without his knowing how to show it). Finally he gets desperate, things begin to happen, and the story ends in an attempt to murder the hero which backfires, killing the hunted man. With a faint enigmatic smile the hero walks out of the story. (He fixed it to backfire—see "The Murder of My Aunt.")

> Ideally this should start with the murder of the hero's wife by an unknown; hero suspected—badly roughed around by cops, finally released with much untold on both sides.[4]

Chandler had a good deal of trouble, especially as he grew older, developing new story ideas and would frequently return to earlier material. He freely admitted that much of the material

for his novels had been "cannibalized" from his earlier short
fiction, much of which was written for *Black Mask* Magazine.
Often the process of reworking the material became so elaborate
that one suspects that it would have been easier for him to have
developed a wholly new idea, but the old material seems to have
given him a useful foundation upon which to work.

Chandler's next film project, *Playback*, which absorbed nearly
all of 1947, seems to have had its origin in "I'll Be Waiting," a
story he published in the *Saturday Evening Post* in 1939. In the
story, Tony Reseck, a hotel detective, becomes suspicious of an
unaccompanied woman who has checked into a tower suite. He
recalls another woman who checked into a tower suite, stayed a
week, and then committed suicide by leaping from her balcony.
This suspicion becomes a false lead, and the story soon takes an
altogether different direction, but the idea seems to have per-
colated within Chandler for the next eight years and provided
the basis for *Playback*.

Playback marks the financial high point and the virtual end of
Chandler's Hollywood career. He was finally able to get, with
Universal International in spring 1947, a screenwriting contract
that only his still growing popularity made possible.

> My next job, however, is to do a job for Universal on one of the
> most unusual deals ever made in Hollywood, or so I am told.
> They pay me a large sum of money and a percentage of the
> picture to write them a screenplay, and they only get the picture
> rights. The unusual feature . . . is that they do *not* employ me,
> but merely agree to buy the motion picture rights to something
> I write in my own way and without any supervision. Of course I
> can't control what they do with it in production. I tried to get
> that, but it was a little too rich for their blood. It is like a studio
> buying the rights to a screenplay a writer has turned out on his
> own time, with the difference that they gamble before I write a
> word. (Letter to Sandoe, March 8, 1947)

Chandler would be working with men whom he had known
and liked at Paramount: William Dozier was now executive
producer at Universal, and Joseph Sistrom was to be the film's
producer. Chandler's salary was to be $4,000 a week—more than
he had ever received—and his working conditions were nearly
all he had ever sought.

The contract was secured on the basis of a five-page story idea
Chandler's agent, Swanson, had submitted to the studio. The

idea is accompanied, in the Chandler archive, by a short note from Chandler to Swanson that reads: "Swanie: I think it stinks. Ray." But this was not an unusual perception of Chandler at the beginning, or at virtually any stage, of the projects on which he worked.

The story idea is little more than a basic situation and various possibilities for plot development. It differs a good deal from the script of *Playback* that Chandler eventually developed and that difference, as well as the projected lines of plot development in the original idea, reveals a good deal about the way Chandler worked out his stories.

The story idea opens with a shot of a covered corpse being removed by hospital authorities from a hotel alley. Much of the story would be told in flashback and would deal with a crucial week in the life of a woman who decides to spend it in the tower suite of a hotel, under an assumed name; to accept what comes; and, at the end of the week, to jump to her death. During that week, the tragedies and frustrations of her life would occur in capsule form, making it appear that she brought her destiny with her.

The woman's drunken husband had died under suspicious circumstances and, although she had been exonerated from any responsibility, her innocence has been questioned. In the situation developed in the story idea, she is escorted to a hotel party by a local masher, a prominent politician's son. At the party, the masher becomes rude, the woman threatens him, and the host throws him out. Later the woman finds the masher dead in her room, with her gun in his hand, and she goes to the host for help. The host is a man of troubled conscience, who lives off the ill-gotten wealth of his father, a crooked politician. His father had possessed evidence incriminating the masher's father, but had been shot in office. The host offers to help the woman, who tells him part of her past and prepares to commit suicide. Instead, she faints and he kisses her.

Chandler's possibilities for resolving the situation include the fact that the audience does not know whether or not the woman murdered her husband; the fact that the masher's father, becoming convinced that the woman was part of a plot to murder his son, is consumed with a desire for revenge; and the fact that the only way the host can clear the woman is to learn more about her past and to do so he must throw in with his father's crooked cronies, something he has long resisted. The woman does not want him to make this sacrifice and feels that the best way out of the situation is to do what she originally came there to do.

Chandler closes the story idea by stating that those are the basic elements of the story, and that the identity of the body originally found in the hotel alley is still unknown.

A significant element of this story idea is the criminal aspect of back-room politics. It is a pervasive theme in nearly all of Chandler's work, and particularly recalls his story entitled "Guns at Cyrano's" (published in *Black Mask* in January 1936), whose main character, Ted Carmody, is also the son of a crooked politician and uncomfortable about living off of his father's dirty money. The film story, as Chandler originally conceived it, would probably have dealt with the infighting of corrupt political groups as a context for a developing romance between two tainted people—the woman tainted by her husband's suspicious death and her own suicidal despair, and the man by his crooked connections. Chandler's full script, however, dropped most of the political implications and took an entirely different direction.

The 224-page typescript, dated September 30, 1947, and described as a first-draft continuity "property of Universal-International Pictures," is in the UCLA Chandler archive. It opens in a North Carolina courthouse on the last day of a murder trial. The brief opening exchange between the bailiff and the clerk, as the jury returns, shows that Chandler had lost none of his skill at writing dialogue:

> CLERK: Verdict?
> BAILIFF: Yes.
> CLERK [*lowering voice*]: Which way?
> BAILIFF: Have to ask?
> CLERK: I'll inform the judge.

We quickly learn that the trial concerns the death of Henry Kinsolving's son, and that Kinsolving, who owns the town, has exerted his considerable influence to have his son's wife declared guilty. A juror objects to Kinsolving's pressure, and using a legal technicality, the courageous judge invalidates the guilty verdict and sets the wife free. The enraged Kinsolving vows to pursue her and ruin her life.

After this powerful opening, the terrified woman assumes her maiden name, Betty Mayfield, and boards a westbound train. A masher learns her secret and follows her to San Francisco, where he demands that she accompany him to Vancouver. Afraid of discovery and caring little about her fate or ultimate destination, she agrees.

In Vancouver, it becomes clear that the masher, Larry Mitchell, has spent much of his life living off women and hopes to blackmail Betty. At a hotel party hosted by Clark Brandon, Larry becomes publicly rude, Betty threatens him, and Clark tells him to leave. When Betty finds Larry dead in her room, she cries: "No, no—dear God, not again." Clark, apparently attracted to her, offers his help. She contemplates suicide, faints; he kisses her, and, numbed, she says: "It's too late for that, too. Too late for everything."

Jeff Killaine, a well-mannered detective of the Canadian police, who had been at the party, is assigned to the case. Despite much of the evidence and despite the fact that Betty refuses to reveal her past, Killaine believes her to be innocent. He gradually falls in love with her.

A sleazy private detective from San Francisco arrives to complicate matters, and is quickly murdered. When a warrant is issued for Betty's arrest, Clark prepares to help her escape by sea in his cabin cruiser. Killaine discovers that Clark killed Larry, who had been blackmailing him (Clark also murdered the private detective), and planned to drown Betty to divert suspicion from himself. In the final confrontation, which comes after a motorboat chase, Betty shoots Clark, who is about to shoot the unarmed Killaine ("This time, it seems I really killed a man"). Betty and Killaine then call one another by their first names and seem headed for true love.

The language in the script of *Playback* frequently resembles that of Chandler's prose, as in the description of a low-life bar: "There isn't a thing in the joint that could be damaged by being dropped out of a third-story window," or in the line of dialogue delivered by a woman attempting to recover from a bad night: "All I want is too much coffee and too many cigarettes."

The script bears an interesting structural relationship to Chandler's last major novel, *The Long Goodbye*, in that both deal with the relationship of three men to one attractive woman:

in the *Playback* script, Larry Mitchell, Clark Brandon, and Jeff Killaine are all attracted to Betty Mayfield; in *The Long Goodbye*, Terry Lennox, Roger Wade, and Marlowe are all attracted to Eileen Wade. Each work also develops a central character who appears sympathetic for much of the story and ultimately turns out to be a villain: in the *Playback* script, it is Clark Brandon; in *The Long Goodbye*, it is Terry Lennox. Killaine can be seen as a kind of Marlowe figure, but beyond the fact that both men are detectives of integrity, there really is not much resemblance. A more interesting area of similarity lies in the fact that both works are set in a kind of postmortem psychic space. Betty clearly believes her life to be over after the trial, and her salvation at the end comes almost as a resurrection; similarly, Marlowe, in *The Long Goodbye*, believes that Terry Lennox actually is dead for much of the novel and does most of what he does out of loyalty to his dead friend. When Lennox turns up alive at the end, what has become a new life for him is a betrayal of the old one for Marlowe.

Chandler used *Playback* as the basis for his last, and least, novel, also entitled *Playback*, and although resemblances between the two works exist, they do not have the resonance of resemblances with *The Long Goodbye*.

By September 14, 1947, Chandler would write Sandoe that "I am on the last leg of this beastly screenplay. I have hated it more than anything I ever did." He goes on to describe that his agent was pressuring him to complete it by the contracted deadline, because Hollywood was in a state of violent retrenchment and the studio would be eager to get out of the expensive contract it had with Chandler, since it was way out of line with contracts then being negotiated. The two letters to Sandoe—the March letter describing the terms of the contract, and the September letter describing its tenuousness—in many ways bracket the pinnacle of Chandler's Hollywood career. In March, he was riding high; in September, amidst evidence of general industry collaspe, Chandler was no longer "hot" and able to dictate his own terms. He was holding on to the remains of a deal the likes of which he would never be able to secure again, and his career was in decline. He was able to get two extensions and worked on the script of *Playback* into early 1948, but the film was never made, and he never again wrote an original film script.

In a letter written a decade later, Chandler explained why the script was never filmed:

> And one of the best films I wrote was never produced, partly because the studio . . . was, as I heard, on the edge of collapse at the time, and partly because the locale, Vancouver, B.C., has uncertain weather and no equipment for protection shots—that is, . . . sets where indoor shots may be made while waiting for good weather outdoors. I tried to buy this thing back, but they would rather write it off their tax returns. They paid me a very large sum of money (I was a "hot" writer then, I am not now) for an original screenplay I hadn't even written, and they paid it whether they liked it or not. It was an unusual sort of deal, I suppose, but the executive producer happened to be Bill Dozier, my first story editor at Paramount, and I imagine he had some confidence in me, because I had (unwillingly) rescued several turkeys for him. I don't regard myself in any way as a really good screenwriter. I am a good dialogue writer, but not a good constructionist.[5]

His assessment of his screenwriting abilities is one generally agreed upon. Toward the end of his Hollywood career and for the rest of his life, he would often express the desire to try his hand at writing plays for the London stage. Part of the reason lay in his affection for England and his belief that he could get a play produced relatively easily, since his critical reputation was higher in England than it was in America; but he also came to realize that his skill at dialogue would be much more central to the success of a stage work than it was to a film. His awareness of the component elements of film had grown in the short time since he had written (in "Writers in Hollywood") that "the basic art of motion pictures is the screenplay; it is fundamental, without it, there is nothing." He now knew that film was a more complex form than he had previously realized and that the screenwriter was not as fundmentally important as he had believed. He expressed this awareness in "Oscar Night in Hollywood," an article that appeared in the *Atlantic Monthly* of March 1948.

"Oscar Night in Hollywood," like "Writers in Hollywood," deals with the behind-the-scenes workings of the film industry. It emphasizes Chandler's perception that Oscars are not really awards for artistic merit, as they pretend to be, but are awards for box-office success. The general indifference to technical achievements and to foreign films is seen as evidence of this. But as he had done in the past and would continue to do, he did not dismiss the form for what he considered its often paltry achievement. In fact, he declared his respect for its potentialities. In this, he demonstrates his much more sophisticated awareness of the nature of film as an art:

> But the motion picture is *not* a transplanted literary or dramatic art, any more than it is a plastic art. It has elements of all these, but in its essential structure it is much closer to music, in the sense that its finest effects can be independent of precise meaning, that its transitions can be more eloquent than the high-lit scenes, and that its dissolves and camera movements, which cannot be censored, are often far more emotionally effective than its plots, which can. Not only is the motion picture an art, but it is the one entirely new art that has been evolved on this planet for hundreds of years. It is the only art at which we of this generation have any possible chance to greatly excel. [6]

By locating many of film's finest effects in such things as scene transitions and camera movements, as opposed to plot, Chandler implies that directors, editors, and cinematographers can contribute as significantly as writers to a film's artistic value. In "Writers in Hollywood," he had placed the screenwriter in an elevated position of aesthetic responsibility; in "Oscar Night in Hollywood," he presents the writer as one of many important contributors, and not necessarily the dominating one.

Early in his Hollywood career he had complained that screenwriters were not awarded the status they deserved in the industry. By 1948, he realized that the writer's status resulted not solely from the artistic insensitivity of the money men but was influenced by the nature of the form itself. Such an awareness could only accelerate his retreat from both the industry and the form. That form simply did not—and perhaps could not—offer him what he wanted.

The appearance of "Oscar Night in Hollywood" coincided with the penultimate stage of Chandler's detachment from Hollywood. When he finished *Playback*, he knew that the kind of money that the industry had recently been able to offer him was no longer as readily available, both because of panic within the industry—attendance was declining, federal antitrust legislation would soon force the studios to sell their theater chains (and thus the assured distribution of their product), and television was about to become a threatening alternative to theatrical films—and because he was no longer as salable a commodity as he had been only a year before. He had developed a reputation for being difficult, had not successfully completed a project since *The Blue Dahlia* three years earlier, and had demanded a salary and working conditions that few people in the industry were willing to meet.

This placed Chandler in a position he seems to have been moving toward for years. He no longer felt he needed Hollywood, and developing circumstances made it less and less likely that he would ever return to it. His work on *Playback* had earned him a great deal of money and had left him financially well off. In addition, his novels continued to sell well and provided a modest income on their own, as well as significant spin-off income. The films based upon his novels had earned him considerable royalty money, and radio and television provided additional markets for the now widely known and extremely profitable Philip Marlowe. In 1947, Swanson sold a Philip Marlowe radio program to CBS as a summer replacement for the "Bob Hope Show." Van Heflin played Marlowe, and Milton Geiger wrote the script. In September 1948, Chandler's new Hollywood agent, Ray Stark, sold "The Adventures of Philip Marlowe" to CBS as a regular radio series, starring Gerald Mohr as Marlowe. It was to run for two years, and later it returned from July through October 1951.[7]

Some projects did not work out for various reasons, but they testify to the access Chandler had to spin-off funds. He involved himself in negotiations for a Marlowe television series. Although television shows were produced based upon individual novels—*The Little Sister* and *The Long Goodbye*, soon after the publication of each—a series did not appear until 1959, after Chandler's death. He also turned down an offer of $1,200 a year to lend his name to a projected *Raymond Chandler's Mystery Magazine*.

Chandler's various income options made him financially independent of Hollywood. Since his style of living remained modest, he would never again have serious financial worries. Furthermore, he made a number of major business decisions in 1948 that indicate a desire to set new directions for himself. He had long been dissatisfied with his American publisher, Alfred A. Knopf, and moved to the Houghton Mifflin Company for his nearly completed *The Little Sister*. His New York agent for years had been Sydney Sanders, and his Hollywood agent was H. N. Swanson. He had broken with Sanders in late 1946 and, in 1948, signed with Brandt and Brandt of New York; whose Hollywood agent was Ray Stark.[8]

By September of 1948, Chandler had finished a first draft of *The Little Sister*. Its publication the following year made it his first novel since 1943 and marked for him a return to what he considered to be his vocation: novelist. This provided him with a good deal of self-justification. He could point to the novel's publication as proof that he had not been corrupted by the film world, that he had used Hollywood to obtain financial security, and that he had not gotten sucked into what he considered its mesmerizing whirl of high living and artistic emasculation.

During this period, he was, more and more, receiving serious attention from figures of literary respectability. There was, after World War II, a growing interest on the part of the literary establishment in the American hard-boiled detective story, which had been virtually under-the-counter material only a decade earlier. Serious defenders of the form most commonly trotted out Chandler and Dashiell Hammett as its masters. Chandler found his work being written about in serious journals by figures of such eminent literary respectability as W. H. Auden, J. B. Priestley, Somerset Maugham, Evelyn Waugh, and Eric Partridge.

Serious acceptance of Chandler's work was by no means universal, but the attention he was drawing at least marked a first step in bridging the gap between "mystery writer" and "novelist" that he found so annoying. Many of his commentators explicitly addressed that issue. Eric Partridge wrote: "The truth is that Raymond Chandler is a much more complex character, a deeper thinker, a sounder moralist and a better, more various writer than . . . several other critics have admitted. . . . Raymond Chandler is a serious artist, and a very considerable novelist."[9]

When *The Little Sister* was published in 1949, then, Chandler found himself not only financially independent of and physically distanced from Hollywood, but also returning after a six-year absence to the literary arena.

The novel's publication, however, was not for Chandler the event of unqualified jubilation that the surrounding circumstances might seem to make it. In fact, Chandler called it "the only book of mine I have actively disliked. It was written in a bad mood and I think that comes through" (Letter to Sandoe, October 14,

1949). The "bad mood" to which Chandler refers may be his unhappiness about what he considered his artistic stagnation in Hollywood, since the book was written during that period of his life. The "mood" may also point to a profound despair about his artistic future. Although he had initiated a number of activities that would appear to point to an artistic renaissance—the changing of publisher and business representatives, removal from Hollywood, the return to serious literary work—the work he actually accomplished may not have fulfilled his expectations.

He had long been aware of the constraints of the mystery genre and claimed to be bored with Marlowe as a character. He had also spoken on different occasions of the value of Hollywood as a topic for a major American novel in the F. Scott Fitzgerald tradition. His years in Hollywood would have given him the needed background to do such a novel himself, and his growing literary respectability would have assured the novel serious attention, but he never attempted it. In *The Little Sister*, he returned to Marlowe as his central character, and, although the novel deals more directly with Hollywood than do any of his other novels, the Hollywood aspect is relatively minor. Although the book marks Chandler's return to fiction, it also may have been for him a return to a tired old formula at a point in his career when he might have undertaken genuinely new artistic directions. His dislike of the novel may have been influenced by the fact that much of it was written during his conflicted Hollywood period, but it may also have represented for him a betrayal of his own artistic potential at a time when he was in a position to nuture it.

The mood of *The Little Sister* is pervasively bitter. The novel places Marlowe in a nearly relentless sequence of nasty and vicious human interactions. He is getting older and no richer, appears to be without friends, and is bored with his job—"the routine I go through is so tired and I'm half asleep on my feet."[10] His comment about policemen and the effect that their environment has upon them seems also to apply to himself: "Civilization had no meaning for them. All they saw of it was the failures, the dirt, the dregs, the aberrations and the disgust" (*The Little Sister*, p. 352). He describes himself as "a blank man. I had no face, no meaning, no personality, hardly a name. I didn't want to eat, I didn't even want a drink. I was a page from yesterday's calendar crumpled at the bottom of the waste basket" (*The Little Sister*, p. 354).

Marlowe realizes that his self-image pervades all he sees: "There are days like that. Everybody you meet is a dope. You begin to look at yourself in the glass and wonder" (*The Little Sister*, p. 241). In chapter 13, Marlowe makes embittered comments about nearly everything he observes: "Screen stars, phooey. The veterans of a thousand beds." He continually braces himself with the comment that provides a kind of coda for the chapter, and the book: "Hold it, Marlowe, you're not human tonight" (*The Little Sister*, p. 268).

Marlowe's bitterness extends to his view of Los Angeles. He says he used to like the town but that now it's a neon-lighted slum whose only distinctive quality, Hollywood, it loathes. Hollywood is not presented as a cause but rather as a symptom of a corrupted world.

At one point, Marlowe finds himself in a garden inside a film studio, talking to an apparently dotty old man with three boxers. He watches the man's boxers tear up the begonias in the garden, and he listens to the man talk of how the dogs frequently urinate all over his office. Marlowe figures "it was just Hollywood" but then learns the man is Jules Oppenheimer, who runs the studio. For no particular reason, Oppenheimer sums up the film industry:

> Fifteen hundred theaters is all you need. . . . The motion picture business is the only business in the world in which you can make all the mistakes there are and still make money. . . . Most expensive talent in the world. Give them anything they like, all the money they want. Why? No reason at all. Just habit. Doesn't matter a damn what they do or how they do it. Just give me fifteen hundred theaters. (*The Little Sister*, pp. 305–6)

Hollywood provides a continual presence in the novel— Marlowe's main client is a film star—and some of the characters have real-life parallels from Chandler's own Hollywood experience. Jules Oppenheimer shares a number of resemblances, including the interest in dogs, with Y. Frank Freeman, the Paramount studio head during Chandler's tenure there. Marlowe observes of an agent: "It could only happen in Hollywood, that an apparently sane man could walk up and down inside the house with a Piccadilly stroll and a monkey stick in his hand" (*The Little Sister*, p. 299). Billy Wilder was known to walk around his office sporting a malacca cane.

But *The Little Sister* can not really be called a "Hollywood novel," certainly not a Hollywood novel as Chandler himself defined one in the above-quoted *Atlantic Monthly* review. The interaction of Marlowe and Jules Oppenheimer is probably the sort of material dealing with the processes of the industry that Chandler would have considered ideal for such a novel, but the scene is an isolated one, and Oppenheimer never reappears. Hollywood is presented as monstrously self-inflating, bitchy, indecipherable, and decadent, although there are occasional instances of surprising decency. Curiously, although Chandler wrote the novel during his active career as a screenwriter, his presentation of the film industry differs little from the way he had presented it long before he had had any first-hand knowledge of it, for example, in his first two short stories, "Blackmailers Don't Shoot" and "Smart-Aleck Kill." If anything, his view had mellowed. In "Blackmailers Don't Shoot," a film star sets up her own kidnapping to generate publicity; she is presented as more cold-blooded than many of the gangsters. In *The Little Sister*, the film star who is being blackmailed turns out to be one of the most decent characters in the novel. This is not to say that the novel presents a positive view of Hollywood; it does not. *The Little Sister* has little positive to say about the film industry, but it says little about it in any case.

At this same time, however, when Chandler's removal from Hollywood was nearly complete, and his interest in it declining, his association with it in the public mind was growing. In the spring of 1949, the British film journal *Sequence* published a major article dealing with Chandler, with the films based upon his fiction, and with what its author, Harry Wilson, considered his substantial influence upon the film industry:

> But Chandler's real contribution to the cinema is in a style . . . to be found in the early films of this genre, notably *Farewell, My Lovely:* the feeling for the squalor and menace of a big city; the poetry of back-street, subway, and beer-parlour; the shine of wet streets after rain. . . . Just as Chandler has had many literary imitators, so has his work exercised a considerable influence on the treatment of crime and violence in the cinema.
>
> Films like *The Dark Corner, Fallen Angel, Cornered, Dead Reckoning, Build My Gallows High,* are all obvious derivatives; while even so relatively unimportant a film as *I Love Trouble* has certain unmistakable affinities with the Chandler methods of characterization, development, and treatment of backgrounds. He

has also helped to bring back to the cinema some of the healthy realism surrendered so carelessly in the early 'thirties to the demands of a minority censorship. What is certain, at any rate, is that since 1944 his work has done much to form the basis of a school of film making as indigenously American as the Western, the social comedy, the musical, and the gangster film of the 'twenties and 'thirties.[11]

At this point, then, Chandler's reputation had clearly outdistanced his own activity, and he was receiving credit for influencing an industry with which he had ceased to be involved. Almost.

He returned once. In 1950, he was asked to write the screenplay for Alfred Hitchcock's *Strangers on a Train*, based upon the Patricia Highsmith novel. He accepted: "Why am I doing it? Partly because I thought I might like Hitch, which I do, and partly because one gets tired of saying no, and someday I might want to say yes and not get asked. (*Raymond Chandler Speaking*, p. 132).

Some of the script had already been blocked out by Hitchcock and Whitfield Cook (who had just written *Stage Fright* for Hitchcock), but it needed tightening and it needed good dialogue. Chandler must have looked ideal for the job. In addition, a major character in the novel is a private detective of great personal integrity who embarks upon a personal crusade to find the murderer of his employer. Perhaps Hitchcock felt that the man who created Philip Marlowe would have a particular affinity with this aspect of the story.

In July 1950, Chandler contracted to write the script for Warner Brothers for $2,500 a week, with a five-week guarantee. He was allowed to work at home, and Hitchcock drove down to La Jolla for story conferences. By July 18, he had finished a first treatment.

Chandler had considerable respect for Hitchcock and as early as 1947 had spoken of him as one of the few intelligent directors in Hollywood. He seems to have looked forward to the collaboration, but, once it began, the pressure became intolerable to him. By mid-August, relations between the two men had begun to deteriorate. Once, while watching Hitchcock climb out of his limousine, Chandler said to his secretary: "Look at that fat bastard trying to get out of his car!" Warned that Hitchcock might hear him, he retorted: "What do I care?"[12] Although he was not always this provocative, the incident points to the anxiety story conferences produced in him. Hitchcock has said of Chandler: "Our association didn't work out at all. We'd sit together and I would say, 'Why not do it this way?' and he'd answer, 'Well, if you can puzzle it out, what do you need me for?' "[13]

Aside from the personality problems involved, their collaboration on the script revealed the radically different approaches to film the two men had. Chandler, as writer, was primarily concerned with story coherence and character development and could not understand Hitchcock's subordination of these things to other elements:

> The thing that amuses me about Hitchcock is the way he directs a film in his head before he knows what the story is. You find yourself trying to rationalize the shots he wants to make rather than the story. Every time you get set he jabs you off balance by wanting to do a love scene on top of the Jefferson Memorial or something like that. He has a strong feeling for stage business and mood and background, not so much for the guts of the business. I guess that's why some of his pictures lose their grip on logic and turn into wild chases. Well, it's not the worst way to make a picture. His idea of characters is rather primitive. Nice Young Man, Society Girl, Frightened Woman, Sneaky Old Beldame, Comic Relief, and so on. (*Raymond Chandler Speaking*, p. 132)

Clearly, Chandler's and Hitchcock's definitions of the "guts of the business" differed, and curiously, Chandler's desire to subordinate "stage business and mood and background" to plot contradicts his own description of film's "finest effects" in "Oscar Night in Hollywood."

But the problem of logic was a major one in the script and was never really solved. Part of it had to do with conflicts between each man's perceptions of the utility of Highsmith's novel as script material, as well as between each man's assumptions about filmmaking and about contemporary censorship codes.

In the novel, Guy Haines, a rising young architect, and Charles Bruno, a rich, pathological mother's boy, meet on a train. Bruno develops a deep but repressed homosexual attraction to Guy and wants to establish a strong friendship. He learns that Guy is unhappily married and comes up with a bizarre idea that they exchange murders, that he will murder Guy's hated wife if Guy will murder Bruno's hated father. Bruno is developed along overtly Freudian lines; he has textbook Oedipal feelings toward his parents and a repressed homosexual desire for Guy. On his own initiative, he murders Guy's wife and is exhilirated, feeling it to be the triumph of his life.

Bruno wants Guy to fulfill his part of the deal. When Guy refuses, Bruno haunts him and threatens to destroy his career as well as his relationship with his fiancée. Gradually, Bruno's desperate, alternately pathetic and threatening, insinuating pressure erodes Guy's self-control. He gives in, almost like a zombie, and murders Bruno's father.

This does not end Bruno's attempts to intrude upon Guy's life. He comes to Guy's wedding uninvited, befriends Guy's new wife, and makes a continual nuisance of himself.

A detective, Arthur Gerard, who had worked for Bruno's father, makes it his personal crusade to uncover his killer. Bruno's self-propelled association with Guy makes the original idea for the murders—that they be committed by strangers without discoverable motive—nonfunctional, and Gerard begins to see the connection. Bruno drowns after making a drunken fool of himself on an outing with Guy's friends. By this time, Guy's personality has almost completely eroded. He feels a desperate compulsion to confess all to his dead wife's lover, and when he does, the man doesn't care. Eventually, Gerard hears Guy's confession. The last words of the novel are Guy's, and indicate his complete submission; he tells Gerard, "Take me."

Chandler had a good deal of trouble accepting Guy as a character. He wrote that "the premise of this story is not that a nice young man might in certain circumstances murder a total stranger just to appease a lunatic. That is the end result. The premise is that if you shake hands with a maniac, you may have sold your soul to the devil" (*Raymond Chandler Speaking*, pp. 134–135). One of the problems with Chandler's perception of the novel lies in his notion of the "nice young man." He seems to have had a relatively fixed notion of character. In his own fiction, characters are generally fixed entities; something concealed or repressed in them may emerge, but they do not generally undergo basic personality changes. Patricia Highsmith, however, often bases her novels upon the assumption that a most extreme personality change can result from what initially appears to be the most haphazard of encounters. It occurs in *Strangers on a Train*, and her remarkable *A Dog's Ransom* provides another example, among many. This personality alteration often occurs under the pressure of a person who makes himself or herself an overwhelming presence, often as a result of intense envy. Highsmith's notion of character, then, is in practice radically different from Chandler's. Her novel is, in many ways, *about* Guy's personality change. Chandler said that he could not accept in the novel the fact that Guy would murder Bruno's father; although that is clearly a keystone in Highsmith's development of Guy's character erosion and alteration. Chandler's disparaging comment about Hitchcock—"His idea of characters is rather primitive. Nice Young Man, Society Girl . . ." might, in this situation, be applied to himself.

But it was not a wholly literary judgment. Chandler read the novel with a film script in mind, and contemporary Hollywood conventions simply would not have allowed the unpunished hero to be a murderer. The hero had to be a "nice young man." The aspect of the novel Hitchcock chose to work with, then, was the initial situation: the dilemma of a man who, without his assent, finds a wife he hates killed by a lunatic who demands that he return the favor or be implicated in his wife's murder. It was this situation, and not Highsmith's notion of character, that Chandler and Hitchcock chose to develop. So, in the film, Guy does not murder Bruno's father, nor does he undergo any significant personality change. He simply must work his way out of a terribly awkward situation, without himself being morally corrupted by it.

Chandler wrote that he nearly went crazy trying to block out the key scene on the train in which the deal is established. His problem was one of situation and character plausibility, as well as audience expectation. In the scene, a perfectly decent young man must appear to agree to murder someone he doesn't know in order to keep a lunatic from tormenting him. The audience must accept the plausiblity of the scene when, because of Hollywood codes, it knows Guy has no intention of killing anyone. Chandler also had to make Bruno's assumption that a deal has been struck believable, while at the same time giving evidence of a lingering suspicion in Bruno's mind that Guy might not fulfill his part of the deal.

Chandler realized that the credibility of the film rested on "the horror of an absurdity become real;" that, however absurd the situation, it had to give the illusion of plausibility in its development. He resented the fact that this script, like those of many Hollywood films, rested upon "this sort of contest between a superficial reasonableness and a fundamental idiocy. Why do film stories always have to have this element of the grotesque?" (*Raymond Chandler Speaking*, p. 134). In the film, *Strangers on a Train*, the troublesome scene is dealt with by making this only one of many of Bruno's crazed but often amusing schemes, and by having the wearied Guy simply nodding an amused but noncommittal "Yes, sure."

But most of Chandler's work on the script was discarded. Relations between the two men seem to have collapsed by the last week in August. Chandler had sent off the final pages of his script on September 26, but Hitchcock found much of what he did unusable and hired Czenzi Ormonde, one of Ben Hecht's assistants, to re-do it. Hitchcock also did a good deal of rewriting himself. In October, Chandler wrote that he thought the film would be acceptable by the time Hitchcock finished it, but by early December, after he had seen the new script, he disowned the project. Feeling that what he had done with the material had been "castrated," he considered removing his name from the film's credits. He eventually decided against such a move only because it had been so long since he had had a screen credit. In December also, after a complicated dispute involving his work on the script, he fired his Hollywood agent, Ray Stark, and returned to Swanson.

Nearly a year later, after Chandler had seen the completed film *Strangers on a Train*, he wrote that it was no worse than he expected, since the final script had been a "botched job." He felt that Hitchcock had refused to face what he considered the basic problem of the story, which is to make the audience believe that a man in the position of the hero would behave as Guy does. Hitchcock, he said, had "the idea that if you move fast enough and make enough noise, nobody will bother to ask where you're going or why" (Letter to Sandoe, September 21, 1951). However, he felt that Hitchcock was probably happy with the film since it was the first of his films in a good while to make money. "The picture has no guts, no plausibility, no characters and no dialogue, but of course it's Hitchcock, and a Hitchcock film always does have something." His sense of his own involvement in the final product is clear: "I don't know why it's a success, perhaps because Hitchcock succeeded in removing almost every trace of my writing from it" (MacShane, *The Life of Raymond Chandler*, p. 177).

The fact that the film succeeded at the box office annoyed Chandler because it represented a kind of failure on his part; it was the last film on which he ever worked. The finished film bears out Chandler's complaints about it, but it also has a great deal to which he may have been blind.

Many of the changes in the novel's plotline had been established before Chandler was hired: Guy is a tennis player, not an architect; the story takes place mainly between New York and Washington, D.C., not all over the United States; Guy becomes engaged to Anne Morton, a senator's daughter, not a millionaire's daughter; and Guy does not kill Bruno's father but tries to warn him of Bruno's insanity.

The time scheme is tightened and structured in such a way that, unlike the novel, the film makes it possible for Guy himself to have killed his wife; in fact, the police suspect him. Bruno possesses evidence, a cigarette lighter, that can incriminate Guy. Bruno's motivation is different: in the novel, he wanted to become part of Guy's life, and the double murder was one way of establishing an irrevocable bonding; in the film, the repressed homosexuality of the novel is not foregrounded, and Bruno's major motivation is to dispose of his father.

There is no pursuing detective in the film, which ends not with Guy's odyssey of self-erosion and exposure but with Bruno's death as he attempts to incriminate Guy. Guy and his fiancée will probably live happily ever after.

Hitchcock's penchant for culturally resonant icons, absent from the novel and one source of Chandler's irritation, is evident in the film. Much of it takes place in Washington, D.C. At one point, Guy receives an unexpected and unwanted call from Bruno. Hitchcock cuts to a shot of Bruno, who is in a telephone booth, with the Washington Monument clearly visible in the background. The presence of the monument is visually striking to the audience and the telephone intrusion is aurally shocking to Guy; both combine to give the scene its jolting quality. At another point, we see a full shot of the Jefferson Memorial and then notice Bruno standing at its base, watching Guy and following. Bruno is frequently associated with images of cultural benignity in an unsettling way that is representative of Hitchcock's habit of creating terror in places and situations not generally associated with evil. Bruno murders Miriam, Guy's wife, on an amusement park "Magic Isle" used by young couples for necking, and is himself killed on a merry-go-round that has gone out of control and become a terrifying, crazed instrument of death.

Much of the film is structured around images and patterns of doubling and of parallelism. Although these are central to the film, their value would probably have been least apparent to Chandler in his work on the script. The film opens at Union Station, and we see two cars pull up, and then the feet of two men emerge successively. One man has two-toned shoes, and the other carries two tennis rackets. The two pairs of feet walk through the station and onto a train. We then see the complex parallel patterns of railroad tracks from the point of view of the front of the train as it moves through the railroad yard. Then

Guy (Farley Granger) meets the psychotic Bruno (Robert Walker) in *Strangers on a Train* (Warner Brothers), Chandler's last screen credit. *(Photo courtesy of Cinemabilia.)*

the two pairs of feet accidentally brush together, and Guy and Bruno meet. While they talk, they sit among elaborate graphic patterns of parallel lines—shadows on the ceiling and walls, blinds, and the like. Guy announces that he is going to Southampton to play "doubles." He has a cigarette lighter with two crossed tennis rackets on it. Bruno decides they should drink and orders "a pair of doubles," joking, "the only kind of doubles I play." When he talks of exchanging murders, he summarizes the activity by saying "Crisscross." Later, when Guy refuses to kill Bruno's father, Bruno says he has been "double-crossed."

The patterns are elaborate, at times Byzantine, and one feels that Hitchcock had as much fun dreaming up endless possibilities for developing them as Howard Hawks claims he did with X's in *Scarface*. They are not used simplistically but they develop central aspects of the film. Although Guy does not carry out the second murder, it turns out that Bruno has, without knowing it, committed a kind of double murder, since Miriam was pregnant when he killed her. When he tells Guy of the murder, a police car comes to Guy's apartment, and Guy hides behind a fence with Bruno. At this point, we see both covered with the parallel shadows of the bars of the fence, resembling jail bars, and Guy says, "Now you've got me acting like a criminal," linking the two men not only formally but thematically: not only is Guy visually covered with the parallel shadows that cover Bruno but he is also involved in the murder Bruno has committed, and he is behaving like Bruno.

Once these patterns of doubling and parallelism are established, Hitchcock begins toying with them. From her very first appearance, Miriam is presented as crass and vicious. Hitchcock photographs her from unflattering angles. We see her break a prearranged agreement with Guy to give him a divorce while grabbing the money he has brought for the lawyer. We learn that although she is carrying another man's child, she intends to remain Guy's wife in order to partake of his recent success. She gloats over the fact that this decision will disrupt his new relationship with Anne.

The prospect of Guy and Miriam as a "couple" at this point in the film is intolerable. The whole notion of coupling as a traditional norm is developed perversely on the night Miriam is murdered. We see two boats traveling through the tunnel of love to the "Magic Isle." If ever there was a situation that traditionally called for couples, this is it. But neither of the two boats contains a couple, and this in itself points to something wrong. One of the boats contains Miriam and two men. We have seen the two men pick her up at her home, and no mention has been made of a second woman. The relationship is overtly sexual. Earlier, as Miriam got popcorn, one man grabbed her shoulder, and she said, "Not now." The other complained as she ate, "Aw, it's no fun necking with a mouth full of popcorn." In the darkness of the tunnel of love, we hear her scream, then laugh, and we see her struggling from the grip of one of the men. What we have in this boat, then, is not a conventional couple but a threesome on their way to a secluded petting spot.

But this is not all. The other boat also does not contain a couple; it contains Bruno, alone and eating popcorn. To increase the perversity of the situation, he has been following Miriam through the carnival. Not only has she been aware of this, but she has repeatedly given him come-hither glances. So she is with two men and wants a third at the same time. The third man arrives alone, kills her on the "Magic Isle," and departs alone. The perversity of the situation, then, is increased within the formal and thematic structure of the film, since the place where the murder happens is so clearly meant for "doubles" and since both parties involved deviate from the pattern.

Interestingly, Bruno begins to lose control of himself later when he sees a "double" of Miriam. Anne's sister, Barbara, resembles Miriam, largely because of the particular kind of glasses she wears. Bruno almost strangles a woman at a party because he obsesses onto Barbara's face, which recalls Miriam's. There is no counterpart for Barbara in the novel, and the logic of the use of two look-alikes is strained—especially when Anne, who had never seen Miriam, intuits that she wore glasses like Barbara's—but it has an apt formal logic. It also points to a major formal linkage in the glasses.

When Bruno strangles Miriam, Hitchcock photographs it as a reflection from a lens of Miriam's glasses, which had fallen to the ground. The lens's shape and visual distortion fill the entire frame, and when Bruno picks the glasses up after the killing, one lens is broken, again a formal parallel to the perverse coupling motif. He brings the glasses to Guy as proof of Miriam's death. This seems to establish them as a major clue, to be used later in the narrative, but they never reappear. Instead, Hitchcock transfers their significance onto Barbara's glasses.

The film has a number of logical problems, of which Chandler spoke. The entire conclusion makes no real logical sense. When Bruno is killed on the merry-go-round, the presence of Guy's lighter in his hand and the recognition of Bruno by an eyewitness as having bought a "Magic Isle" ticket at the time of Miriam's murder are presented as if they were conclusive proof of Guy's innocence, which is absurd. In addition, there is a serious continuity error: just prior to the crash, when the merry-go-round is whirling wildly out of control, Bruno and Guy are involved in a savage fistfight and we see both of Bruno's hands holding onto a bar. It would be impossible for him, in the elapsed time, and during the impact of the crash, to get the lighter into his hand as he dies.

Strangers on a Train has a number of such problems, but as Chandler observed, Hitchcock's pacing tends to obscure them. But there is another kind of elision in the film that points to a much more complex development of Guy than Chandler's "nice young man" theory suggests.

Guy is clearly the "hero" of the film. He is young, handsome, athletic, upwardly mobile, and in love. His situation arises out of his kindness to a lunatic on a train. But the more closely we examine what he does, and does not do, the more questionable his heroic status becomes. Interestingly, Hitchcock was not happy with Farley Granger as Guy. He wanted an actor of greater "strength" to play the role and would have preferred William Holden, but such "strength" would have obscured the problem even more.

Many of Guy's activities are ambiguous. He appears to be in love with Anne and is working in some capacity for her father, a senator. He states that he wants a political career after his tennis career ends. The possibility exits that opportunism, and not true love, lies at the basis of his feelings for Anne, and early in the film, Bruno, who has followed Guy's career in the newspapers, openly states this possibility: "You're smart—marrying the boss's daughter—that, that makes a nice shortcut to a career, doesn't it?"

Part of Guy's dilemma after Miriam's death lies in the fact that he had really wanted her dead. Bruno immediately realizes this. In fact, Guy had told Anne that he wished to strangle Miriam. Curiously, he does not show any remorse or grief at her death. All of his thinking focuses on the position in which it places him. For form's sake, he suggests that he cancel an upcoming tennis match, and the senator says, "My boy, wouldn't it look rather awkward if you suddenly canceled all your plans?" Anne adds, "He's right, Guy, you musn't do anything that looks suspicious. You must go on acting as if nothing had happened." This is rather curious advice and behavior when one's wife, even if estranged, has only that evening been murdered. Guy never considers doing the "honest" thing, that is, telling the police and assuming truth will out. He is too calculating.

A final example comes on the night Guy has agreed to murder Bruno's father. According to plan, he goes to the house with the gun Bruno has sent him. However, once in the father's bedroom, he begins to explain that Bruno needs psychiatric help. Unfortunately, the occupant of the darkened room turns out to be not the old man but Bruno.

The scene has little credibility. It is set up to look as if Guy will, in fact, kill the old man, but, due to his "hero" status, the audience knows he will not. But Bruno does not know this, although he suspects it, and placing himself in his absent father's bed—a Freudian delight—is a nearly suicidal risk. But even more central, why does Guy go through with it up to the last minute? If he were not going to kill the old man, there would have been no need to follow exactly the plan set up for it, even to the extent of carrying a loaded gun. He could have visited the old man at home or in his office and not have placed himself in danger by illegally entering the house with a loaded gun. The only explanation for this scene's presence in the film, aside from audience titillation, is to indicate that Guy did, in fact, entertain the idea of killing Bruno's father, even though he may have changed his mind at the last minute. The purity of Guy's "nice young man" status is questionable indeed.

The debacle of Chandler's involvement in *Strangers on a Train* resulted in his abandoning film work forever. It also confirmed for him what he considered the inadequacy of a writer's role in film. He realized that "a really creative writer ought to become a director." He had learned that what he

wanted to develop of his own talent was not compatible with
work in films.

> A preoccupation with words for their own sake is fatal to good
> film making. It's not what films are for. It's not my cup of tea.
> . . . The best scenes I ever wrote were practically monosyllabic.
> And the best short scene I ever wrote, by my own judgment,
> was one in which a girl said "uh huh" three times with three
> different intonations, and that's all there was to it.[14]

Although Chandler was through with Hollywood, he had not
finished commenting upon it. In the *Atlantic Monthly* of February
1952, he published an article entitled "Ten Per Cent of Your
Life," which deals with agents, particularly Hollywood agents.
Like his earlier articles, its main concern is the process of the
film industry. He speaks nostalgically of the personal care and
loyalty of old-time literary agents, but he admits that the fast-
paced nature of the contemporary film industry has made their
type obsolete. A central notion of the article is that big money
changes the very nature of the business. Chandler describes the
new breed of agents as crass, heartless, and fast-moving hucksters.
(Part of the impetus behind the description may have come from
his break, in December 1950, with Ray Stark.) He considers the
new agents monopolistic and overwhelming. They were often
involved with their clients' hiring corporation and therefore
profited from both ends. "He wasn't working for you: you were
working for him." Chandler presents this as a necessary outgrowth
of the increasingly lucrative entertainment industry, but he
regrets what has been lost in the process: "Where the money is,
there will the jackals gather, and where the jackals gather,
something usually dies."[15]

When "Ten Per Cent of Your Life" appeared, Chandler was
working on *The Long Goodbye,* his most ambitious, and, many
would argue, best, novel. Soon after he finished it, his wife,
Cissy, died, and he lived much of the rest of his life in alcoholic
despair. He seems to have lost most of his interest in Hollywood.
Helga Greene, his agent, heir, and the woman he was to have
wed just before his death, has written me that he seldom spoke
of his Hollywood career in the last years of his life.

Harold Hecht, then a partner in the Hecht/Hill/Lancaster
company, approached Chandler in mid-1958. He had long
admired Chandler's work and hoped to lure him back to Holly-

wood. The incident was pathetic. Chandler was drinking heavily, chain-smoking, coughing, and barely responsive. After twenty or thirty minutes of seeking ideas and suggesting possibilities, Hecht left in tears. He was probably the last Hollywood producer who tried to deal with Chandler. Chandler died in less than a year.[16]

Near the end of Chandler's time in Hollywood, he wrote an article entitled "A Qualified Farewell." Never published during his lifetime, in many ways it sums up his career, or at least his own perception of it. It situates the screenwriter within the Hollywood process, and himself within the role of screenwriter. He admits, as a producer once told him, that he was not a "sole screenwriter," that he simply was not that good at screenwriting. He also admits that most of his career intersected with a period of unrivaled success in Hollywood, and that the success of films he worked on was not necessarily due to his work. In addition, he confesses that he often made impossible demands.

At base, he describes his problem as he had described it in "Writers in Hollywood." It concerns the role and status of the writer in the filmmaking process: "My real concern is that those among them who *are* writers and have proved it in other fields simply can't get any real fun out of screenwriting. All they can get is money, and if money satisfies them, they are not writers."[17] He objects to the lack of freedom, to what he termed the mid-Victorian censorship codes, to the producer's control over the writer's work, and to the presumption on the part of directors and cameramen that much of what a writer puts into a script is irrelevant and to be disregarded. But he strikes a balance. He admits that Hollywood has produced some brilliant work and declares film an art form of unquestionable value. He also realizes that he, with his notions of integrity and of vocation, simply did not fit in: "The qualifications for permanent success in Hollywood, which I lack, are a tremendous enthusiasm for the work at hand coupled with an almost complete indifference to the use which will be made of it."

His closing paragraph summarizes his view of his position:

> I bid you farewell. I have enjoyed writing this piece, although essentially I know it is a testament of failure. If it were merely a personal failure, the piece would not be worth writing. I think it is much more. A man does not deliberately turn his back on what

I could get out of Hollywood from motives of personal pique or overinflated vanity. Such moods pass. Mine has been with me for a long time. I have a sense of exile from thought, a nostalgia of the quiet room and the balanced mind. I am a writer, and there comes a time when that which I write has to belong to me, has to be written alone and in silence, with no one looking over my shoulder, no one telling me a better way to write it. It doesn't have to be great writing, it doesn't even have to be terribly good. It just has to be mine. ("A Qualified Farewell," p. 76)

Part III

FILMS BASED ON CHANDLER'S FICTION

6 | BEGINNINGS: *THE FALCON TAKES OVER, TIME TO KILL,* and *MURDER, MY SWEET*

From almost the very beginning, Chandler's novels interested Hollywood. His first novel, *The Big Sleep,* appeared in 1939; his second, *Farewell, My Lovely,* in 1940; and his third, *The High Window,* in 1942. By 1942, there were two films based upon two different Chandler novels. Although he only wrote seven novels in all, by 1982, there were ten films based upon six of them. Undoubtedly, more will follow.

As with Chandler's screenwriting career, the timing was ideal. The novels appeared just as Hollywood was developing a serious interest in their type. They quickly became the subject of major studio deals. One suspects that, had Chandler, like Edgar Allen Poe, never done any screenwriting himself, his name would still be associated with a particular type of film.

Chandler took pride in his belief that he had elevated in critical opinion the fictional genre in which he wrote. He felt he left it better than he found it. The film genre that used Chandler's novels also underwent significant changes at precisely the time it was drawing from Chandler's fiction. *Film noir* was receiving serious attention, and the Hollywood reputation of its fictional sources rose accordingly.

Until the mid-1940s, detective films, like Westerns, were largely cheaply made "B" films that seldom received serious critical attention. Unlike Westerns, however, they had not become a significant genre until the sound era. This is not to say that the character of the private detective was not a presence in films until that time or that there had not been "A" detective films. The first detective film was probably American Biograph's *Sherlock Holmes Baffled* in 1903, the same year of *The Great Train Robbery*. In 1916, the year after *The Birth of a Nation* helped establish the feature-length format, Essanay produced a feature-length *Sherlock Holmes*, starring William Gillette, who had played the role with great success on stage. In 1922, Samuel Goldwyn produced *Sherlock Holmes*, starring John Barrymore. There were many others, and other detectives aside from Sherlock Holmes, but it was not until the sound era that the genre took off.

In his *The Detective in Film* (1972), William K. Everson suggests a number of reasons for this development. One is the relative newness of the fictional genre from which the films drew extensively. The detective had only become a significant figure in literature—primarily with Sherlock Holmes—in the last quarter of the nineteenth century. Many popular detectives did not appear in fiction until after 1925; examples are Hercule Poirot, Philo Vance, Ellery Queen, Charlie Chan, the "Saint," and Sam Spade.

The magazine most associated with the development of the hard-boiled story, *Black Mask*, first appeared in 1920. Dashiell Hammett first published in it in 1922 and Carroll John Daly introduced his popular private eye, Race Williams, to *Black Mask* in 1923. The American private eye, then, was only beginning to appear in fiction in the closing days of the silent era. Since the character type was original with that fiction, it took a while for its counterpart to appear in film. Furthermore, sound allowed this genre greater scope for complex verbal argument.

Early in the sound era, mystery and detective films experienced a boom in popularity. Many cinematic detectives became so popular that they were made the basis for a series, often continuing with the same actor, but at other times switching the lead actor in the series. William Powell enjoyed great success as Philo Vance, and later as Nick Charles in the *Thin Man* series; Ronald Colman became identified with Bulldog Drummond; and, of course, starting in 1939, Basil Rathbone was the classic Sherlock Holmes.

As these series progressed, they often slipped from "A" to "B" status, sometimes, as with Sherlock Holmes, even changing studios. Many, indeed most, other detective series existed only in "B" formats. They were made cheaply, using a readily identifiable formula, and were given only perfunctory critical attention. By the 1940s, detective films had largely become synonymous with "B" films; examples are the Ellery Queen and Boston Blackie series at Columbia; Charlie Chan, Mr. Moto, and Mike Shayne at Twentieth Century-Fox; the "Saint" and the "Falcon" at RKO; Philo Vance at Warner Brothers; and Bill Crane and Sherlock Holmes at Universal. The world of crime did little more than provide a context in which the brash, intelligent, elegant or two-fisted (sometimes both), and witty central character proved himself a hero. Many of the films were comedies with violence thrown in. Nearly all had as a central characteristic the ability of the hero to unravel complex mysteries, often after plodding police detectives had failed at the task. The films, however, seldom developed a sense of a genuinely evil or corrupted environment, and certainly did not present the hero as significantly jaded or even partially broken by that environment. Such was the context within which the first two films based upon Chandler's fiction appeared.

In July 1941, Chandler sold RKO the film rights to *Farewell, My Lovely* for $2,000. *Film noir*, with which Chandler's fiction would later come to be seen as particularly compatible, had not yet developed, and this novel's story line became the basis for a film in RKO's Falcon series.

The series (ostensibly based upon a Michael Arlen character) had begun in 1941 with *The Gay Falcon*. Chandler's novel provided story elements for the third film in the series, *The Falcon Takes Over*, which appeared in May 1942. Interestingly enough, this series had a kind of origin in another RKO series, the Saint series. George Sanders had played the "Saint" in five films, starting with *The Saint Strikes Back* in 1939. After *The*

Saint in Palm Springs in 1941, RKO used Sanders to begin the Falcon series, which was heavily indebted to the Saint series, not only for its star but also in style and format. In *The Falcon Takes Over*, Sanders plays Gay Lawrence, the "Falcon," as a rich, debonair socialite, also an amateur sleuth, with an eye for the ladies.

The Falcon Takes Over, as do many series films, presents a number of situations and relationships as already established, and they remain stable at the film's end, ready for continued use in the next episode. The "Falcon" is widely known for his interest in crime, and when, at the beginning of the film, he just happens to be at a nightclub when a man is killed, the press assumes he will pursue the case. A running gag in this and in other films in the series is the fact that he is engaged to be married and yet continually becomes involved with attractive women, and often quickly abandons them to move on to others. He has a bumbling, and often terrified chauffeur, Goldy (Allen Jenkins), who provides direct comic contrast to the elegant Gay Lawrence. Goldy's trademarks are his Brooklyn accent and continual malapropisms such as "corpus delicious" and "miscarriage of injustice." Gay Lawrence also has a relationship of genial antagonism with a wisecracking police detective, O'Hara (James Gleason) and his dullard assistant Bates. The setting for much of the action is the posh world of society nightlife in which all of the regulars except Lawrence are laughably out of place. The opening credits foreshadow the film's style: they appear over a silhouette of an elegant-looking man with top hat, overcoat, and walking stick.

This format at first appears curious, since the setting and tone of the series differ so extensively from those of Chandler's novel, but it provides an interesting example of the way a work with clearly defined genre patterns can appropriate elements of another that appears unrelated. And in many ways it was. The Falcon series embodied much of what Chandler hated about the detective genre, particularly the notion of the debonair, amateur detective who solves the crime between brunch and cocktails and the notion of the world of murder and crime as little more than a context for a puzzle to be wittily solved.

Both novel and film begin with similar plot events, but differences in the contexts constructed around those events point to thematic differences in the works themselves.

The bumbling Goldy (Allen Jenkins) and the debonair Gay Lawrence (The Falcon—played by George Sanders) in *The Falcon Takes Over* (R.K.O. Radio Pictures). This film was the first to be based upon a Chandler novel. *(Photo courtesy of the Museum of Modern Art.)*

In both, Moose Malloy, a giant of a man just out of prison, is searching for his former sweetheart, Velma. He enters a bar in which he is clearly out of place and which has changed considerably since Velma worked there years before. He easily defeats men in the bar who try to throw him out and winds up killing the manager, Mr. Montgomery. It is not a premeditated murder but simply the unfortunate result of Montgomery's trying to oppose a man who does not know his own strength. The central detective simply happens to be there when it happens and becomes involved in the events more from idle curiosity than from anything else.

In Chandler's novel, the bar—Florian's—is in a run-down section of Los Angeles that has become a black ghetto during the eight years Malloy has been in prison. Marlowe happens to be nearby on a petty case he neither solves nor gets paid for. Malloy is out of place not only because of his size and ostentatious clothes but also because he is white. Intense racial antagonism causes a bouncer to attempt to eject Malloy from the bar, and the manager tries to shoot him, leading to his own death. Nulty, the police detective assigned to the case, is resentful about it, calling the assignment "another shine killing." He feels, rightly, that because a black is the victim the case will get no publicity for him and that no one cares very much whether or not it is solved.

The film *The Falcon Takes Over* opens as Malloy (Ward Bond) approaches the "Club 13." It is not a run-down bar in a Los Angeles ghetto but a stylish Manhattan nightclub at Seventh Avenue and Fifty-second Street. The "Falcon" is not there on a fruitless job but is a well-known patron. The doorman tries to eject Malloy not for racial reasons (everyone in the club is white) but because evening clothes are required. Malloy stands out not because he is white but because he does not wear a tuxedo. When Detective O'Hara arrives, he is not resentful because the racial implications of the assignment indicate that his superiors hold him in low esteem; rather, he engages in witty banter with the "Falcon," saying, "Oh, the great Falcon. Haven't seen you around for about a half dozen murders." While they talk, an attractive woman approaches the "Falcon," calling him "Homer Bilky." He tells her she must be mistaken, that his name is "Dittenfriess," and quickly moves away from her, exchanging sly grins with O'Hara. This points to his habit of seducing women under false names while his fiancée is out of town.

In both novel and film, the murder victim (the manager) is virtually ignored, but for very different reasons. In the novel, the victim is black in a racist society. Marlowe even comments that the police treat his murder like a misdemeanor. The absence of concern over the man's death points to a profound social problem. In the film, however, the victim receives scant attention simply because his death provides little more than a catalyst for the plot and an excuse for verbal banter between O'Hara and the "Falcon."

The central detective characters in the two works are radically different. The "Falcon" is a tireless *bon vivant*, for whom everything, including this case, is a lark. He is rich and famous, apparently has no need to work, has a stylish apartment and servants, a fiancée, and as many other women as he wants. Marlowe, on the other hand, has not worked in a month and needs money. A lonely man, he has few friends and no sweethearts—until he meets Anne Riordan. He exists in an atmosphere of depravity and of failure and has little more than his sense of integrity to sustain him.

Curiously, some elements of the film stylistically resemble elements that would later be foregrounded in *noir* films. Moose Malloy is generally photographed from a low angle and is often lit from below in ways that anticipate *noir* photography of sinister characters. He moves in a lobotomized, zombie fashion and is— although a killer and a constant terror to Goldy—essentially a lost man who experiences one betrayal after another until he is killed. He seeks information about Velma from the widow of the former owner of Florian's bar, Jessie Florian, whose seedy life, ill-kept house in Brooklyn, and murder also anticipate the kinds of incidents and settings that later become important to *noir* films. They seem somewhat alien to the style of *The Falcon Takes Over* and are little more than diversions from the clearly dominating style of well-lit interiors, romantic flamboyance, and witty banter.

In May 1942, the same month *The Falcon Takes Over* opened in New York, Chandler's most recent novel, *The High Window*, was sold to Twentieth Century-Fox for $3,500. It provided the story line for *Time to Kill*, which opened in New York in December 1942. Like *The Falcon Takes Over*, *Time to Kill* was also part of a detective series: the Mike Shayne series, based on the Brett Halliday character.

The two series were very different in style and format, and they appropriated elements from Chandler's fiction in very different ways. Interestingly, the studios—RKO Radio and Twentieth Century-Fox—that had purchased the novels for "B" series detective films would, within the next five years, each make a second film based upon the respective novels, only this time in clearly identifiable—and now fashionable—*noir* style.

The film *Time to Kill* opens with a shot of a desk top, from which the soles of two shoes with holes worn in them dominate the frame. Mike Shayne (Lloyd Nolan), to whom they belong, is nearly penniless but cocky in spirit and fast-talking. After he receives his first payment on the case, we see a similarly framed shot of him with his feet on the desk top, only this time the shoes are newly soled. His unstable financial status might, at first glance, appear to make Mike Shayne more like the Marlowe of the novels that the "Falcon," but in fact they are equally distant from Chandler's protagonist. The two matched shots of the feet, done as sight gags, point to the film's presentation of Shayne's poverty; it is something to be laughed at, not taken seriously, and certainly without degrading psychic effect on the central character.

In both the novel and the film, the detective is hired by the nasty, overbearing Mrs. Murdock to recover a valuable coin, a Brasher Doubloon, left her by her dead husband. She suspects that her son's showgirl wife has stolen it, and she not only wants the coin back but also wants a divorce arranged for her son. A number of people are soon murdered, and the detective eventually learns that the showgirl is innocent, that the son has been involved in a plot to counterfeit the coin, and that the old woman had acquired it in the first place by murdering her husband.

At the thematic center of Chandler's novel is a notion of justice thwarted. Marlowe is bitterly aware of an almost universal injustice and of his own inability to do much about it. This awareness affects even his choice of descriptive similes: "The white moonlight was cold and clear, like the justice we dream of but don't find."[1]

When the police try to pressure Marlowe into dealing with the case according to their rules, he refers to what he calls the Cassidy case of some years before. Cassidy was a multimillionaire, whose son, according to the newspapers, had been murdered by his secretary during a drinking spree. The secretary then committed suicide. Marlowe and the police know that the official version was a lie, that Cassidy's son had murdered the secretary and then committed suicide. However, the elder Cassidy had been sufficiently influential to have the official version of the facts changed in order to protect the family reputation. For Marlowe, the Cassidy case indicated that justice is in the hands of very imperfect and corruptible institutions, to which he feels no presumptive loyalty.

In the Murdock case, the official version also differs from the facts as known to and partially manipulated by Marlowe. When Mrs. Murdock's son, Leslie, kills Vannier, who had been blackmailing his mother with evidence that she had murdered her husband, Marlowe rearranges the death scene to make it look as if Vannier had committed suicide and the police accept that conclusion. Marlowe also frees the psychically disabled Merle

Davis from the clutches of Mrs. Murdock, who had held the girl
in bondage by convincing her that she (Merle) had killed Mr.
Murdock while repulsing his sexual advances. Having proven to
Merle that Mrs. Murdock is the murderer, Marlowe then
apparently destroys the evidence against his erstwhile employer.
At the novel's end, then, Marlowe leaves two killings unre-
ported. He simply lets both of the killers know that he knows
the truth, and, for his own reasons, leaves them to their fates.
The police have always believed that Mr. Murdock's death was
an accident, and they never prove that Vannier's death was
anything but a suicide. This gross discrepancy between actual
and official truth is presented as representative of the workings
of the justice system. The novel closes with a stated awareness
of this problem by Marlowe and the chief police detective dealing
with the case. Both have an implicit agreement to do whatever
they can to help the "little guy" whenever possible.

Marlowe spends much of the novel in a desperate state. His
credibility as a private detective depends on his ability to maintain
confidentiality for his client's interests. When murder becomes
an issue, however, the police demand to know his client's name
and the details of the case and threaten him with loss of his
license unless he reveals information that would make his client's
affairs public. In either case, his ability to function as a professional
is seriously endangered.

In the novel, Marlowe is deeply disturbed by these threats to
his livelihood. In *Time to Kill*, similar threats are leveled at Mike
Shayne, but he laughs them off. His self-confidence is never
threatened by his situation or by police threats. Perpetually
wisecracking and justifying his reputation as "a terrible wolf with
the ladies," he breezes through it all.

Shayne's financial problems are primarily topics for jokes and
are not used to establish any real tensions within the character.
In addition, the film makes no attempt to parallel the novel's
almost lyrical atmosphere of sleaze:

> The small dark narrow lobby was as dirty as a chicken yard. The
> building directory had a lot of vacant space on it. . . . There were
> two open-grill elevators but only one seemed to be running and
> that not busy. An old man sat inside it slack-jawed and watery-
> eyed on a piece of folded burlap on top of a wooden stool. He
> looked as if he had been sitting there since the Civil War and

had come out of that badly. . . . I got out at my floor and started along the hallway and behind me the old man leaned out of the car and blew his nose with his fingers into a carton full of floor sweepings. (*The High Window*, pp. 44–45)

More significantly, the film makes no use of the novel's pervasive sense of universal injustice. In *Time to Kill*, the police are in on the final events, and there is no ultimate discrepancy between what Shayne learns and the official version of the case. No murders go unpunished, a situation that would have been a clear violation of the Production Code, and all loose ends are neatly tied up. Mrs. Murdock's son is subdued by Shayne and arrested by the police, and an outrageous *deus ex machina* takes care of Mrs. Murdock. She has been established throughout the film as perpetually eating T-bone steaks. After participating in the capture of her son, Marlowe learns that the mother choked to death on a piece of steak. The death is treated as little more than a joke, and Merle is presented as cured. The film closes with the indication of an impending affair between Shayne and the attractive Linda Conquest, Leslie Murdock's soon-to-be ex-wife.

Dashiell Hammett's *The Maltese Falcon* served as the basis for two films before the famous 1941 John Huston version starring Humphrey Bogart. Both earlier versions, the first, *The Maltese Falcon* (1931), directed by Roy del Ruth and starring Ricardo Cortez and Bebe Daniels, and the second (called *Satan Meets a Lady*, 1936), directed by William Dieterle and starring Warren Williams and Bette Davis, while not series films, presented the world of crime and detection as primarily a backdrop for a clever, witty, dashing hero who throughout remains unaffected by the world with which he deals. The Huston film, on the contrary, presents the central character as both jaded and threatened by his environment.

The notion of a world gone bad, of a genuinely, as opposed to only an apparently, threatening environment, is central to what would come to be known as *film noir*. When that style became fashionable, filmmakers would seize upon aspects of fictional sources that developed this perception. In the early 1940s, therefore, Hollywood's treatment of Chandler's fiction, as well as Hammett's, clearly showed the shift in taste. Both novelists worked in a genre that assumed a corrupted environment and made it essential to their novels. But when those novels were used for films, the films drew from them what the dominant codes of the times prescribed. *The Falcon Takes Over* and *Time to Kill* provide clear examples. They preceded the shift in taste and appropriated from their source novels only what fit their carefully coded template. *The Falcon Takes Over* somewhat cracks the template in its treatment of Moose Malloy and Mrs. Florian: in a very minor way, it points to things to come. But essentially, both are pre–*noir* films using source material firmly associated with *noir* films. Both films show how genre conventions affect choices in adaptation.

Curiously, both films marked terminal points of a kind in their series. *The Falcon Takes Over* was the last Falcon film to actually star George Sanders: in the next installment of the series, *The Falcon's Brother*, Sanders's character spends most of the film in a coma and is killed battling Nazis at the end; the "Falcon's" brother, Tom Lawrence (Tom Conway, Sanders's real brother) engages in most of the action. *Time to Kill* was also Lloyd Nolan's last Mike Shayne film.

A much more significant shift occurred in the way Chandler's fiction came to be seen as source material. The next film to use it, *Murder, My Sweet*, would elevate the Hollywood status of Chandler's fiction, and would both reflect and help initiate major stylistic changes in film history.

Murder, My Sweet opens with an unoriented shot of what we later learn is the reflection of a lamp on a desk top. We soon hear dialogue, and it becomes evident that Marlowe (Dick Powell) is being interrogated by the police. His eyes are bandaged. The room is unevenly lit: we see harsh, stark contrasts from an overhead bulb and murky shadows in the background. When Detective Randall, whom Marlowe seems to respect, enters, Marlowe says, "The boys tell me I did a couple of murders. Anything in it?" Randall's face is grim, and he quietly advises Marlowe to tell the whole story from the beginning. "With Malloy, then," replies Marlowe. "Well, it was about seven. Anyway, it was dark." As he talks, the camera moves past him to, and then out of, the window to a montage sequence of Los Angeles at night.

On the sound track we hear Marlowe tell of how he had been working on a petty case that he had accepted because he was broke. He never solved the case. "I just found out all over again how big this city is." At the end of the city-at-night montage, we see Marlowe in flashback, alone, without the eye bandages, in his dark office. He says that he had been depressed, that his office bottle hadn't helped, and that he had called "soft shoulders" for a date. She already had a date, but thought she could break it, and Marlowe was waiting for her return call. The camera moves in on him as a flashing light outside intermittently illuminates the office in an eerie, lonely way. We hear Marlowe's voice-over: "There's something about the dead silence of an office building at night—not quite real—the traffic down below was something that didn't have anything to do with me."

Marlowe sits looking at the city below through a large window, and whenever the dully flashing light appears we see his reflection in it. Suddenly we also see the reflection of a huge, sinister-looking man who seems to have come from nowhere. It is Moose Malloy (Mike Mazurki). He appears, disappears, and reappears with the flashing light. Marlowe sees him, represses his shock, and ultimately goes off with him to look for Moose's lost sweetheart, Velma. As Marlowe leaves, his telephone is ringing, but he does not pick it up.

This sequence establishes major patterns of formal and thematic disorientation for both the characters in the film and the audience. The very first shot, of the lamp's reflection, is impossible to situate until the camera moves away. The audience literally does not know what it is looking at—lamp, reflection of a lamp, blank wall, or abstract space.

Marlowe is confused. Most obviously, he is blinded. Initially, he literally does not know whether or not Randall is in the room. We also learn later that he does not know how the major events of the story he relates turned out, since he was blinded and knocked out by gunfire at the climax. He is literally and metaphorically "in the dark." And when he refers to the inceptive moment of the series of events by saying, "Anyway, it was dark," the dialogue underlines the fact that the darkness extends far beyond the interrogation room in which the film opens.

Later in the film, Marlowe's plight is capsulized when he stumbles into Ann Grayle's house for refuge after having been beaten and drugged. She tells him: "You go barging around without a very clear idea of what you're doing. Everybody bats you down—smacks you over the head and fills you full of stuff, and you keep right on hitting between tackle and end. I don't think you even know which side you're on!" Marlowe accurately replies: "I don't know which side anybody's on. I don't even know who's playing today." When in the opening scene, he jokes to Randall, "The boys tell me I did a couple of murders. Anything in it?" it is not entirely a joke. At this point, he does not even know who has been killed.

This disorientation is not confined to the character in the film. When Marlowe begins to tell his story and the camera moves out of the window for a series of shots of the city at night, there is no clear cue as to the temporality of the images of the city. At the end of the sequence, we see Marlowe's flashback of himself at an earlier time in his office, but the point of transition is uncertain. The audience does not know whether those images show the city at the time of Marlowe's interrogation or at the time his story began. This lack of temporal specificity makes the images of the nocturnal city a continuous presence. Marlowe's statement, "I just found out all over again how big this city is," points to how easily one can lose one's bearings in it, as the audience just has. Such disorientation appears to be the permanent state of affairs.

Early in the film, Lindsey Marriott, an effeminate client of Marlowe's, is murdered. Marlowe discovers the body and looks at Marriott's driver's license. We see a shot of the license in a man's hand. Then the camera cuts to show that it is Randall, and not Marlowe, who is looking at the license, and that we are no longer looking at the murder scene but are in a different time and place altogether. We see Randall looking out of a window at nighttime Los Angeles. Since it is in the same room as the film's framing story, since it is at night, since Randall is dressed similarly and speaks in the same tone of voice, we are led to believe that the film has jumped back from the murder scene to the initial interrogation scene from which Marlowe is narrating the entire film. But it has not. Randall moves across the room and the camera pans with him. Suddenly we see Marlowe without bandaged eyes, and this fact places the scene not within the frame story but immediately after Marriott's death. These two minor dislocations of audience expectation, as well as the early lack of temporal specificity in the city montage, point to a continual strategy within the film of introducing the unexpected or the confusing, of continually knocking the viewer slightly off guard.

Another such scene occurs at the home of the drunken Mrs. Florian. She is seated across from Marlowe and has just given him a picture that is supposed to show the missing Velma. The camera moves in to a close shot of her as she takes another drink and continues to talk to Marlowe. Then the camera pulls back, and we suddenly see that Marlowe is no longer in the chair he sat in only seconds before. The audience and Mrs. Florian are surprised at about the same time. Marlowe has, in a way, fooled both the camera and Mrs. Florian by sneaking into the room from which she got the picture to search for another.

At times, both the viewer and Marlowe are disoriented simultaneously. A prime example is the early appearance of the reflection of Moose Malloy, seemingly from nowhere and with shocking suddenness at the film's beginning. Malloy's image is reflected in Marlowe's window and consequently is superimposed over the city at night. When Marlowe describes "the dead silence of an office building at night—not quite real," and says, "the traffic down below was something that didn't have anything to do with me," he establishes the city as a location for a highly subjective awareness of dark and disconnected forces. The association of the sudden appearance of Malloy—this doomed, apelike, strange man—with the image of the city at night indicates that the unreal things that Marlowe feels have nothing to do with him will, in fact, have a great deal to do with him.

Malloy's reflected and ghostlike image is visible only when the eerie outside light flashes. A major disorienting strategy of the film is its use of lighting, especially low-key lighting, stark contrasts, and often visually jarring shadows. The film frequently suggests, by means of its visual textures, a strange, threatening, nightmarelike world. Watching the film, one is reminded of the lighting in German expressionist films of the 1920s and of *Citizen Kane,* made at the same studio (RKO Radio) only three years earlier.

When Marlowe and Malloy enter Florian's bar, for example, one side of the bar is visually dominated by the sharp, crisscrossed shadows of stacked chairs reflected on the wall and ceiling. The shadows seem more substantial than the objects that cast them—

and infinitely more sinister. Most of the film occurs at night, and its strange, and at times jarring, shadows suggest a greater darkness beyond.

When, early in the film, Marlowe accompanies Lindsey Marriott to ransom a stolen necklace, the meeting place resembles nothing urban but rather a primeval forest. It is wooded and murky, and mist rolls over the damp earth. The camera pans to follow the ghostly mist across the weird landscape. Marlowe is startled by a deer. He has no idea what lurks in the darkness and, as he looks around, is suddenly knocked unconscious. When he awakes, an unknown woman is shining a light in his face. She runs off. He finds Marriott beaten to death. It all seems like a crazed nightmare. The place at first appears very different from the city at night, and yet it also is dark, and the darkness contains unknown threats. But it is more than dark; it has an intensely subjective quality to it.

Most of the story, it must be remembered, is told from Marlowe's point of view. We see not so much what happens, as Marlowe's perception of what happens: things that occur only within Marlowe's mind are presented as though they were real events. When he hallucinates in a drugged state, we see the crazed and paranoiac images his mind conjures up. When he is knocked unconscious and describes the sensation—"A black pool opened up at my feet. I dived in. It had no bottom"—we see the frame slowly covered by spreading blackness, like an oil slick.

The audience knows that this is not an actual black pool, even though it appears to be one on screen, but its tangible presence underlines the fact that we see nearly everything in the film from Marlowe's recollected point of view. Just as that point of view does not discriminate between "objective" occurrences and clearly hallucinatory perceptions, so there is no assurance that even the "objective" events may not be highly colored by Marlowe's perception.

Marlowe's personality dominates the film. Not only do we constantly see him on screen—almost nothing is shown in which he is not directly involved—but we continually hear his narrating voice. The narrative comes to us not as an independently existent sequence of events but filtered through Marlowe's remembrance.

This fact points to a major break with the two earlier film

treatments of Chandler's fiction: *The Falcon Takes Over* and
Time to Kill. They treated their source novels as series of plot
events to be appropriated. *Murder, My Sweet* attempts to
appropriate not only the story line but also the mood and verbal
textures of the novel. All of Chandler's novels are told in the
first person by Marlowe. Much of their value lies not in their
story lines, but in their portrayal of Marlowe's perceiving
personality—his evocative descriptions, his rambling associations, and often joltingly apt similes. *Murder, My Sweet* attempts
to foreground the personality. By placing most of the story in
flashback, the film develops Marlowe's perception of events as
much as the events themselves. It uses a great deal of description
and dialogue taken either directly or in slightly altered form
from Chandler's novel.

Alain Silver and Elizabeth Ward, in *Film Noir: An Encyclopedic
Reference to the American Style* (1979), refer to *Murder, My
Sweet* as an archetypal *noir* film because it was one of the very
first films to employ many of the strategies associated with the
noir style. Central to these strategies is the film's presentation
of personality. Both of the earlier films based upon Chandler's
fiction presented their events as occurring in an objective world.
The camera served merely as an invisible recorder of "reality."
Here, however, we do not see "reality" but one person's
subjective impression of it, and that one person's perception is
confused, at times questionable and incomplete. Marlowe is
frequently beaten unconscious; he is drugged, blinded, wearied,
and manipulated. How reliable an observer can he be? As in
much of *film noir*, we explore with him a reality he does not
fully—and may never—understand.

One function of the sinister and murky environment is to
remind us that it is *his* sinister and murky environment. His
world, unlike the worlds of the "Falcon" and Mike Shayne,
cannot be breezed through gaily; it is fraught with great dangers
for him. Clearly poor and compromised by his poverty, he
accepts jobs against his better judgment because he needs the
money. In his dealings with the police and others, he frequently
becomes almost hysterical with rage, desperation, and confusion.
He is not able to right all wrongs by means of an effective right
cross to the jaw of the villain. In fact, in violent situations, he is
more often beaten up than victorious. When we see his world

crisscrossed by sinister and threatening shadows, we do not know how much of what we see is his world, and how much is his perception of it, but we do know that he exists in an environment that is erosive and to which he is highly vulnerable. Unlike the "Falcon" or Mike Shayne, he can be beaten, and he knows it.

The film not only develops patterns of disorientation by means of strange camera angles, unexpected editing, and lighting strategies that evoke sinister forces but it continually places Marlowe in situations that are exotic or perverse. The settings for these situations seem to have very little in common. They vary from sleazy low-life dens—Mrs. Florian's house and Florian's bar—to the dwellings of the ultrarich—the high ceilings, wood paneling, and cavernous interiors of the Grayle mansion; the overlit, ultramodern apartment of the suave professional psychic Jules Amthor; the shadowy sensuality of the Grayle beach house— to Marlowe's shabby apartment and office; from Los Angeles at night to the primeval canyon where Marriott is killed.

Many of the settings into which Marlowe moves convey a sense of something gone wrong or perverse. Amthor's apartment and Dr. Sondegard's house are supposed to be medical establishments. However, Amthor suavely admits that he is a "quack," and we learn that he uses his psychic consultations to blackmail his patients; Dr. Sonderborg permits his house to be used as a prison for the drugged detective. Both men clearly pervert their professions.

The thread connecting all of these diverse locales, and itself smacking of the perverse, is sexual manipulation. Like much of *film noir*, and like *Double Indemnity* in particular, the locus for the film's events is the black widow, in this case, Mrs. Helen Grayle (Claire Trevor), who is also Moose's lost Velma.

Murder, My Sweet presents her as intensely attractive, and deadly. We see her as Marlowe sees her, and she constantly does all she can to entice him. When he first meets her, her dress is low-cut and has a bare midrift and, at precisely the right moment, she allows her skirt to fall away from her shapely leg so that Marlowe can observe it. We next see her when she boldly comes to Marlowe's apartment. She comments on his good build and invites him to an exotic nightclub. In the beach house scene near the end, she is frequently photographed before a large and luxurious bed. During Marlowe's first time there, she disrobes before him to reveal a clinging slip, asks him to murder Amthor for her, and pleads with him to spend the night. She soon tries to kill him, and we learn that she had tried to kill him before they met. On the one hand then, she fits Chandler's description in the novel of "a blonde. A blonde to make a bishop kick a hole in a stained glass window."[2] On the other hand, the closer Marlowe gets to sexual fulfillment with her, the more obviously deadly she reveals herself to be. And we gradually learn that she has always been deadly.

Marlowe is the only major male character in the film (excepting detective Randall) to resist her allure, and live. All others are destroyed. Moose had been involved with her years before and still loves her; her husband's desperate love for her necessitates his continual humiliation and suicidal despair; Marriott had had an affair with her but had outlived his usefulness. All of these men, as well as Jules Amthor, who were powerfully attracted to her die as a direct result of their involvement with her. The nature of Amthor's involvement with her is unclear. She claims to have gone to him for psychic consultation and to have been blackmailed by him. Whether or not they ever became sexually involved is never established, but it is not unlikely.

The film develops a strong association of unnaturalness and perversity with sexuality. All of Mrs. Grayle's sexual partners are unlikely choices for her: Moose is a grotesque gorilla of a man, whose dim-wittedness and criminal background would not fill her social needs; her husband is at least twice her age and frail; Marriott is foppish and ineffectual, with hints of homosexuality (his affected mannerisms and heavy use of cologne). Mrs. Grayle's association with these men is clearly manipulative. She uses her sexuality to get what she wants from them, and then moves on to others.

The film casts a dark shadow over all of its sexual interactions, even what at first seem to be throwaway sexual jokes. When Marlowe visits the drunken, filthy Mrs. Florian in an effort to trace Velma, her ragged bathrobe falls open, and as she closes it she coyly rebukes Marlowe with "No peekin'," as if he were, or would want to. Like the unsuitability of Mrs. Grayle's sexual partners, there is something extremely unpleasant about this pleasantry. It points to what is not there: the likelihood of mutual attraction. Marlowe is presented as sexually attractive, and the notion of the aesthetic compromises he would have to make to sustain sexual involvement with the withered, slobbering Mrs. Florian, as well as the self-deception involved in her presumption of her own sexual desirability, reflects upon the comparable nature of Mrs. Grayle's unlikely and manipulative sexual involvements.

This pervasive aura of sexual manipulation affects the one normative relationship in the film—that of Marlowe and Ann Grayle. After her father nearly commits suicide in humiliation over his wife's treachery, he pleads with Marlowe to abandon the case. Marlowe tells him he will but then goes with Ann to explore the beach house for evidence, telling her that things have gone too far to be dropped. At the beach house, they become affectionate and kiss. Suddenly Marlowe suggests that, since her father could not buy him off the case, "you decided to be nice to me." She becomes insulted and bitter. Marlowe retracts the suggestion, but it still remains a possible motivation and taints the purity of her sexuality. It also points to Marlowe's pervasive suspicion of all sexual motives. And he is quickly justified, since Mrs. Grayle has been watching him and Ann, and will soon attempt to seduce Marlowe and get him to murder Amthor.

Ann Grayle's counterpart in Chandler's novel *Farewell, My Lovely* is Anne Riordan, and the decision of the filmmakers to make her not the daughter of an honest policeman but of Mr. Grayle points to their development of sexual taint as universal, as affecting even the "good girl." As Mr. Grayle's daughter, she is profoundly upset by his sexual humiliation at the hands of his wife, Helen. When Ann first meets Marlowe, she takes pains to establish the fact that her father's wife is not her mother. When Marlowe comes to their mansion, she watches in agony as Helen flirts with him. Her pain comes from a dual sexual jealousy: she is developing a fondness for Marlowe, and she has an intense, possibly neurotic, desire for her father's affection. Here she watches as her stepmother flirts with Marlowe to the abject humiliation of her father.

Ann feels that she and her stepmother are rivals for the affections of both her father and Marlowe—and that she is losing. When she and Marlowe find her father preparing to commit suicide because he thinks his wife has spent the night with

Dangerous sexual interactions. Philip Marlowe (Dick Powell) eyes the seductive Mrs. Helen Grayle (Claire Trevor) as her husband (Miles Mander) and stepdaughter, Ann (Anne Shirley) watch him in *Murder, My Sweet* (R.K.O. Radio Pictures), the first Marlowe film. *(Photo courtesy of the Museum of Modern Art.)*

Marlowe, he pathetically explains. "I am an old man. You can see that. I only have two interests in life—my jade and my wife." Although he quickly adds, "And, of course, my daughter," it is obviously little more than a polite afterthought and indicative of a domestic situation that has caused his daughter anguish. Then, increasing her humiliation, he desperately pleads with Marlowe to agree with him that Helen is "beautiful and desirable."

Ann has lived, then, in the middle of a Freudian nightmare—one without parallel in Chandler's novel—and the climax of the film makes it worse. She sees her stepmother shot dead by her father, then her father and her stepmother's former lover kill one another, and then the man she cares for blinded. She soon appears at the police station to exonerate Marlowe, whose blindness we learn will only be temporary, and the film closes as they kiss in a taxicab.

Although the ending appears to be a happy one, a number of perverse touches undercut it. First, Ann has recently undergone a major domestic trauma—including seeing her father degraded and killed—and the longevity of her pert stability at the end, as well as her relationship with her father's rival, is questionable. Secondly, the film contrives, by means of a joke, to introduce elements of sexual deviation into the final embrace. Marlowe is being led out of the police station by Detective Nulty, and Ann, who has told the police not to reveal her presence, quietly follows. Marlowe speaks glowingly of her to Nulty, and, when Marlowe gets into a taxi, Ann, instead of Nulty, gets in with him. Marlowe continues to talk, and we see him sniffing, obviously smelling her perfume and realizing the exchange. He does not let on, however, and says, "Nulty, I haven't kissed anybody in a long time. Would it be all right if I kissed you, Nulty?" They kiss. The film contrives, at the very moment of relatively unhindered heterosexual communion, to facilitate that communion by means of a homosexual joke that suggests an unlikely couple. And finally, as Marlowe and Ann begin to embrace, he suddenly pulls back, removes a pistol from his inside jacket pocket, and only then embraces her. This closing moment of the film recalls his close call with death at the hands of Ann's stepmother. Helen had held a gun on him and told him not to reach for his inside jacket pocket: "I've kept forgetting to tell you that you shouldn't kiss a girl when you're wearing that gun. It leaves a bruise." He had replied, "I'll try to remember that." And he does, while kissing her stepdaughter at the end.

The film's "happy" end, then, recalls serious problems in Ann's past, recalls the pervasive tone of manipulative and deviant sexuality throughout most of the film, and recalls the one relationship that nearly destroys both Ann and Marlowe. It also shows us Marlowe with the large bandage around his eyes. It gives evidence of the physical and psychic wounds that these characters have suffered as a result of the dangerous and perverse world they inhabit. Although the overall tone of the ending is optimistic, those wounds to which it refers will not quickly disappear, and there is no assurance that others will not follow.

The film's atmosphere of tawdry, manipulative, and deadly sexuality, with overtones of incest, prostitution, and homosexuality, joins with other factors in suggesting a very disturbed world. And that atmosphere was a major reason why *film noir*, as had hard-boiled fiction a decade earlier, first challenged and then stretched censorship codes of the time. New territory was being explored. Things were being hinted at and even explicitly stated that had not previously been allowed.

The film opened as *Farewell, My Lovely* in December 1944, but early reactions indicating audience expectations of a Dick Powell musical caused the studio to change the title to *Murder, My Sweet*. Well reviewed and a box-office success, it opened up a whole new career for Powell as a mature actor.

Adrian Scott, a former writer newly turned producer, had come upon the property and had determined to make his mark with it. RKO Radio Pictures already owned Chandler's novel, having used it as the basis for *The Falcon Takes Over* only two years before. To Chandler's outrage, the studio did not even have to pay him additional moneys to make the second film. Scott hired John Paxton to write the script and Edward Dmytryk to direct. The latter had directed *The Falcon Strikes Back* only the year before, and he was acutely aware of the differences in approach between the Falcon series and the kind of film he was now attempting.

All three men were eager to make a name for themselves in "A" films and were consciously trying to break new ground.[3] The film they made, based upon a Chandler novel that had been used only two years before as the basis for a film at the same studio, was stylistically light-years away from the earlier film. The filmmakers sought very different things in their source novel, and the resultant film not only reoriented Hollywood's perception of the usability of Chandler's fiction but reflected and helped create a new sensibility, an emerging style. *Double Indemnity* had opened a few months before; the New York opening of *Murder, My Sweet* at the Palace directly followed Fritz Lang's *The Woman in the Window;* and *The Blue Dahlia* and *The Big Sleep* were in production. The style was catching on, and *Murder, My Sweet* had many of the major ingredients: retrospective narration; obsession with personality and the haunted past; a sinister atmosphere; a pervasive sense of loss, of fear, of de- pravity—of a world gone bad.

It also introduced Philip Marlowe to the screen. It appeared when both Chandler's name and that of his detective were becoming widely known and was to be the first of many attempts to appropriate that distinctive fictional character for film.

7 | THE BIG TIME: *THE BIG SLEEP, LADY IN THE LAKE,* and *THE BRASHER DOUBLOON*

In 1939, Chandler noted that the *Los Angeles Times* review of his first novel, *The Big Sleep*, saw it as the basis for a film starring Humphrey Bogart, "which I am in favor of also. It only remains to convince Warner Brothers" (*Selected Letters*, p. 4).

More than seven years later, Warner Brothers did indeed release *The Big Sleep*, starring Humphrey Bogart. The early choice of Bogart is most curious. In 1939, he was either starring in "B" films or playing second leads or villains in "A" films. Still to come were the films—*High Sierra* (1941), *The Maltese Falcon* (1941), and *Casablanca* (1943)—that would make him a major star. *The Big Sleep* (1946) was to become one of Warner Brothers' biggest hits, as well as the most widely praised and discussed of all films based upon Chandler's fiction. Bogart became Chandler's favorite screen Marlowe.

Warner Brothers purchased the screen rights to the novel for $10,000 in mid-1944, when *Murder, My Sweet* was in production at RKO and Paramount's *Double Indemnity* was nearly ready for release. Howard Hawks was to produce and direct it, and he hired William Faulkner, Leigh Brackett, and Jules Furthman to write the script. Early versions were ready by September 1944. Chandler could not work on it because of his Paramount contract, but he did consult informally with Hawks. An early version of the film was shot by January 1945. This was not released domestically but was shown to servicemen overseas, a common practice at the time. Changes were later made in the film: new footage was shot, and the story line altered. The completed film was finally released in August 1946.

Much of the rationale for the film had nothing to do with Chandler's novel. Howard Hawks and Warner Brothers had had a major success with *To Have and Have Not*, shot in 1944 and released in January 1945. It starred Bogart and Lauren Bacall, a Hawks discovery, in her first film. Even before the film's release, the word was out that the Bogart-Bacall star chemistry was remarkable, and Hawks prepared a follow-up for the team: *The Big Sleep*.

It was shot at the same studio. Hawks again produced and directed, Faulkner and Furthman were again used as writers, Sidney Hickox again photographed, and Christian Nyby again edited. Interestingly, and representative of both Hawks's thinking and of Hollywood tradition, *To Have and Have Not* had in turn been greatly indebted to a 1943 Bogart success, *Casablanca*.

The strong response to the Bogart-Bacall team upon release of *To Have and Have Not* made the studio realize how hot a property the early version of *The Big Sleep* was likely to be, and new footage was shot of Bogart and Bacall. The off-screen, highly publicized romance and 1945 marriage of the two stars only reinforced the studio's desire to highlight their on-screen romance.

Studio advertising of the film concentrated upon romance ("The Screen Smash They Were Born For") and violence ("The Violence—Screen's All-Time Rocker-Shocker"). The posters emphasized either shots of the couple about to kiss or a shot (not in the film) of Bogart about to smash a kneeling and groveling man on the head with a pistol. Many ads emphasized both: "Baby, you asked for action and you're gonna get some!" and "A story as violent as their love."

The credit sequence of the film indicates its priorities. The opening Bogart-Bacall credits, as well as the title, appear over a silhouette of the two stars. Bogart lights a cigarette for Bacall, and both put their cigarettes into an ashtray; the camera tilts down to the ashtray with the smoldering cigarettes as the rest of the credits appear. This cigarette shot is repeated for the closing "The End" credit. The mutual lighting and smoking of cigarettes were, in the 1940s, a highly coded romantic convention, brought possibly to its most overtly stylized level in *Now, Voyager* (1942), in which Paul Henreid repeatedly lighted two cigarettes and gave one to Bette Davis. Frequently, the lighting of a cigarette by one character for another provided an excuse for close eye contact, and the process of smoking presumably soothed eruptive romantic tensions. The focus here upon the cigarettes smoldering together sets up a parallel for the two stars smoldering with passion throughout the film. From the opening credits, then, we know that this will be a film dealing primarily with the romance of its two stars.

In the same 1939 letter in which Chandler mentions Bogart as a star for a possible film based upon *The Big Sleep*, he also registers distress that early reviewers of the novel seemed unduly concerned with its "depravity." The accusation of depravity was not an unusual response to hard-boiled fiction of the 1930s and became an issue when that fiction began to be used as film sources. Chandler's novel overtly deals with homosexuality, nymphomania, pornography, and drug abuse—all of which were touchy themes even for contemporary fiction and certainly violations of Hollywood's Production Code. The film's use of this material from its source novel was the basis of a major criticism leveled against it, that of incomprehensibility.

The *New York Times* review (August 24, 1946) is, on this issue, representative: "If somebody had only told us . . . just what it is that happens in the Warners' and Howard Hawks' *The Big Sleep*, we might be able to give you a more explicit and favorable report. . . . But with only the foggiest notion of who does what to whom—and we watched it with closest attention—we must be frankly disappointing about it."

The famous story about how neither Faulkner nor Hawks was able to figure out who killed the chauffeur, leading Hawks to wire Chandler, who replied that he did not know either, would appear to support this criticism of the film. Hawks has defined a good film as one that has five good scenes and does not annoy the audience. When asked how much the plot of *The Big Sleep* mattered to him, he replied: "It didn't matter at all. As I say, neither the author, the writer, nor myself knew who had killed whom. It was all what made a good scene."[1]

It can be argued that Hawks's interest in good individual scenes, combined with his cavalier indifference to overall narrative logic, accounts for the confusion viewers often attribute to the film. To these possibilities can be added the fact that the mystery genre itself uses initial viewer confusion as a basic aspect of its appeal, just as the horror film uses shock. Perhaps the threads in this film simply became too tangled and Hawks's indifference to overall narrative logic allowed them to remain that way.

It can also be argued that the production history of the film put strains upon its coherence. The alterations made in the early version in order to build up the Bogart-Bacall romance may have knocked other elements of the film out of coherent balance. From script to final print, a number of endings were considered, including one reportedly devised by Hawks and Chandler. The final choice was largely made simply to shorten the film's closing. A good deal of footage featuring Martha Vickers, playing Bacall's younger sister, was deleted and replaced with footage featuring Bacall. This factor also helped to determine the ending.

The complexity of the source novel, Hawks's stated indifference to overall plot coherence, the built-in confusion of the mystery genre, and the film's tangled production history might all be seen as contributing to the now famous labyrynthine confusion of Hawks's film, but the issue goes deeper.

Many of the factors cited are misleading. Whether or not something is explained in a film's fictional source has little relation to its use in a film. Major story elements from the novel were changed or deleted in the construction of the film's story line. Lauren Bacall's role is a prime example of this. It would have required little more than an inserted line of dialogue to clear up the "Who killed the chauffeur?" issue. The obvious question is: "Since Hawks was aware of the problem, why didn't he clear it up?"

The answer does not lie in Hawks's attitude toward narrative coherence, because the issue is more complex than Hawks presented it. He was, in fact, known not for narrative chaos, but

Philip Marlowe (Humphrey Bogart) and Vivian Rutledge (Lauren Bacall) exchange ominous glances in *The Big Sleep* (Warner Brothers). Publicity for the film capitalized upon the romance of the two stars as well as that of the characters they played. *(Photo courtesy of the State Historical Society of Wisconsin.)*

for his narrative austerity and clarity. The coherence problems that arise with relation to *The Big Sleep* do not arise in his other films, including *To Have and Have Not*, the film he made prior to *The Big Sleep*, and *Red River*, the film he made after it. Why does *The Big Sleep* stand apart?

Neither the demands of the genre nor the film's tangled production history accounts for the situation. Hawks had directed films from 1926, had successfully mastered an almost unmatched variety of genres, as well as production circumstances. A thoroughgoing professional, he could easily have produced a film that would have escaped charges of being an incomprehensible mess.

Some of the film's confusion has a good deal to do with censorship. Film codes were still too rigid to allow direct presentation of many of the topics important to the novel. Rather than discard them—as did *Time to Kill*, for example, with many of the topics covered in *The High Window*—Hawks's *The Big Sleep* obliquely suggests them in an elaborate subtext. This tactic was not new in films, but it was becoming a major one in *noir* films of the 1940s and was being used in new ways. Much of *film noir* hints at the forbidden, at dark motives and interactions, and the *mise-en-scène* became an increasingly important way of developing this. A great deal can be suggested without actually being stated. The aura of censorable sexuality, for instance, can be established without the actual fact.

For example, when Marlowe (Bogart) first meets Vivian Rutledge (Bacall), the meeting occurs in her bedroom. We see them framed against a large and luxuriously ornate bed. Although nothing sexual develops on the level of plot or dialogue, the visual association of them with the large bed adds a sexual dimension to the scene. Similarly, in *Murder, My Sweet*, the framing of Mrs. Grayle against the large bed in her beach house, even though we never see her in it, provides comparable associations, which are, however, supported by both plot and dialogue: we know she had met other lovers there, and she invites Marlowe to spend the night with her. In *The Big Sleep*, the bed is never used, nor are there serious suggestions about its use, but the associations are established.

Other associations are less clear. Audiences of the day were not generally confused by such traditional tactics as cutting away to the fireplace or to the sunrise during a love making scene— what such elisions suggested, but did not show, fell within the range of the acceptably forbidden, but in the early 1940s, films began to refer to things much more culturally unacceptable, even incomprehensible, to mainstream audiences.

For example, in John Huston's *The Maltese Falcon* (1941), Joel Cairo (Peter Lorre) is presented as dandified, contemptuous of women, and morally perverse in ways that could be interpreted as exotically homosexual, although he never engages in explicitly sexual interactions. In addition, there is the relationship between the obese Casper Gutman (Sidney Greenstreet) and his young "gunsel" Wilmer (Elisha Cook, Jr.). The word *gunsel* means "gunman," and that is clearly Wilmer's role in the film. However, the word also means a "boy" used in pederasty and points to aspects of the Gutman-Wilmer relationship that are not otherwise developed in the film but add an ever so subtly indicated touch of perversion to an already sinister pairing.

The Production Code explicitly forbade the presentation of homosexual relationships on screen, but veiled hints at a variety of manifestations of forbidden evils became important to many *noir* films of the 1940s—and associations were often layered. If you have a villain like Caspar Gutman, why not make him repulsively obese, why not make him homosexual, why not associate him with exotic foreign places of unimaginable evils? God knows what else drives the man. One could move beyond traditional imperatives for evil, such as greed and heterosexual lust, into murky and mysterious areas that would boggle the minds of majority audiences.

Once more, the dark shadows of the genre conceal, and suggest, much. They hint at "otherness" of all kinds—otherness that often encroaches upon and threatens cultural norms of the 1940s, such as heterosexuality, whiteness, and Anglo-Saxon values. *Film noir* often deals with the erosive effects of the foreign upon the American norm. The Maltese falcon, for example, is of foreign origin and associated with sinister events in foreign history, and Gutman and his unsavory band have been chasing it all over the world. Now their sinister mission pollutes America. Sam Spade is presented as a rather unsavory American, but in the end morally superior to Gutman's crew.

Jacques Tourneur's classic *noir* film *Out of the Past* (1947) opens with images of idyllic rural American life in Bridgeport, California. The dark past of Jeff Bailey (Robert Mitchum) catches up with him, and much of the film depicts his retrospective narration of his search for a gangster's runaway girl friend, Kathie (Jane Greer). The first place he looks is in a Negro nightclub, then he goes to Mexico City, then to Acapulco, where he finds her. Acapulco is established as the place where you can catch the boat farther south, and consequently farther away from the centers of American civilization. He falls in love with Kathie and brings her north, but her poisonous evil destroys everyone involved with her.

The film carefully establishes the woman's evil not only by

her explicit acts of betrayal but by linking her with various forms of racial and cultural otherness. The linkage is implicit, not explicit; it is part of a subtext of associations rather than a causal chain. Little narrative explanation is given as to why a black nightclub would be the first logical place to look for her, but it is, and the fact links her with people who are racially different. Then she literally leaves the country for exotic Mexico, and under this culturally alien influence, Jeff Bailey determines to betray his employer.

There is no strong narrative reason for the inclusion of either the black nightclub or Mexico. Kathie could have been sought in any number of hangouts and could have fled to a remote area of the United States, but these two culturally "other" environments create more than background "atmosphere." They establish a bold contrast to the all-American environment of Bridgeport, California, where Jeff works in a gas station, goes fishing, and has a sweetheart. We see no blacks in Bridgeport, and everyone speaks English. The sense of racial and cultural otherness compounds by association the villainess's evil and her threat to the good life of Bridgeport, California.

In Hawks's *The Big Sleep*, Marlowe is hired by General Sternwood to stop A. G. Geiger from blackmailing him about gambling debts run up by his daughter, Carmen Sternwood (Martha Vickers). Marlowe learns that Geiger deals in rare books, but also that the woman in charge of his store knows nothing about rare books. He follows Geiger home and watches; he sees Carmen arrive. After some time, he sees a flash from inside the house, hears a scream and then shots. As he runs to the house, two cars drive away. When he enters the home, he finds Carmen in a dazed, doped state and dressed in an Oriental-looking gown. Geiger is dead on the floor. He finds, concealed in a Buddha-like sculpture of a head, a camera from which the film has been removed. He leaves with Carmen, but later returns to find Geiger's body missing. He returns once more to find the body, now in exotic-looking fabrics, laid out as if for funeral services.

Very little of this sequence is satisfactorily explained in the film. We learn that Owen Taylor, the Sternwood chauffeur, had followed Carmen to the house and had shot Geiger, presumably because he was in love with Carmen and outraged at what was going on. But what was going on? Presumably Geiger was taking some sort of pornographic pictures of Carmen, and Carmen was too doped-up either to resist or care. But when Marlowe bursts in on the scene, seconds after the flash for the pictures has gone off, she is fully clothed in an Oriental-looking dressing gown. And yet, those pictures are soon used to blackmail her. Since nudity was clearly forbidden by the Production Code, the exoticism of the gown and Carmen's doped-up state seem used to suggest that unspeakable things have gone on, without giving a very clear idea of what they are. One might say that they make subtextual associations to account for what cannot overtly be shown.

We learn later that Joe Brody, who had once seduced Carmen and blackmailed her father, had followed Owen Taylor from the Geiger house, had stolen the photographs from him, and tried to use them for blackmail. It is likely that he is the answer to the question "Who killed the chauffeur?" When he denies any contact with the chauffeur, Marlowe produces evidence that Brody got the pictures from the chauffeur, and Brody, extremely nervous and avoiding eye contact with Marlowe, revises his story, saying he got the photos from Taylor, but left him alive. It is quite likely that he is still lying, but before Marlowe can press him further, Brody is killed by Carol Lundgren. The mystery of "Who killed the chauffeur?" is not quite as unresolved as reputation has it, but it tends to obscure other unanswered questions.

Marlowe captures Lundgren and tells him he shot the wrong man, that Brody did not kill Geiger. They return to Geiger's house, where Marlowe now discovers Geiger's body ornately laid out on a bed with a lighted candle on either side of him. He calls the police, who ask Lundgren, "What did you hide Geiger's body for? Do you admit shooting Brody? Do you?" Lundgren grunts his refusal to answer, and Marlowe says, "He doesn't have to admit it. Here's his gun." Case closed. Or is it?

We know that Lundgren killed Brody, but why did he first remove and then replace Geiger's body? Why was he so fiercely loyal to Geiger that he would kill to avenge him? Why should he have keys to Geiger's house? The film never explains this. In fact, the whole sequence of events is bizarrely shrouded in mystery. The chauffeur, who killed Geiger and is himself murdered, never appears on screen. Marlowe finds at Geiger's place a "sucker list" in code, which Brody was eager to have. We never learn what it signifies. What are the "suckers" suckered into, and what does it have to do with Geiger's books? There is a good deal of mystery surrounding furtive activity around Geiger's bookstore, and boxes of books are removed quickly, after his death, but the woman running the store knows nothing of rare books. What is going on? Is the store more than a front for a blackmail racket? These questions are never answered.

But there are hints, and it is in them that major effects of the film lie. In many ways, the mystery both begins and climaxes in Geiger's house. The dominating motif is Oriental, with sculptured Buddhas, oriental-looking decorated fabrics, beaded curtains, and the like. The decor is presented as exotic, matching the activities that occur there. Like the camera concealed within the sculptured head or the list in code, much is concealed, unexplained, perhaps unexplainable. Marlowe seems to understand much of it but says little. He looks in the sculptured head for the camera, then in the camera for the missing film. He sniffs the empty glass near Carmen and seems to understand what it contains. Later, he seems to know why Geiger's body is so carefully laid out, but he never verbalizes it. The film develops a major gap between what Marlowe understands, which enables him to solve the case, and what the audience understands, which leaves it in the dark. The audience can only search for clues to whatever it is that Marlowe does not, or cannot, reveal. Those clues exist only on a subtextual level.

The Oriental furnishings of Geiger's house and the veiled activities that go on there associate it with death, sex, blackmail, exotic drugs, and pornographic activity. This association extends to Geiger's store, which is decorated with Oriental objects—a Buddha-like head, a statue—similar to those in Geiger's house. Geiger himself, whom the viewer never clearly sees in life, is described as having a "Charlie Chan moustache," amid other characteristics presented as distasteful: he is "fattish, soft all over," and has a glass eye.

Geiger is associated with things Oriental, and in this film, things Oriental suggest mysterious, unexplained, and perverse evil. This is not at all surprising, considering the racism inherent in many American films of the period, and especially considering the fact that most of the film was shot when the United States

Marlowe in Geiger's house. The corpse on the floor is only one aspect of the sinister mise-en-scène (*The Big Sleep*, Warner Brothers). *(Photo courtesy of the Museum of Modern Art.)*

was at war with Japan, when anti-Oriental feeling was particularly strong. Although Hawks could not explicitly show many of the things the story line suggested—nudity, drugs—he could suggest that anything was possible simply by using an exotic Oriental atmosphere. The implicit reasoning is that a man who surrounds himself with Oriental objects is capable of anything.

As Marlowe first enters Geiger's store, he pauses, smirks to himself, pushes his hat brim up, places sunglasses on the bridge of his nose, and affects a fluttery, peevish manner. It is a comic bit, and Bogart does it well, but why is it here? After Geiger's death, Marlowe returns to the store, reprises the fluttery act, and sees Brody and Lundgren packing up the books in the back room. Lundgren watches Marlowe, Brody calls out, "Come on, Carol," and Lundgren returns. Later, Lundgren shoots Brody, and Marlowe brings him to Geiger's house, where he discovers Geiger's carefully attended body.

Marlowe's fluttery act in Geiger's store impersonates popular views of homosexuals, and the fact that he does it upon entering Geiger's store indicates that he feels it has some sort of appropriateness for this Orientally decorated locale. He soon learns that Lundgren is Geiger's "shadow," or assistant. Another suggestive hint comes when Brody calls Lundgren "Carol," a sexually ambiguous name. If there were a homosexual attachment between Lundgren and Geiger, then Lundgren's killing of Joe Brody in mistaken revenge and his concern and peculiar ritualizing over Geiger's body would be explained, and Marlowe's homosexual mimicry at Geiger's store would also be appropriate.

But all of this is obliquely suggested rather than stated in the film. Marlowe clearly knows more than he ever reveals: although he comes to the right conclusions, much of what occurs remains unexplained to the audience. It must accept Marlowe's conclusion on faith.

The fact that things that are opaque and unestablished in the film are explicitly established in the novel is not really relevant to the film. In Chandler's novel, Carmen is nude when Marlowe enters Geiger's house; Geiger and Lundgren are explicitly described as homosexuals; and Geiger's store is explicitly established as trafficking in pornographic books. The film does not establish these things as certainties, only as vague possibilities in an exotic environment, and this aspect of uncertainty seems more the result of careful crafting than incompetent plotting. A great many of the film's subtextual associations overshadow what it unequivocally presents, but they also strike a balance between the dark, pervasive uncertainties in the world Marlowe encounters and the specifics of those uncertainties.

Much about the film has a curiously unresolved quality to it. One example is that Marlowe appears to exist in a world of almost limitless sexual opportunity. He is not sexually aggressive, but women repeatedly come on to him. In his very first scene, Carmen falls into his arms, and she later comes to his apartment. We learn that she is not only promiscuous, but a drug user and potentially homicidal. Marlowe resists her advances, but other opportunities constantly open up to him.

After he first investigates Geiger's store, he goes into a bookstore across the street to ask about Geiger. The proprietress, played by Dorothy Malone in a scene that helped make her

famous, becomes attracted to him so quickly that she closes the
store, pulls down the window shade, removes her glasses, lets
down her hair, and drinks rye with him for an indeterminate
time until the rain stops. When he leaves, she clearly does not
want him to.

When Marlowe follows Brody from Geiger's store, he climbs
into a taxi with an attractive woman driver and tells her it's a
"tail job," and she replies, "I'm your girl, bud." When he leaves,
she suggests he might want to use her again and gives him a
card with her telephone number on it. He asks, "Day and night?"
and she replies, "Night's better. I work during the day."

There are many other examples, such as the giggly hostesses
at Eddie Mars's nightclub or the counter girl at a coffee shop,
from which Marlowe makes a brief telephone call. He asks her
to light his cigarette, and she suggestively looks into his eyes as
she does.

Most of these interactions are very brief, and have little direct
bearing upon the main relationship between Marlowe and Vivian.
They are not the result of flirtatious behavior on Marlowe's part
(as, say, many of the encounters in James Bond films) and
Marlowe is not even presented as especially attractive—in fact,
one of the first things Carmen says to him is that he is not very
tall and his height becomes a kind of running joke in the film.
There is also no hint of sleazy sexuality in the encounters, but
rather, Marlowe is simply established as having virtually unlimited sexual opportunity. Almost every time he turns around,
another attractive woman is smiling longingly at him.

The encounters establish his attractiveness to women, but
point to directions not taken. There are so many interested
women around that they almost become confusing—literally so
at Eddie Mars's nightclub where the women are twins. Each
one is a potential diversion, an allurement that could divert him
from his pursuit of the case, and it becomes a measure of his
integrity that he resists all temptation. Even when he remains
in the bookstore with the Dorothy Malone character, he leaves
the moment Geiger drives up. This action reflects upon a central
moment in the film, when, after Lundgren's capture, Vivian tries
to "sugar" Marlowe off the case, with money and with the
prospect of an affair. Instead of pursuing her seduction attempts,
he stuns her with the central question of the film "What's Eddie

Mars got on you?" His priorities are clear; sex will have to wait until his job is done.

In the second part of the film, the basic conflict becomes clearly defined, and it builds to a man-to-man confrontation between Marlowe and Eddie Mars (John Ridgley). We learn that Mars has been behind nearly everything sinister in the film. He had killed Shawn Regan, who had become involved with Mars's wife, and had led Vivian to believe that Carmen had done it. Much of Vivian's suspicious behavior in the film results from her attempt to cover up the fact that she thinks her sister has killed Regan, possibly after Regan, like Marlowe, spurned her sexual advances. Carmen did not kill Regan, but her nymphomania, drug use, and involvement with pornography and Geiger indicate that she is capable of it. The film's pervasive atmosphere of sexuality points to dangers as sinister as those suggested by Geiger's Oriental surroundings.

Marlowe and Vivian declare their love for one another after Vivian helps Marlowe kill Mars's "best boy," the killer Canino (Bob Steele). Marlowe tells her, "I didn't have a chance to thank you for what you did back there. You looked good, awful good!" This admiration of competence is central to Hawks's ethic, and in most of his films, a central question is invariably whether or not someone is "good," a kind of Hemingway understatement. Early on, Marlowe expresses his respect for Shawn Regan, because "he was a good man at whatever he did." He brags to Mars, after he has killed Mars's hired gunman, "Canino's a pretty good boy. You'll have trouble getting another as good." He had earlier asked Eddie whether or not he killed Regan, and when Eddie asks if he is kidding, Marlowe replies, "All right, I'm kiddin'! You didn't do it yourself, and none of your boys are good enough to do it. I used to know Regan." Once he realizes that Mars did, in fact, kill Regan, a direct confrontation between the two men becomes inevitable. Marlowe outwits Mars, who is killed by his own men. The film closes as Marlowe asks Vivian, "What's wrong with you?" and she replies, "Nothing you can't fix."

In many ways, the film's plot is much more a closed system than that of the novel. In the novel, the only woman to whom Marlowe is attracted is Eddie Mars's wife, but no significant relationship develops between them and he remains alone at the conclusion. Although he kills Canino, Eddie Mars remains alive at the end, with Marlowe suggesting he will "take care" of him in due time. In fact, little that he has dealt with has been resolved in any significant way. In the film, however, Marlowe has everything. He has defeated not only Canino but also Eddie Mars, and he is in love with a woman who is "good." His relationship with her would also, since her sister is mad and her father dying, give him access to the Sternwood fortune.

Earlier endings of the film featured Carmen. In one, as in the novel, she tries to shoot Marlowe and thus proves she killed Regan; in another, she accidentally commits suicide with the compliance of her father's butler; and in another, she is killed by Eddie Mars's men after vicious behavior towards Marlowe. In the film as it was finally released, she disappears from the second half, as does her father, and the focus becomes Marlowe, Vivian, and Eddie Mars.

Chandler felt that Carmen's disappearance from the film was the result of the studio's desire to expand Bacall's part. That factor certainly contributed, but an examination of Hawks's other work (although Hawks reportedly at one point threatened to sue the studio because of the cuts in Carmen's role) would lead one to sense that he would have been happy with the final ending, in which the three central characters (Marlowe, Vivian, and Eddie Mars), all of whom are "good," resolve things among themselves.

The film ends on notes of both entrapment and salvation. Marlowe and Vivian are inside Geiger's house, Eddie's body is on the floor, and his killers may still be outside. Marlowe had, just prior to forcing Eddie's death, shot and shattered the sculptured Oriental head that had hidden the camera—symbolically shattering a focal point of the subtextual world of evil—but he and Vivian are still surrounded by sinister Oriental artifacts inside and by killers outside. As they gaze into one another's eyes, we hear a police siren. The film ends, and we see the two cigarettes smoldering in the ashtray.

It is likely that they will be freed, but it is also possible that they will be killed, an ambiguity rather appropriate for a film so heroic in its assumptions, on the one hand, and so sinister in its implications, on the other.

Chandler was quite happy with the film, especially with

Hawks's taut direction and Bogart's on-screen toughness. He commented that unlike Alan Ladd, who he felt was a small boy's idea of a tough guy, Bogart could be tough without a gun. He also felt that Bogart was superior to Dick Powell, although later he was to say that there was a great difference between his Marlowe and Bogart playing Marlowe.

And there is. The film also differs in many ways from dominant *film noir* modes. It has no retrospective narration, no flashbacks,

A dark and dangerous world. Marlowe, after having been beaten by thugs in an alley, meets Harry Jones (Elisha Cook, Jr.), someone else he doesn't know (*The Big Sleep*, Warner Brothers). (*Photo courtesy of the State Historical Society of Wisconsin.*)

no sense of a haunted, lonely, or vulnerable central character, and no black widow. The film does not attempt to jab the viewer off balance with unexpected camera angles or unusually harsh lighting or limitless murky shadows. Marlowe is not poor or desperate, and although he is twice badly beaten, he retaliates effectively and shows no scars, physical or psychic. He certainly inhabits a sinister world but remains above it, as the heroes of Hawks's films do, and triumphs completely at the end. However, *The Big Sleep* has become a classic *noir* film, largely because of its presentation of a very sinister, very perverse, very mysterious world, charged with eroticism, uncertainty, and death.

Soon after most of *The Big Sleep* had been shot at Warner Brothers, and while Chandler was writing *The Blue Dahlia* at Paramount, M-G-M, in February of 1945, purchased the film rights to Chandler's most recent novel, *The Lady in the Lake,* for $35,000. The price, three and one-half times what Warner Brothers had paid for *The Big Sleep* less than a year earlier, indicates the growth of Chandler's popularity. All of his four existing novels had now been purchased by four different major Hollywood studios, and he was writing an original screenplay for a fifth.

Chandler was hired to write the screenplay based upon *The Lady in the Lake* and worked on it for thirteen weeks in the summer of 1945. Neither he nor the studio was satisfied with what he produced, and Steve Fisher was called in to re-do it. Chandler refused screenwriting credit on the film.

Robert Montgomery, who had been a major M-G-M star of the 1930s, starred in John Ford's *They Were Expendable* (1945) after naval service in World War II. When Ford became ill towards the end of shooting, Montgomery took over some of the directing and liked it. He wanted to direct his first postwar film. He also wanted to experiment with point of view and proposed doing an entire picture from the point of view of a single character. After complex negotiations, M-G-M allowed him to try the technique with Chandler's novel, as long as he also starred in the film.

Lady in the Lake was the first Hollywood film to be presented almost completely from a single point of view. It is particularly appropriate that a Chandler novel should be chosen as the basis of such a film. Much of *film noir* was obsessed with individual perception, and with its distintegration, and *Murder, My Sweet* had already broken new ground in the development of the hard-boiled perspective in films. *Lady in the Lake* would push that experimentation further. Curiously enough, Chandler, all of whose novels are presented in the first person, had little interest in first-person point of view in his major film scripts and wrote most of them using a third-person, "objective" viewpoint. When he learned that Montgomery was going to use a first-person technique in *Lady in the Lake*, he mocked the idea.

Most discussion of the film has centered upon this technique, whose stated rationale is to make the viewer the detective. The film opens with Montgomery, playing Philip Marlowe, directly addressing the camera: "You'll see it just as I saw it—you'll meet the people, you'll find the clues—and maybe you'll solve it quick and maybe you won't." Marlowe then tells the story of the case in flashback, but, in contrast to *Murder, My Sweet*, in which we see Marlowe in his flashback tale, in *Lady in the Lake*, Marlowe is generally invisible, because the camera—the viewer—*is* Marlowe. We see things as Marlowe sees them. Characters stare directly into the camera and speak; Marlowe's voice responds. If someone slaps Marlowe, that preson slaps at the camera. When Marlowe lights up a cigarette, smoke intermittently fills the frame as he exhales and speaks. If something catches his eye, the camera pans to observe it. At one point, an attractive, blonde receptionist walks past when Marlowe speaks with Adrienne Fromsett (Audrey Totter). While Fromsett is still talking, the camera pans to follow the seductive-looking receptionist. We then hear the voice of the outraged Miss Fromsett asking Marlowe to refocus his attention upon her, and the camera pans back to her.

This point-of-view technique required a number of basic deviations from Hollywood conventions. For obvious reasons, the shot–reverse shot method of shooting and editing had to be abandoned, and much of the film gives the initial appearance of having been done as a series of long takes. But many of the moving pan shots that represent Marlowe's surveying of a room or moving from one place to another incorporate quick, almost invisible cuts. Montgomery had to spend a good deal of time retraining the actors, because performing in the film involved direct violation of a basic rule of Hollywood acting: do not look at the camera. The actors had to look at the camera, talk to it,

Marlowe's (Robert Montgomery) image reflected in a mirror as he speaks with a suspicious Adrienne Fromsett (Audrey Totter). This is one of the few times the audience is able to see the subjectively-presented main character in *Lady in the Lake* (Metro-Goldwyn-Mayer). *(Photo courtesy of Cinemabilia.)*

even hit it. To facilitate this retraining, Montgomery frequently crouched under the camera during takes.

We only see Marlowe when he directly addresses the camera (four times in the film) or when, within his point of view, he passes a mirror. Because of their deviation from Hollywood practice, both techniques make of him and his personality an almost monolithic presence. Whether he addresses us or whether "we" are "he," his point of view is dominant, almost oppressive. The change from "inside" to "outside" the character does not diffuse his presence, but doubly imprints it.

Following the practice in previous Marlowe films, and in Hollywood adaptations of fiction in general, the story is largely structured around the romantic involvement of the major characters. Like *The Big Sleep* (and somewhat less like *Murder, My Sweet*), the film gives central status to a romance that is much less important or even nonexistent in the source novel, and it ends on a note of romantic fulfillment absent from the novel.

A basic organizational principle for the film is the occasionally jarring combination or juxtaposition of things that initially appear incompatible. The opening credits, for example, appear on Christmas cards, and Christmas songs are sung on the sound track. When the last card is pulled away, we suddenly see a small black pistol. One does not generally associate guns with Christmas, but this film establishes a Christmas atmosphere that counterpoints the sinister events in the story (the basic story line begins three days before Christmas and ends on Christmas Day). The main characters are depressed, lonely, and fed up with their lives, at a time when everyone about them is celebrating communion and happiness. At a particularly low point in the film, on Christmas Eve, when there have already been a number of killings, when more are inevitable, and soon after Marlowe himself has nearly been killed, we hear a radio announcer proclaim that death has taken a holiday. For the first Christmas Eve in years, there have been no deaths in the area, according to the announcer. The film frequently juxtaposes apparently incompatible settings and emotional environments. After Marlowe discovers the body of a murdered man crumpled in a bullet-riddled shower, Montgomery cuts to a Christmas party. Later, after Marlowe himself is nearly murdered and has blacked out on an isolated roadside, he awakens in the elegant apartment of the woman he will love. This structural principle of surprise and incongruity also applies to the film's character development.

At one point, Marlowe is in the office of the tough police captain Kane (Tom Tully), who is the only one capable of controlling the corrupt and brutal Lieutenant DeGarmot (Lloyd Nolan). Kane suddenly receives a telephone call from his young daughter. He speaks about her Christmas stocking and recites a Christmas poem to her. Obviously a doting father, he periodically looks sheepishly at Marlowe (the camera), realizing the incongruity of his roles as no-nonsense police captain and sentimental father.

Such surprising, but relatively minor, incongruities parallel the central character oppositions in the film. DeGarmot is a good policeman become corrupt, largely because of his degrading love for Mildred Haveland (Jayne Meadows), who is responsible for most of the murders and who had left him some time ago. In the climactic scene, he tells Mildred and Marlowe that once he kills them, he will be free both of her and of Marlowe's knowledge of his involvement with her, and will, consequently, be able to return to being an honest cop again. Marlowe comments, "First you cover up a murder for her and then you kill her. Doesn't make sense, does it?" DeGarmot asks him, "How does it feel to die in the dirty middle of somebody else's love affair?" He then tells Marlowe: "You're in the same boat I'm in, but you're gonna be in it dead."

DeGarmot's explicit comparison of his own fate with Marlowe's appears accurate at the time he makes it, because it appears that Marlowe has also been betrayed by a woman he loved and trusted: Adrienne Fromsett.

Adrienne initially appears to have all the qualifications for a villainess. She edits a series of sleazy-looking magazines, with titles like *Lurid Detective*, *True Horror Tales*, *Monster Stories*, and *Murder Masterpieces*. When we first see her, she is discussing the layout of one of the magazines with an assistant, telling him, "No Vic, it won't do—not enough gore, not nearly enough gore." When Vic argues, "Well, that's because you don't see it in color," she replies, "Color or no color, there's not enough blood. Take it out and put more blood in."

From early on, she is portrayed as "unfeminine" according to contemporary codes. This first sight of her shows her in a position of power and ordering a man around, as well as proving herself even more extreme than the man on issues—blood and gore—generally considered unfeminine. She clearly does not know her "place" and threatens the culturally presumed masculine position of dominance.

She is also in a superior position to Marlowe. He has come to her, hoping to start a career as a writer because he is fed up with being a detective. She has little interest in his story but has cleverly manipulated his literary aspirations to acquire his services as a detective. He feels betrayed when he learns this and initially refuses to work for her, but she quickly outbargains him. When he implicitly agrees to take the case, she coldly tells him, to his humiliation, that every man has his price.

Adrienne soon demonstrates other highly suspicious characteristics. She is admittedly a gold digger, who wants to marry her rich but bland boss, Derace Kingsby (Leon Ames), and has already established a relationship of some intimacy with him.

She hires Marlowe to track down Kingsby's missing wife, hoping to precipitate a divorce. Later, when murder becomes an issue, she gleefully hopes to incriminate Kingsby's wife. When Marlowe informs Kingsby of his involvement in the case, Kingsby becomes outraged and tells Adrienne to stay out of his private life. She bitterly tells Marlowe, "So you lost me my million dollars. Aren't you smart?" The comment clearly indicates her perception of her relationship with Kingsby.

An additional strike against her potential as a heroine is that she is presented as sexually experienced. She has probably had an affair with Chris Lavery, a gigolo also involved with Mildred Haveland. Her relationship with Kingsby is not explicitly defined, but we do know that she wants to legally dispose of his wife and that she also has a Christmas present for him, a bathrobe, at her apartment. The nature of the gift, combined with the fact that Kingsby is married, points at least to the fact that Kingsby has spent time in her apartment and that they may have become intimate. Her hopes of supplanting his wife support this.

She is the type of woman who, according to the codes of the time, had either to be tamed or destroyed by a man. If not, she would destroy him. When DeGarmot tells Marlowe that they are "in the same boat," he refers to the fact that Mildred has destroyed his life. He kills her, hoping to be free of her, but things have gone too far, and he is soon destroyed as a result of his relationship with her.

Marlowe is in a comparable position. He has become involved with a dominating, castrating woman. Although a number of interchanges have led him to believe that he may have "tamed" her, the final test involves his supposed meeting with Kingsby's wife. Marlowe knows that the meeting is very possibly a trap laid to kill him. To protect himself, he asks Adrienne to wait a short time and then to tell Captain Kane how to find him and, if it is a trap, to save him. But DeGarmot arrives instead, indicating to Marlowe that Adrienne has betrayed him. Just as DeGarmot is destroyed by his relationship with Mildred, so Marlowe appears doomed by his trust in Adrienne.

Much of the film involves Marlowe's efforts to "right" the sexual imbalance between himself and Adrienne Fromsett. After she insults him during their first meeting by proving that he can be bought, he tells her that her lipstick is on crooked. She rushes to a mirror, and Marlowe smugly comments, "Vain female, aren't you?" She immediately becomes less aggressive and asks for his help. When Marlowe comes to her apartment at night, we see her for the first time in traditionally "feminine" attire (a flowing nightgown), rather than in her business clothes. Marlowe tells her what he has learned, and she starts to puzzle it out. He abruptly cuts her off: "Why don't you just look beautiful, and quit worrying about guns, and dead females, and missing ones, and that million bucks you want to marry?" His priorities are clear: a woman's role is not to think but to "just look beautiful," and Adrienne will be better off when she learns it.

She soon comes to his apartment to abase herself and to swear that she has not murdered anyone and did not have an affair with Chris Lavery. Clearly under the influence of his self-righteous masculinity, she tells Marlowe that she is all mixed up. Marlowe curtly tells her, "The girl I like won't be editing a string of magazines or looking for a quick million bucks or trying to hang a murder on another woman." When she asks, "What will this girl do?" he replies, "Take care of me. Unglamorous, isn't it?"

This treatment of her is evidently successful, because, in her apartment on Christmas Eve, she tells him, "I want to take care of you. Maybe it isn't glamourous. I don't know. I want to be your girl. That's what I want for Christmas." They spend Christmas Day together in apparent postcoital bliss (she has changed her clothes, he is smoking, she is telling her life story).

The final showdown resolves not only the case but also their relationship. Marlowe risks his life on her loyalty. She begs him not to go, but he tells her he must, because, if he never learns the answers to the case, "I'd never be sure about you, would I?" Both repeat what has become a code phrase for their relationship: "I'm scared, but it's wonderful."

When confronted with DeGarmot and certain he has been betrayed, Marlowe says, "I'm scared, but it isn't wonderful anymore." At this point, DeGarmot declares that they are both "in the same boat." But they are not. Adrienne has been faithful, and Kane arrives to kill DeGarmot. In the closing scene of the film, we see Marlowe and Adrienne preparing to travel to New York together. He asks, "You scared?" and she replies, "Yes, but it's wonderful." They kiss, in the only scene violating the point-of-view format of the film.

In many ways, the question of Adrienne's sexual role is more central to the film than the unraveling of the murder mystery. Until the very end, the possibility exists that she may be a black widow, like the frenzied, psychotic Mildred Haveland. Adrienne's "salvation" at Marlowe's hands may, after all, be only an act, and that is why the final "all or nothing" gamble on Marlowe's part is so important. He risks his life on the hope that she has finally learned her "duty," which is to help her "man." Nothing else—not her career, not any other aspect of her personal life—is important.

Her final line "Yes, but it's wonderful" resembles Vivian Rutledge's final line in *The Big Sleep:* "Nothing you can't fix." In both films, the central female character is a potential black widow—Vivian, because she is working with Eddie Mars in an attempt to cover up what she believes to be her sister's murder of Regan; and Adrienne, because of her castrating, "unfeminine" past. In both films, the Marlowe character forces the woman to switch her allegiance (from Eddie Mars; from Derace Kingsby) to him, to "come clean" and accept his domination. Both films end with a clear declaration of their acceptance of this role. Love has survived mortal danger, a mortal danger and web of murders that have largely been caused by another woman (Carmen Sternwood; Mildred Haveland) who did not know her "place" and, consequently, wreaked havoc.

The Marlowes of both films are dominating males, but their circumstances differ a good deal. Bogart's Marlowe seems happy with his work and reasonably successful. Montgomery's, however, is much more down-and-out; he works for only ten dollars a day (Bogart's makes twenty-five dollars a day) and wants to abandon the detective business: "I was tired of being pushed around for just nickels and dimes, so I decided I'd write about murder." He appears poor, bitter, and alone. Like Bogart's Marlowe, he is arrogant, but he does not have that character's wit and verbal resilience, and most of his wisecracks come across as coarse, smug retorts. He is much more of a brute.

But both films, unlike the novels upon which they are based, have romantic "couple" endings. In each film, a female character whose counterpart in the book had no real romantic involvement with Marlowe serves as the basis for Marlowe's central romantic interest. Whereas Marlowe ends each novel alone, at the end of each film, he is happily in love with a woman much wealthier than he. This conclusion also occurs in *Murder, My Sweet,* with

Marlowe's happy romantic involvement with Ann Grayle, now sole heir to the Grayle fortune.

Chandler's *The Lady in the Lake* has as a central theme the decay of human relationships and of individuals. Marlowe describes the body of the lady found in the lake as the "thing that had been a woman."[2] In the novel's last line, Marlowe describes DeGarmo (the basis for the film's DeGarmot), who has just committed suicide after his life has fallen apart, as "something that had been a man" (*The Lady in the Lake*, p. 217). In the film, the decay of Mildred Haveland and DeGarmot as individuals and as a couple is used to counterpoint the rising and restorative romantic relationship of Marlowe and Adrienne Fromsett. In this film, as in the earlier Marlowe films, contemporary cinematic codes had much more to do with shaping the direction of the narrative than did Chandler's novel.

The same can be said for director John Brahm's *The Brasher Doubloon*, based upon *The High Window* and released four months after *Lady in the Lake*. As with *Murder, My Sweet*, the studio (in this case, Twentieth Century-Fox) had made a film based upon the same novel only a few years earlier. It would now use the novel for a second film, one not in the happy-go-lucky mode of *Time to Kill* but influenced by the dark, somber style that had emerged in the intervening years.

The Brasher Doubloon marks an end point in this first cycle of Chandler-based films. All four of the then existing Chandler novels had been the basis for a Marlowe film; *The Brasher Doubloon* was to be the last made in Chandler's lifetime. It was less obviously ambitious than any of its predecessors. *Murder, My Sweet* had experimented with techniques new to American audiences and signaled an emerging style; *The Big Sleep*, made with major stars by a major director at a major studio, put big money into this new style; and *Lady in the Lake*, also with a major star, made a narrative experiment quite appropriate to the *noir* mode that was radical for a Hollywood film.

The Brasher Doubloon came along when the style had already been established, so established that it was being parodied in films like *My Favorite Brunette* (1947). It had neither a large budget, major stars, nor a "hot" director, and it generated none of the critical enthusiasm that surrounded the earlier Marlowe films.

Interest in the private detective genre was declining and being deflected into other media. In the summer of 1947, the first Marlowe radio series appeared; in 1948, another followed. There were a number of negotiations for a television series, but in a letter to Sandoe, Chandler wrote simply: "Private dick stories are dead" (February 26, 1951). He was right. After *The Brasher Doubloon*, more than twenty years were to pass before the appearance of another Marlowe film.

Like its predecessors, *The Brasher Doubloon* is structured largely around a romance with little basis in the source novel. In the voice-over introduction, Marlowe (George Montgomery) tells us, "It was the voice of the girl on the phone that got me." The voice belongs to Merle Davis (Nancy Guild), and Marlowe flirts with her as soon as they meet. After Mrs. Murdock (Florence Bates) tells him about the missing doubloon, he decides not to take the case because he feels Mrs. Murdock is withholding information. Only after Merle pleads with him does he agree to take "both cases—yours and Mrs. Murdock's."

Marlowe's motivation is romantic from the beginning. The actual mystery of the missing doubloon and the murders that follow hold less interest for him than Merle does. The case becomes an impediment to be removed so that he can get to the "real" business at hand: Merle.

The film links romance with danger, in much the same way earlier Marlowe films did. It also contrives to present that linkage as an historically verifiable fact of human nature. Marlowe announces, after discovering the first murder victim, "I got into this thing on account of a pretty face. The ancient Trojans were sucked into a ten-year war for the same reason, but they didn't regret it any more than I did." Marlowe is not the only one to give this linkage of romance and violence an historical context. Elisha Morningstar summarizes the history of the Brasher Doubloon in terms without basis in the novel, but reminiscent of Casper Gutman's history of the Maltese falcon. He says the coin "has a romantic and violent history. . . . First, the man who coined it was murdered and robbed through the treachery of a female, and since then, at least seven other owners of the coin have come to abrupt, unhappy ends."

Like the earlier films, *The Brasher Doubloon* ends with the heroine declaring her love for, and faith in, her savior, Marlowe. Merle sits in Marlowe's lap and says, "You said you were taking both cases—Mrs. Murdock's and mine. Mine isn't solved yet."

Marlowe replies, "It will be. I got a feeling you're going to graduate with honors." Fade-out.

The film's narrative is rather simple, probably more so than any film yet based upon a Chandler novel. It uses retrospective narration, but the narration does little more than provide narrative linkage and motivation; it does not develop a complex, perceiving personality as was becoming representative of the genre by this time. Much of the film's value lies outside of its narrative structure and in its carefully developed *mise-en-scène*.

In the opening shots of the film, as Marlowe approaches the Murdock house, his voice-over narration tells us of his hatred for the hot summer wind, and we see large palm trees around the house blown by that wind. Once inside the dark, cluttered Victorian mansion, Marlowe is led into a large sun room to meet Mrs. Murdock. The shadows from the waving palms outside pervade the room. We see these shadows only upon Marlowe and upon the walls behind, not upon Mrs. Murdock. They so dominate the shots of Marlowe that they suggest something threatening, warning him of danger to come.

Marlowe (George Montgomery) and the sinister Mrs. Murdock (Florence Bates) in her sunroom in *The Brasher Doubloon* (Twentieth Century-Fox). *(Photo courtesy of the Museum of Modern Art.)*

The first three major sets we see—the Murdock house, Marlowe's office, and Elisha Morningstar's office—all have sinister aspects to them. Brahm at times photographs them from unconventional angles and frequently places objects between the camera and the focus of dramatic attention—a hat rack in Marlowe's office, scales in Morningstar's office, statuary in Mrs. Murdock's house—that loom unsettlingly large in the frame and cumulatively generate the sense of something ominous.

The lighting contributes to this sense. Not only do we see the shadows of the waving palms inside the Murdock house but the house itself is crisscrossed with dark objects and heavy shadows. We see heavy beams across the ceilings, and obscured statuary and alcoves throughout. Similarly, both Marlowe's and Morningstar's offices are lighted either too harshly or too dimly: we see harsh blinds slashing the daylight outside or huge shades obscuring it, and distorting shadows everywhere, even in the hallways immediately outside the offices.

After visiting Morningstar's office, Marlowe goes to the rooming house of the first murder victim, George Anson, where many of the earlier lighting motifs intensify. Before entering Anson's room, Marlowe walks down a long hallway with a large window at the far end. It looks like a path to doom because it combines the harsh exterior light with the heavy, chaotic interior shadows. Once inside the apartment, Marlowe comes to a closed bathroom door. As he pushes it open, Brahm cuts to an overhead shot, and we look down upon Marlowe and upon Anson's crumpled body next to a bathtub. We then see a closer shot, from inside the bathroom, of Anson's head next to the curve of the tub. It is shot in such a way as to make the tub look like a toilet. The Production Code would not allow toilets to be shown in films in 1947, but the camera work suggests what it cannot show and adds to the grotesqueness of the image. When the police come to question Marlowe, Brahm photographs them in huge low-angle close-ups that give them a monstrous appearance.

Once murder has become involved, Brahm reprises the first three sets in even more sinister ways, thus demonstrating his skill at making the environment central to the film's development. These sets had all been photographed in daylight; now we see them at night. Marlowe returns to Morningstar's office to find him dead on a cluttered floor. A neon light from outside flashes dully into the room and accentuates rather than disperses the darkness. Marlowe returns to the Murdock mansion. From outside, it now looks like a haunted house, and inside, it is even darker than before. The shadows of the waving palms in Mrs. Murdock's sun room seem huger and more dominating.

Then Marlowe returns to his office. Again, it is darker, more shadow-dominated. Inside, the dull neon light from the "Broadway Hollywood Hotel" goes on and off. An intruder enters and threatens to shoot Marlowe. The sets of the film become more sinister as the events of the story become more deadly.

We soon see Marlowe go to his apartment, where Merle awaits. It is virtually the only fully lit, nonthreatening set in the film, and it is a surprising change of pace. The lighting is soft; everyone and everything are visible. Merle has come, under orders from Mrs. Murdock, to entice Marlowe into giving up the coin. For the first time, we see her in black and erotically clothed. When enticement fails, she pulls a gun and orders Marlowe to undress. Her actions are more suspicious than anything she has previously done. Marlowe disarms her and wins her over. One might say the very lighting of the apartment indicates that it is a place for salvation. Merle has entered it at her lowest point of degradation, but once in it, she begins her recovery. When she sleeps there, Marlowe, against her protestations, chivalrously leaves to sleep in his office.

He is kidnapped and brought to an underground gangster's den adjoining a nightclub. It looks like something out of *The Blue Angel*. Brahm, in fact, was a German immigrant, who had worked in Weimar Germany, and much of the film shows strong German expressionist influence, nowhere more so than this sequence, when Marlowe comes closest to being killed. The ceilings are low, and the rooms shadow-ridden and claustrophobic. When Marlowe is beaten, a shot from his point of view on the floor shows the heads of the thugs looking down; it is like a ball's view of a football huddle. Marlowe escapes by crashing through a window, and his flight through the low-life area of the city recalls sets in Fritz Lang's *M*. At one point, he rushes into a saloon and screams, "There's a busted wine barrel in there," and the whole degenerate mob rushes after it. The dark alleys and degenerate lost souls of the night he encounters in his brief flight form a classic *noir* environment.

The next day, Merle calls Marlowe to Vannier's house, where Vannier (Fritz Kortner) lies murdered. As Marlowe approaches, the hot wind still blows, and the trees and shrubs virtually obscuring the house move as though alive, recalling the palms outside the Murdock mansion. Even when Marlowe is inside, we continually see the almost frantic and sinister movement outside.

Inside Vannier's house, Marlowe finds the evidence with which Vannier had blackmailed Mrs. Murdock. It is film footage showing Mrs. Murdock shoving her husband out of a window to his death. Marlowe then gathers virtually the entire cast in his office, shows the film, and proves Mrs. Murdock guilty of killing her husband as well as Vannier. He also proves her son, Leslie (Conrad Janis), guilty of killing Anson and Morningstar. Leslie had killed the two men to get the film, not in order to free his mother from danger but rather to get money for settling gambling debts from gangsters who would use the film to blackmail Mrs. Murdock.

Mrs. Murdock's family is perverse. She murders her husband for infidelity, but she loves her son. Her son, also a double murderer, hopes to betray her. The perversity in the film does not end there. Vannier's prime goal was not blackmail but the Brasher Doubloon. He had a fetishist's desire for the coin. Marlowe asks him, "Why so frantic, little man?" when he showed him the coin, and Vannier virtually drooled over it. Vannier has a German accent and appears a repressed wreck. Marlowe comments on the abnormality of his interests: "The guy had been a collector all right. He apparently collected whatever normal people threw out when they cleaned up their attics."

But abnormality strikes much closer to home. A major aspect of Mrs. Murdock's perversity is that she consciously tries to drive Merle insane and beyond the arena of sexual desirability. Mr. Murdock had tried to seduce Merle and had given her a pathological aversion to being touched by men. When Marlowe speaks of "educating" her and of her graduating "with honors" at the end, he means educating her out of this phobia. Apparently, although the film is unclear about this event, Mr. Murdock made a particularly offensive advance towards Merle on the day his wife murdered him. Merle was presumably so disoriented that Mrs. Murdock convinced her that she had killed Mr. Murdock. Mrs. Murdock then let Merle believe that she paid Vannier's blackmail to protect Merle and not herself. This ensured Merle's lifetime loyalty and service and allowed Mrs. Murdock to work over a long period of time to make Merle frigid and, consequently, undesirable to men.

But she also uses Merle's sexuality for her own ends. When she learns that Marlowe has the coin, she orders Merle to get it from him, saying, "Didn't you see the way he was looking at you? . . . Capitalize on what you've got, child. It would have been no problem for me when I was your age." At this point, under Mrs. Murdock's influence, Merle goes to Marlowe's apartment. But it is there that Marlowe's influence triumphs over Mrs. Murdock, and Merle starts on the road to mental health and sexual ecstasy.

This new direction for Merle thwarts Mrs. Murdock's jealous and destructive desires. At the end, after her two murders have been discovered, after she learns her son had planned to betray her, and after Merle learns of her plan to drive her insane, Mrs. Murdock clings to her one remaining accomplishment. She screams, "You'll never steal another woman's husband! But I've had my revenge. Just look at you—you shiver and shudder every time a man so much as lays a finger on you! What man would fall in love with a lunatic?" As the police drag her out, she continues to scream, "A lunatic!" But even in this prediction, she will be thwarted. Marlowe will soon continue Merle's "education."

Like the three earlier Marlowe films, *The Brasher Doubloon* ends with Marlowe "saving" a troubled woman he has come to desire. Like the earlier films also, the cause of much of the evil is the action of a genuinely evil woman who threatens familial and social stability. In the earlier films, the villainess was a desirable woman capable of luring men to their doom; in *The Brasher Doubloon,* the woman has lost her desirability and wants not to entrap and destroy men, as she may have done in her youth, but to obliterate desirability in a woman who still possesses it.

Although *The Brasher Doubloon* is narrated from Marlowe's point of view, there is never any real threat to that point of view. Although he is beaten up, he is never especially befuddled, or existentially weary; he never hallucinates and never has reason to question his own perceptions, as happens with the Marlowe in *Murder, My Sweet* and the Marlowe in *Lady in the Lake*, and as was becoming pervasive in *noir* films.

The pattern of mental breakdown and uncertainty, however, appears in Merle. She clearly believes she did what she did not do: kill Mr. Murdock. She is capable of acting in ways wholly opposed to what the film presents as her "nature," that is, in dressing seductively in black and in trying to seduce or murder Marlowe. She lives in psychic bondage to Mrs. Murdock, wholly confused as to her own identity. It requires Marlowe to restore her mental coherence. His role moves beyond the clearing away of situational impediments to romance, as in earlier Marlowe films, to one of partial psychic restoration and partial psychic creation. She will owe not only her salvation to him but her very identity. In this role, Marlowe not only reinforces, as the Marlowe of the other films had done, the patriarchal social structure by participating in the destruction or containment of one evil woman and in the salvation of one good one, but he virtually assumes the role of Jehovah Himself.

This elevated role has a curious analogue in the film's final sequence. To prove Mrs. Murdock's guilt, he shows the incriminating film in his office. Interestingly, it is a film, and not a still picture, as in the source novel and even in *Time to Kill*. At this point, the audience watches a film that the characters within the film are watching. It is being projected by Marlowe: he sets up the screen: he runs the projector. We see most of the viewers clustered as they watch, and then we see isolated shots of Marlowe against a blank wall, controlling all. He shows the film that shows Mr. Murdock, from a great distance, falling from a building. Mrs. Murdock says that it shows what she already knew, that Merle pushed her husband from the window. Merle agrees with her, and the police prepare to arrest Merle.

Suddenly, Marlowe tells everyone to sit down. He says, "That was too far away for you to see anyone clearly. These are the films that Vannier used for blackmail, all right, but they don't prove anything. Now here's an enlarged version of the same film." He has the lights again turned out, and the enlarged version of the film clearly shows Mrs. Murdock in the window. It is possible that even Vannier had not seen this and that the police would have accepted the original film as proof that Merle, and not Mrs. Murdock, committed the murder—and Merle would have agreed with them. Marlowe, by seeing what no one else can see; by forcing others to see what they had earlier seen, but had not seen; by using the very medium in which he is presented to the audience; and by controlling the image (turning it on and off, enlarging it) assumes godlike stature—dispenser of truth—not only to the characters in the film but also, by his control of the film form, to the audience.

8 | LOOKING BACKWARD: MARLOWE, THE LONG GOODBYE, FAREWELL, MY LOVELY, and THE BIG SLEEP

Marlowe (1969) was the first film based upon a Chandler novel (*The Little Sister*) after *The Brasher Doubloon,* and the twenty-two–year gap between the two films had seen a great many changes in the film industry and in American culture. Since *Marlowe,* three other films have appeared based upon Chandler novels: *The Long Goodbye* (1973), *Farewell, My Lovely* (1975), and *The Big Sleep* (1978). All reflect those changes.

In the 1940s, *film noir* reflected a contemporary sensibility. Chandler's novels were set in contemporary Los Angeles, and the Marlowes of the films were men of their time: tougher, more honest, and less financially successful than others, but men of their time. By the late 1960s, the romanticized private eye, like the cowboy, was considered part of a past age. He was associated with value structures and styles of filmmaking that were as anachronistic as the fedora or Lucky Strike Green. Even when presented as contemporary men dealing with contemporary problems, they could not help but recall a past age, like modern-day cowboys in pick-up trucks.

154

An instance of overt recognition of this anachronism was the NBC television series "Faraday and Company" (September 1973– August 1974). Frank Faraday (Dan Dailey) is a private eye in the Marlowe mode, who, in the late 1940s, had been imprisoned in South America. He emerges in the 1970s to learn that his son has grown up to become a private detective, and the two join forces. Much of the humor in the series results from Frank's stunned reactions to the modern world, as well as from the fact that his two-fisted, hard-boiled detection methods, his vocabulary and world view are now comically out-of-date, especially when contrasted with the more modern procedures and assumptions of his son.

The new Marlowe films had to confront the fact that they were dealing with "dated" material and adopted a variety of strategies. The most obvious was to present Marlowe as an anachronism, as a man impelled by values themselves out-of-date. The films make Marlowe more of a man alone than do any of the 1940s films. In the 1940s, all of the adaptations developed a central romance for Marlowe that appeared successful at the film's end; all of the post-1960 Marlowe films end with Marlowe alone and having suffered great disappointment. In all but *Marlowe* (1969), he has no romantic involvement at all.

Richard T. Jameson has coined the term "son of noir"[1] to deal with a new, post-1960 type of film that has antecedents in the 1940s style. But the antecedents are more thematic and emotional than formal. The filmmakers respect the older genre, and their films try to approximate its effects—but for a contemporary audience. Examples are Blake Edwards's *Gunn* (1967), Roman Polanski's *Chinatown* (1974), and the post-1940s Marlowe films, especially Robert Altman's *The Long Goodbye* (1973). They deal with a private detective involved in a complex, perverse, and deceptive world, and the investigation often centers upon an alluring and dangerous woman.

This new type of film tends to be in color, as are all of the post-1960 Marlowe films. Instead of the murky darkness and ominous shadows of the 1940s films, they frequently use comparably sinister, too-bright, glossy, color surfaces. In this respect, they owe a debt to many melodramas of the 1950s, such as those directed by Douglas Sirk.

The detective often appears in most scenes, thus allowing

audiences to puzzle out a case more or less confined to his point of view. But there seems less of an imperative in such films to retrospective narration than in the 1940s. Many of the directors served their apprenticeship in television, and television codes may not only have influenced shooting techniques (the use of the zoom lens in *Gunn,* for example, or the split screen in *Marlowe*) but also narrative structure. Although many television detective series use voice-over narration, the filmmakers, in attempting to "update" Marlowe films, may have chosen to discard the technique as being too stylistically "dated."

The suggestion of censorable, "forbidden" material was a major factor of the 1940s *noir* films. By the late 1960s, the Production Code no longer functioned, and the reigning structure of censorship did not prevent the showing of material considered morally dangerous, but it did influence the rating (P, PG, R, X) the completed film was assigned and the minimum age of the audience. In addition, American culture had changed so much since the 1940s that many of the things that had then been considered shocking were no longer so.

Now the "son of noir" films could explicitly show material that previously could only be hinted at. *Gunn* deals explicitly with transvestism; *Chinatown* with incest. Almost as a direct reference to this new freedom, the very first action of *Marlowe* is the untying and removal of a woman's bikini top by her lover.

Transvestism, incest, and nudity are still considered of questionable morality, however, and their use in film, while permitted, gives that film associations of shocking (however mild) or of borderline morality. Such morality is still associated with hard-boiled film sources: witness the advertising campaign for *The Postman Always Rings Twice* (1981), presenting it as a film showing uncontrolled, animalistic sexuality—a "daring" film. All of the recent Marlowe films have received "R" ratings or their equivalent. They now can draw from their source novels in different ways than their 1940s counterparts could; they can now show what in the 1940s they could only obliquely suggest. But, curiously, the change in mores is such that the recent films are not popularly considered nearly as shocking as were their 1940s counterparts.

The credit sequence of *Marlowe* shows a woman surface at the side of a swimming pool and kiss a man, who removes her bikini top. Suddenly the screen splits, and on the right-hand side, we see a young man hiding in the nearby bushes and photographing the lovers.

This sequence sets the action of the film in motion. The woman is Mavis Wald (Gayle Hunnicutt), a television star; her lover is Sonny Steelgrave (H. M. Wynant), a gangster. The photographs are being taken by Orrin Quest (Roger Newman), Mavis's brother, and will be used to blackmail her. We have, then, before the credits disappear, the explicit depiction of nudity and of a voyeurism that is especially perverse because it is intrafamilial.

In the last major action of the film, the villainess, Dolores Gonzales (Rita Moreno), is shot dead by her ex-husband just after she has removed her brassiere in a strip-show. Once more, we have nudity, voyeurism, and betrayal shown in ways unthinkable for a 1940s *noir* film. The two actions provide the inception and the resolution of the story.

The film is not set in the late 1940s, as was its source novel, *The Little Sister,* but in the 1960s. Mavis Wald is not a film star, but the star of a television series. Marlowe (James Garner) does not wear a trench coat and fedora, but a sports jacket or a contemporary suit; he goes hatless. Although he looks modern, the film makes it apparent that the times are changing around him, that he really carries the values of an older time with him.

In his very first scene, he looks for Orrin Quest in a rundown hotel called "The Infinite Pad." Various "flower children" lounge outside the place. Marlowe's dress and vocabulary link him with an older, "over-thirty" generation. He later tells Orrin's sister, Orfamay (Sharon Farrell), that Orrin will someday "shuck his sandals and cut his hair and return home." His disdain for modish 1960s life-styles is evident; he associates himself with an earlier time.

This becomes more explicit later in the film when he speaks with a business representative of Mavis's, Mr. Crowell (William Daniels), at a television studio. They stand in the control booth as a show is being shot. Before them, we see the actual performers through a large window. We also see five different television monitors, four of which show the action being filmed onstage in color; the fifth, in black and white, shows a scene with Greta Garbo from *Grand Hotel* (1932). Marlowe watches the film and comments to Crowell, "She was great, wasn't she?" and adds, with directional emphasis, "on the film." Crowell is mildly perturbed and comments that "the show we're doing is out there."

Marlowe is surrounded by five separate contemporary images—the actual performance and four separate television images of it—all in bright color and with razzle-dazzle movement. He prefers the "old-time" image. The form itself is significant. Marlowe emphasizes that the image that interests him is "on the film"—the black-and-white film—not on color tape or on the stage, live. Chandler's novel dealt with the film world, which was culturally dominant in the 1940s. The film, in "updating" the story line, transposes the action to the world of television, which by the 1960s had surpassed film in popularity. The very form to which Marlowe is drawn raises associations of a time gone by. We later learn that he doesn't even know what "sitcom" means and has not seen Mavis Wald's show, the highest-rated sitcom in the country.

Marlowe is associated with older values in other ways. At one point, Winslow Wong (Bruce Lee), one of Steelgrave's henchmen, comes to Marlowe's office to intimidate him. Wong puts on an elaborate kung fu performance, in the process smashing up Marlowe's office. As Wong becomes more ferocious and destructive in what was perceived in the late 1960s as a mysterious, "foreign" method of combat, Marlowe appears mortally endangered and unequipped to deal with this threat. Suddenly he produces a pistol and aims it at Wong. Marlowe has turned the tables by using a more traditionally American method of self-defense.

Later, Marlowe is lured onto the roof of a high building by Wong, who again puts on a threatening kung fu display, maneuvering Marlowe closer and closer to the edge. When Marlowe stands on the edge itself, he taunts: "Why you're light on your feet, Winslow. Are you just a little gay, huh?" This infuriates Wong, who makes a flying leap. Marlowe jumps aside, and Wong goes sailing to his death.

Marlowe represents a cluster of Anglo-Saxon values that, in the 1960s, found themselves increasingly threatened. The traditional American action hero fought with his two fists or his gun or his wits, and took on all comers. He was not intimidated by exotic "foreign" methods of combat. A scene in *Raiders of the*

Marlowe (James Garner) turns the tables on the threatening Winslow
Wong (Bruce Lee) in *Marlowe* (Metro-Goldwyn-Mayer). *(Photo courtesy
of Cinemabilia.)*

Lost Ark (1981) works in a similar way to those scenes between
Marlow and Wong. Indiana Jones (Harrison Ford) is confronted
in an Egyptian marketplace by a tall, sinister-looking Arab
carrying a huge sword. As the crowd clears away in terror, the
Arab starts whirling the sword in a dazzling display of virtuosity.
He appears deadly. Jones, who has not once moved during this
entire performance, finally assumes a look of bemused and
contemptuous dismissiveness, casually draws his gun, and kills
the man with a single shot before dashing on to his next adventure.
As in the scenes between Marlowe and Wong, we have someone
clearly "American" threatened by someone clearly "foreign," and
defeating him. Victory, as presented in both films, brings with
it associations of cultural and racial superiority.

In the 1960s, various Oriental martial arts, such as karate and
kung fu, were becoming popular in the United States and were
seen as more effective than traditional American modes of combat,
such as boxing. The popular ABC television series of the 1970s
Kung Fu (October 1972–June 1975) stressed the Eastern origins

of the discipline, as well as its superiority to American modes of combat. The hero, Caine (David Carradine), would often confront cowboys, the most classic of American heroes, and defeat them. (Bruce Lee was to become a representative figure of this kind of fighting, and a "Bruce Lee film" *means* a film dealing with deadly forms of Oriental combat.)

In *Marlowe*, Marlowe confronts Wong twice and wins. The film depicts Wong as all form with little substance. For all of his virtuosity, Wong is clearly no match for a bullet, and even when Marlowe does not use his gun, he can easily outwit Wong. Marlowe tells him, "You're very impressive, Winslow, but I've seen dogs do better on television," thus, by implication, reducing the skills needed to master kung fu to those of a trained dog. Marlowe then proves Wong's inferiority by provoking him to leap to his death.

He provokes him by suggesting that Wong is "a little gay." Not only is the word "little" a pun on Wong's height compared with the taller Marlowe but the association of homosexuality with exotic foreignness provides a double counterpoint to the all-American Marlowe, clearly white, American, heterosexual, and superior.

The racism implicit in the two Winslow Wong scenes is reinforced in the scene following his death. There have been two deaths earlier in the film, both involving white criminals. In both cases, Marlowe views the bodies of men, for whom he had no particular respect, with respect for death. These deaths sober him.

Director Paul Bogart, however, never shows Wong's body. The last we see of him is his foolish sailing off of the rooftop, almost like a cartoon character. Unlike the two white victims, we do not get a sobering look at him in death. Rather, we see Marlowe reenter the restaurant and walk past Steelgrave, who appears surprised to see Marlowe unharmed. Marlowe says nothing but makes a humorous "sailing" gesture with his hand. We never hear of Wong again in the film, and none of the deaths to come is treated so lightheartedly. Consequently, in both its presentation to the film's audience and in the response of the characters within the film to it, Wong's death is little more than a joke.

The other major "foreign" character is Dolores Gonzales, the major villainess. She is a friend of Mavis Wald and a direct contrast to her. Mavis is presented as an all-American girl from Manhattan, Kansas, who is now the clean-cut star of the country's number-one situation comedy. She is vulnerable to blackmail because of the purity of her public image. Crowell tells Marlowe, "Can you imagine what would happen if it got out that our pure little Mary was shacking up with Public Enemy Number One?" But although she is having an affair with Steelgrave, she is presented as basically decent, while beset by a vicious, black-mailing family, whom she nevertheless continues to assist. One senses that her public image is closer to the real Mavis, regardless of indiscretions in her private life.

With Dolores, there is a violent opposition between her public and private self. It surfaces in her strip act. Although she is clearly Hispanic, with dark hair and skin, her stage costume is a parody of "whiteness." She wears a platinum wig and an all-white gown, studded with glittering rhinestones, which she peels off to reveal her darker, naked self.

Her final strip act, the last major scene in the film, is revealing on a number of levels. Marlowe has discovered that she murdered Steelgrave and has tried to frame Mavis for the killing. He stands in the stage wing while she is performing and confronts her with this information. As they speak, she not only undresses before the audience, removing the all-white clothing and revealing her body and, to an extent, her ethnicity, but she also reveals her moral duplicity. She has presented herself as an "old friend" of Mavis's and acted throughout the film as if she actually were. She now reveals that she is homicidally jealous of Mavis, for whom Steelgrave had spurned her. She not only killed Steelgrave but has tried to frame Mavis for the killing. Not only does her physical striptease uncover a body quite different from what her costuming suggests, but she also reveals that her role as Mavis's companion was the opposite of what she presented it to be. When Marlowe first met her, he asked if her name, Dolores, was "Spanish for pain." Subsequent events reveal his associations to be apt.

Dolores only admits what she has done because she knows that Marlowe secretly loves Mavis and would not bring about a public disclosure that would ruin her career. Her last words to Marlowe are, "And there's nothing you can do about it, is there?

Unless you want to destroy her—and you wouldn't want to do that, would you? You dream of those great big eyes of hers." Immediately after this statement, as she stands naked before the crowd, she is murdered by her sexually degraded and abandoned ex-husband, who then commits suicide.

A major cut preceding the strip-show sequence capsulizes many of the values of the film. Marlowe is shown comforting Mavis at his home. Realizing what a savior Marlowe has been, she affectionately tells him, "You're something else, Philip Marlowe." Marlowe quietly kisses her on the forehead. The film then cuts to a mirror shot showing Dolores starting her striptease, the film's final sequence.

What we have, by means of the cut, is the juxtaposition of two very different approaches to sexuality. Marlowe intensely desires Mavis, but acts, even when a likely opportunity presents itself, with restrained, old-fashioned decency. He does not reveal what he feels. Dolores, on the other hand, is making a sexual spectacle of herself in her public life and is soon murdered for sexual excesses in her private life.

The cultural associations are also apparent. The two major "foreign" characters in the film, both villains, are presented as sexual deviations from the American norm. Winslow Wong, as unlike as can be from the strapping six-footer ideal, is called "gay" by Marlowe. He engages in what might be termed overcompensating demonstrations of his skill at "manly" combat, only to be proven ridiculous when confronted by the all-American Marlowe. Dolores is a sexual exhibitionist, abandoned by the man she wanted, whom she lost to the all-American Mavis. Dolores murders him and is, in turn, murdered by a man she abandoned. She provides a direct contrast to Mavis, whom Steelgrave appears to have loved, whose public life is not one of sexual exhibitionism but of respectable purity, and whose private life is not one of seething betrayal but of decent support for a vicious family that holds her in contempt but takes her money.

In a departure from the earlier films, Marlowe ends up alone. We see him leave the club in which Dolores has just been murdered and drive off into the night by himself. He has a girl friend, Julie, with whom he periodically sleeps, but her true role is not to fulfill him emotionally, but to serve as an occasional escort or to gather information. She even jokes about it, saying at Steelgrave's nightclub, "Here's to a late breakfast, or am I

penciled in for the eight to twelve shift?" The only genuine
romantic feelings Marlowe seems to have are those that he
represses for Mavis. Had this film been made in the 1940s, it
would probably have ended with Marlowe kissing Mavis, who
might have just signed a multipicture contract. Times had
changed.

Marlowe presents its protagonist as heroically embodying old-
fashioned values but also as lonely and subject to depression.
The refrigerator in his office contains only a bottle of whiskey,
and when we see him drink, it is not the bolstering shot of liquor
a Humphrey Bogart might take, but rather the quiet, sad drinking
of a lonely man.

The film does not try to approximate the pervasive despair of
Chandler's novel, but it does have moments of despair and
isolation unlike anything in earlier Marlowe films. At one point,
Marlowe returns to the office that Wong has wrecked. He stands
in the dim light and mournfully observes the debris. He gets
the pictures used for blackmail, sets them afire, and simply stares
at the flame with a look of infinite sadness on his face. Dolores
enters, and he tells her, "I've been stabbed, snubbed, generally
snookered. I ache all over. My office qualifies for urban renewal.
The cops envy my successes—they're trying to take my license
away. I'd say that's an average day. I'm almost afraid to ask why
you're here." She replies, "I'm almost afraid to tell you." What
she winds up revealing to him is bad, but it's a lie, so things get
worse.

The Marlowe of *Marlowe* is a noble man living by values that
much of the world has abandoned. He is out of step and suffers
for it, but he maintains his integrity and earns a good deal of
respect.

The Long Goodbye (1973) opens as the camera roves through
Marlowe's apartment at 3 A.M. Fully dressed in wrinkled clothes,
his shoes still on, Marlowe (Elliott Gould) is asleep on his bed.
His cat leaps upon his stomach and awakens him. Realizing that
the cat wants to be fed, and unable to get it to eat anything in
the kitchen, Marlowe stumbles out to an all-night supermarket
for a particular brand of cat foot (Curry-Brand) the supermarket
doesn't have. He buys a substitute and enacts an elaborate
subterfuge to convince the cat it is Curry-Brand. The cat won't
eat it.

Terry Lennox (Jim Bouton) arrives, tells Marlowe that he is

in trouble, and asks to be driven to Tijuana immediately. Marlowe does it. When he returns the next morning, his cat is gone, and he is thrown in jail.

This film begins not by plunging Marlowe into the confusing events of the case, but with a long, seemingly aimless, cat-feeding sequence characterizing him, and it points to a Marlowe developed according to assumptions different from those underlying any other Marlowe, before or since.

He has a cat and goes to extraordinary lengths to keep it happy—going out at 3 A.M. to get a particular brand of cat food and then, when that brand is unavailable, placing a substitute into an old "Curry-Brand" can, then letting the cat see him take the food out of the "Curry-Brand" can so it will eat it. It doesn't matter, the cat refuses to eat it, and soon abandons him.

The importance of the cat is established in a joking exchange in which Marlowe asks if a man has a cat, and the man replies, "What I need a cat for? I got a girl." Marlowe mutters to himself, "He's got a girl, and I got a cat." Regrettably, it's all he has, and he doesn't have it for long.

Marlowe then makes a similar middle-of-the-night journey for his friend, later winds up in jail trying to protect that friend, and goes to extensive lengths to prove that Terry did not commit a crime which, in fact, he did commit. Terry has betrayed Marlowe. At the end, when Marlowe confronts Terry with the fact of his betrayal, Terry says, "Nobody cares," and Marlowe replies, "Yeah, nobody cares but me." Terry says, "Well, that's you, Marlowe. You'll never learn. You're a born loser." Marlowe pulls a pistol out, says, "Yeah, I even lost my cat," and shoots Terry dead.

Throughout the film, Marlowe continually says, "It's OK with me," in response to nearly everything he encounters. The line implies the kind of laid-back, southern Californian indifference to which Terry refers when he says, "Nobody cares," but Marlowe's actions throughout the film prove the line to be more of a cover than truly representative of his emotions. His murder of Terry blows his cover.

The Long Goodbye is one of the most complex of the films based upon Chandler's fiction, but many lovers of Chandler's fiction regard it with ontological loathing. Terry's description of Marlowe as "a born loser" is accurate in a way many Chandler enthusiasts find revolting. Robert Altman, the film's director, has said, "I see Marlowe the way Chandler saw him, a loser. But a *real* loser, not the false winner that Chandler made out of him. A loser all the way."[2]

In the novel, Marlowe tells an old friend:

> I'm a romantic, Bernie. I hear voices crying in the night and I go see what's the matter. You don't make a dime that way. You got sense, you shut your window and turn up more sound on your TV set. Or you shove down on the gas and get far away from there. Stay out of other people's troubles. All it can get you is the smear. The last time I saw Terry Lennox we had a cup of coffee together that I made myself in my house, and we smoked a cigarette. So when I heard he was dead I went out to the kitchen and made some coffee and poured a cup for him and lit a cigarette for him and when the coffee was cold and the cigarette was burned down I said goodnight to him. You don't make a dime that way.[3]

Much of the appeal of Chandler's Marlowe as a character comes from his romanticism. He lives by his own set of rules and values his integrity. In *The Big Sleep*, Chandler compares Marlowe to a medieval knight in a world in which knights no longer have meaning. Chandler presents Marlowe's value as resulting from his refusal to compromise, from his isolated idealism. Many characters in the novels have much more than Marlowe ever will, but they envy his integrity. He may be alone, but he is Byronically alone. He lives in a better world than this one.

For Altman, there is no better world. His Marlowe is not a man to be admired but to be pitied. He is a romantic child who has never grown up. His generosity is misguided, resulting from a perception of others and the world that has little basis in reality. Soon after his cat wakes him up, it claws him, but he nevertheless goes out to the supermarket, muttering, "Cat gets me up at three o'clock in the morning to get him a special kind of food. I've got to be out of my fucking mind." And he is.

Altman's Marlowe is hopelessly out of step with his environment. The film is set in the early 1970s, and most of the characters are casually dressed, well-tanned southern Californians. Not Marlowe. He is virtually the only character in the film to wear a suit—a shabby, ill-fitting one—as well as a white shirt and tie. It is the only outfit we ever see him in. His skin is pasty white, and he frequently needs a shave, badly. He is the only character in the film who smokes, and he does it perpetually, choosing unfiltered cigarettes.

It is significant that we first see him asleep. Altman has called the character "Rip Van Marlowe" and wanted Gould to play him as a man who has been asleep for thirty years, who barely knows that times have changed, and who certainly has not changed with them.

Altman's Marlowe has no relationships that are not manipulated to his disadvantage. For the first time in any of the films, he has no romantic attachments or possibilities. This is especially interesting since the source novel gives Marlowe an explicit sexual relationship. Earlier Marlowe films placed their hero in romantic relationships without parallel, or with muted parallels, in the source novels. Here, although the source novel places Marlowe in a number of romantic situations, none is developed or even used in the film. Altman's Marlowe is, as far as we can see, asexual.

Even worse, he is early on called a "fag" during a police investigation. And near the end, he is nearly castrated by the gangster Marty Augustine (Mark Rydell). Not only does he lack an evident sexual life, but the police accuse him of sexual deviance, and gangsters come close to eliminating all possibility of sexuality in his life.

This asexuality of Marlowe is striking, since he lives in a sex-drenched environment. Every other major character has multiple sex partners. Terry Lennox murdered his wife soon after his affair with Eileen Wade (Nina Van Pallandt) was discovered. Eileen Wade's drunken husband, Roger Wade (Sterling Hayden), had had an affair with Sylvia Lennox. The gangster Marty Augustine speaks proudly of his wife and spends much of his time with his mistress.

Marlowe's apartment adjoins one shared by a number of young women who appear perpetually spaced-out on drugs. At all hours of the day and night, we see them dancing or exercising on their veranda, frequently topless or naked. Most of the men who visit Marlowe's apartment can barely keep their eyes off the women. Marlowe never leers at them and acts only as a vaguely friendly neighbor, uninterested even when they invite him over.

Chandler's novels and the earlier Marlowe films present Marlowe as having great sexual attractiveness. The film *The Long*

Goodbye does not. No women leer at him, and his scruffy appearance and mannerisms make him unlikely to attract any.

The beautiful Eileen Wade at one point appears to be sexually interested in Marlowe. Marlowe has rescued her husband from an alcoholism clinic, and Eileen, grateful, asks him to return to her house sometime for a visit. Later in the film, after her repulsively drunken husband has passed out in his den, she asks Marlowe to stay with her and prepares an elaborate meal for him. They spend hours together.

After the meal, they walk through the darkened house, and the camera moves slowly with them. The setting is romantic.

A scruffy Marlowe (Elliott Gould) who is *not* being seduced by the attractive Eileen Wade (Nina Van Pallandt) in *The Long Goodbye* (United Artists). *(Photo courtesy of Cinemabilia.)*

The house is candlelit, and we see the dark surf in the background through the large panel windows. She asks him to call her "Eileen." They stop, and the camera moves in slowly to what appears to be a close shot. It shows them in profile at opposite ends of the Panavision frame. Suddenly Marlowe asks her about her husband's involvement with Marty Augustine and Sylvia Lennox, breaking the potentially romantic mood. Clearly, Marlowe is more interested in the Terry Lennox case than he is in being seduced by Eileen Wade.

During this time, the camera has been moving closer. Inexplicably, it seems to be moving too close, almost going between them instead of stopping on a big close shot of them. Suddenly, between them, we see something white going into the surf in the distance. It is Roger Wade committing suicide, and this new presence in the shot is jolting to the viewer. As Marlowe asks, "Where was your husband the night Sylvia Lennox was killed?" the sound track switches to the roar of the surf. Soon Marlowe and Eileen see Roger, but it is too late.

The sequence is complex and representative of much of the film. The atmosphere is increasingly sexual, but Marlowe seems neither to notice nor to care. There is a comparable scene in Howard Hawks's *The Big Sleep* in which Vivian Rutledge and Marlowe exchange witty, *double entendre* banter. Vivian compares herself to a racehorse who will only perform properly if the right person is "in the saddle," the right person obviously being Marlowe. Suddenly Marlowe breaks the mood by asking, "What's Eddie Mars got on you?" showing that a relationship between them will have to wait until the case is solved. But Bogart's Marlowe is clearly interested in Vivian. Elliott Gould's Marlowe never gives Eileen Wade appraising glances or makes romantic advances. Sex is in many ways a glaring absence in the film: it is constantly prepared for, but never happens.

The sequence between Marlowe and Eileen Wade shifts twice. At first, it seems to be laying the ground work for a relationship between Marlowe and Eileen. Then, it seems to be "about" Marlowe's perception of Roger Wade's involvement in the case and suddenly is "about" Roger Wade's suicide.

The first shift comes through dialogue. The second by means of camera movement—and the camera work is tremendously important in the film.

Vilmos Zsigmond's camera moves in virtually every scene in the film, and, like many *noir* camera techniques of the 1940s, it is unsettling. Quite often, the focal point of a shot is uncertain; often a shot has a number of focal points. In the first sequence, when Marlowe walks through his apartment, the camera appears to be following him, but slowly it moves past him, and we see through windows the half-naked women in the apartment beyond. It is unexpected. They had simply appeared to be part of the background, and suddenly they are the focus of the shot. The shot is no longer "about" Marlowe in his apartment; it is "about" his neighbors.

The next morning we see a veranda shot of two of these neighbors from inside their apartment. One is exercising and one is quizzing the other on state capitals, most of which the other gets wrong. The camera moves slowly in on one woman and seems to move down to focus on her crotch, but it moves through her legs, and suddenly we see, in the street below, Marlowe emerging from his car, the new nonsexual focus of what appeared to be a sexually oriented shot.

The camera almost never stops moving. It seems constantly roving, constantly looking for new things to turn up. Often the movement is a very slow zoom shot, commonly used as an intensifying shot: moving closer to the scene's dramatic center. At times it serves that function here, but at other times, it has a wholly different purpose, as in the Roger Wade suicide shot or the shots of Marlowe in his apartment and of the neighbors in theirs.

Even when the camera is relatively still, there are often a variety of competing focal points. When Marlowe is being questioned about his role in Terry Lennox's disappearance, he sits in a police interrogation room. The camera looks at him through a one-way mirror from an adjacent observation room. Marlowe knows it is a one-way mirror and has placed a black handprint on the glass.

The shot has five different focal points. In the interior room, we see the seated and alternately enraged and wisecracking Marlowe, responding both to the policeman in the room and to those he knows are watching on the other side of the one-way mirror. We see also the abrasive interrogation officer who circles and attempts to provoke Marlowe. On the intervening window, we see the ridiculous, black handprint Marlowe has placed there. And in the observation room, two racially antagonistic police-men—one white, one black—are watching and arguing among themselves. One hardly knows what to watch, and of course, throughout all of this, the camera continues to move.

This camera restlessness makes the viewer continually scan the frame for unexpected occurrences. Such events are common in the film and part of its design. Many of the events of the film come virtually out of nowhere, wholly unexpected, like Roger Wade's suicide, and have a jolting effect on the viewer.

Terry Lennox had left town with $355,000 of Marty Augustine's money. Augustine comes to Marlowe's apartment to intimidate Marlowe, hoping to learn something about the money. He at first appears an almost comical gangster. Jewish and shorter than his multiethnic henchmen, he constantly demands that they agree to whatever he says. He talks incessantly about his possessions, including his mistress. Marlowe seems bored with it all, apparently viewing Augustine's nonstop, self-inflating patter as petty theatrics. Augustine speaks of his love for his mistress, asks Marlowe to observe her delicate beauty, on which the constantly moving camera lingers. Suddenly, the camera stops. Augustine shatters a Coke bottle into her face, gouging it into a bloody mess. Even Augustine's henchmen are horrified. Augustine tells Marlowe, "Now that's someone I love, and you I don't even like. Find it, cheapie, find my money."

The scene is terrifying. The cutting and framing make the bottle appear to come out of nowhere and virtually to explode in the woman's face and the camera. And the action is wholly unexpected, coming after so many caressing shots of the woman's face. It is also thematically horrifying to see a man so mutilate someone he cares about simply to intimidate someone else.

The scene reverberates throughout the film. Soon after it, we see an argument between Roger and Eileen Wade. He has started to drink again and she refers to the fact that he is impotent. Conversation stops and he suddenly grabs her chin with his left hand and moves slowly back, his arm extending. It is a terrifying moment, because Roger, a hulking ape of a man, appears to be holding her head in place for a virtually decapitating roundhouse punch. The previous Marty Augustine scene has sensitized the audience to the film's ability to present appalling violence. Wade never punches his wife, but the audience is unsettled nevertheless.

Near the end of the film, Marlowe is brought to Augustine's office. The volatile Augustine shows him his mistress. Her face is grotesquely wired with reconstruction devices and bandages. Marty kisses her tenderly. Marlowe says, "Look I get the point," obviously terrified that Marty will suddenly smash all the reconstruction devices into her face. Like the possibility of Roger Wade's punching his wife, the possibility of Marty's becoming violent does not happen, but Marty's early brutality has made it a very real possibility.

Immediately after this scene, Marlowe is hit by a car and rushed to the hospital. We see a hospital room and a man bandaged from head to toe. It is apparently Marlowe, but it is not. Altman cuts, and we see Marlowe in the next bed. He says, "You're OK. I've seen all your pictures too." It's a perverse joke.

On the most obvious level, it is another example of the film's unsettling strategy, its shifting of expectations and directions. On another level, it refers to Hollywood genres. The bandaged man looks like the "Invisible Man." Hence Marlowe's joke. The film frequently refers to Hollywood films. A gateman Marlowe drives past continually does imitations of film stars: Barbara Stanwyck (from *Double Indemnity*), Walter Brennan, Cary Grant, James Stewart. Marlowe calls a white dog that stops in front of his car "Asta." While being interrogated by the police, he smears ink on his face and starts singing "Swanee." At the film's end, after he has killed Terry Lennox, he walks away from the camera. Suddenly we hear a scratchy recording of "Hooray for Hollywood" on the sound track, and Marlowe dances. The song is particularly noticeable not only because of the evident age of its recording but because the only other songs in the film are seemingly infinite arrangements of "The Long Goodbye"—as a soulful ballad, a funeral march, among many others.

In many ways, the film itself is a long goodbye to Hollywood, certainly the Hollywood that created the classic private detective. The Hollywood references are to old stars, old films, not to present-day ones, and even the aural antiquity of the recording of "Hooray for Hollywood" identifies it as the product of an outmoded technique that now calls attention to its inadequacies.

So it is with Philip Marlowe, Altman appears to be saying.

When we hear the recording, Marlowe has just murdered a former friend for not living up to the notions of friendship Marlowe holds dear. The former friend has sent Marlowe $5,000 in recompense, but he has broken Marlowe's code, and Marlowe kills him. Altman associates that code with the illusions of the old Hollywood. Marlowe is deeply hurt because Terry appears to be his only friend, aside from his cat, and one suspects that that very lack of friends is in itself indicative of Marlowe's inability to deal effectively with the world as it is.

Altman has frequently launched frontal assaults on established genre traditions. In *M*A*S*H* (1970), he showed real carnage in a service comedy. In *Buffalo Bill and the Indians* (1976), he presented Buffalo Bill as a drunken fraud. Some country and western music enthusiasts hated *Nashville* (1975) because it presented a vision of that industry different from theirs.

Many of Altman's films have been called antinostalgic, because they often work in a form with built-in nostalgic resonance, while they undercut the traditional basis for nostalgia. It has been claimed that *McCabe and Mrs. Miller* (1971) undercut the Western in this manner. *The Long Goodbye* certainly undercuts the detective film. Probably the main reason for the venom with which so many Chandler enthusiasts regard *The Long Goodbye* is the fact that it contrives to make of Marlowe not a romantic rebel but, as Altman describes him, a "real loser." Central to this view of Marlowe is the association of Marlowe and private-eye films with the 1940s. Altman attacks the view of that era as a "better time." He does not imbue the present with greater value—he presents it as corrupted and largely devoid of value—but he refuses to romanticize the past.

Few films differ more in their approach to the recent past than do *The Long Goodbye* and Dick Richards's *Farewell, My Lovely* (1975). *Farewell, My Lovely* does not "update" Marlowe into the mid-1970s, but is a "period" picture, set in 1941. It is the first Marlowe film to recreate a past era rather than to depict a contemporaneous one.

Richards's film made its source novel the only one of Chandler's novels to be used for a pre-*noir* film (*The Falcon Takes Over*), a *noir* film (*Murder, My Sweet*), and a "son of noir" film (*Farewell, My Lovely*). *Farewell, My Lovely* employs a story line and a style of filmmaking that in the 1940s evoked the underbelly of the contemporary world, but this story line and style in the 1970s are used to recall the past nostalgically. This style had originated in attempts to shock contemporary standards and desentimentalize content. In the 1975 film, those very techniques and styles are put to sentimental and nostalgic purposes.

Farewell, My Lovely appeared when nostalgic "period" films set in the 1930s and 1940s—*Chinatown* (1974), *The Sting* (1973), *Paper Moon* (1973), *Summer of '42* (1971)—and films reprising genres associated with that time—*That's Entertainment* (1974), *What's Up, Doc?* (1972), *Young Frankenstein* (1975), *The Three Musketeers* (1974)—were popular. *Farewell, My Lovely* does both: it is set in 1941 and clearly reprises 1940s *film noir* techniques.

Much about the film aside from the obvious period costuming, sets, automobiles, and other props recalls 1940s *noir* films. Most obviously, it stars Robert Mitchum in a trench coat as Marlowe. Not only was Mitchum an important star in the 1940s, but he starred in *noir* films such as *Undercurrent* (1946), *Crossfire* (1947), *Out of the Past* (1947), and *Macao* (1952). Charlotte Rampling (who plays Mrs. Grayle/Velma) is made up and costumed and acts in a way that recalls Lauren Bacall in *The Big Sleep*.

Both Mitchum and Rampling recall presences from the history of film, and because they do, their use in this film works in a different way from those presences in the original films: they cannot help but evoke a discrete historical period about which audiences might feel nostalgic. The very difference between Altman's casting of Elliott Gould and Richards's casting of Robert Mitchum points to very different strategies for dealing with the past.

Like what happens in *Murder, My Sweet* and in many 1940s *noir* films, and unlike what happens in either of the earlier post-1960 Marlowe films, the detective tells much of the story in a voice-over retrospective narration. Not only do the device and the language recall the earlier era but we also have Robert Mitchum's voice, used as it was in *Out of the Past*.

The film's use of color differs radically from that in *The Long Goodbye*, in which the color is harsh, cold, often unflattering and bleached, especially in outdoor scenes. For the latter film, Vilmos Zsigmond, the cameraman, used a technique called *post-*

flashing, exposing the negative, after shooting but before developing, to additional light that reduces color intensities to pastel levels. In contrast, *Farewell, My Lovely* was one of the first American films to use Fujicolor, which can emphasize pastels. Cameraman John Alonzo used "warm," intense colors—deep reds, browns, yellows—and a good deal of neon-type lighting. The color textures of the film resemble those of old color photographs and advertising posters from the early 1940s.

Farewell, My Lovely opens with processed color shots of Los Angeles traffic and a shot of a neon marquee showing a woman's face. The cars, the colors, the depiction of the woman all recall older styles, but the colors are a bit too intense, the movements a bit too slow, the stylization a bit too extreme—it recalls a dream of the past rather than a naturalistic depiction. The camera tilts up to show Marlowe looking out of a hotel window. His voice-over says, "This past spring was the first that I'd felt tired and realized that I was getting old." He says that things are now worse for him than they were in the spring and that his only pleasure comes from following the hitting streak of the 26-year-old Joe DiMaggio.

DiMaggio's streak is a central motif in the film; it gives Marlowe something heroic to believe in, in the face of almost universally depressing events, one of which is his own age. Throughout most of the film, he is confused and endangered by the events of the case, and world events provide no relief. At one point, a news vendor asks him, "Whaddya think of this guy Hitler? He invaded Russia." Marlowe replies, "So did Napoleon, and that's not as hard as hitting forty-two straight."

We frequently see Marlowe pick up a newspaper, ignore the world events on the front page, and turn to the back to learn of DiMaggio's progress. Georgie (Jimmy Archer), the ex-boxer newsvendor, comments, referring to the increasing pressure upon DiMaggio during the streak, that he also knows what pressure is, that he once won nineteen straight fights.

This pressure parallels the pressure on Marlowe. Things go poorly for him throughout the film, and, at the end, they look worse. His clients and a man with whom he sympathized are dead, DiMaggio's streak has been broken, and American involvement in World War II is imminent. He even gives away the money he earned.

The film would seem to present Marlowe as a "real loser,"

fitting Altman's description, but of course it does not. Marlowe is romanticized, maintains admirable integrity in the face of great danger and loss, and the very extent of his loss amplifies the courage it takes for him to go on.

Although he identifies with DiMaggio, who is younger than he is and a "winner," he sympathizes with Tommy Ray (John O'Leary), even more of a "loser" than Marlowe. He involves Tommy Ray in the case by asking him about Moose Malloy's lost Velma. Soon, Tommy Ray is murdered. This event profoundly upsets Marlowe. Tommy Ray was white and married to a black woman, a fact that ruined his show business career. He and his wife seem devoted to one another, and Marlowe strikes up a friendship with their mulatto son, also a baseball fan.

The film climaxes on the gambling boat of Laird Brunette (Anthony Zerbe), a rich racketeer who wants Marlowe to bring Malloy (Jack O'Halloran) to him. Marlowe realizes that Brunette probably intends to murder them both if they go onto the boat, but he also realizes that only by taking that risk can he solve the case. He takes it because "otherwise that kid of Tommy Ray's will haunt me for the rest of my life for letting them kill his father."

Marlowe's act of altruistic heroism inspires a comparable one from Detective Nulty (John Ireland). Nulty at first refuses to help Marlowe because Brunette has enormous political power. Suddenly Nulty tells his driver to head for Brunette's boat. His thoroughly corrupt assistant, Billy Rolfe (Harry Dean Stanton), refuses to go, and Nulty screams, "Seven people are dead, Rolfe, seven, and the police are driving away." He risks his career, is morally rejuvenated, saves Marlowe's life, and scores a major triumph on the case.

At the end, Marlowe reads of the breaking of DiMaggio's streak. He still has money he got from Brunette and says, "I had two grand in my pocket that needed a home and I knew just the place." He goes to give the money to Tommy Ray's wife and son, and the film ends.

Even the DiMaggio loss does not bring him to despair, but rather to a sense of admiration for the unexpected achievements of so-called losers: "Bagsby and Smith, a couple of run-of-the-mill pitchers stopped DiMaggio. Perhaps they had a little extra that night, like Nulty had tonight."

Marlowe is presented as a man of prodigious integrity, an old-fashioned hero who gains nothing for himself but helps the underdog and inspires moral strength. There are no analogues to either Tommy Ray's family or Nulty's rejection of his corrupt past in either of the earlier films or in Chandler's novel, but they are central to the structure of this film.

The paralleling of the two is important. Marlowe's kindness to the family is not presented as stupid, as is Marlowe's kindness to Terry Lennox in *The Long Goodbye;* rather, it is part of his radiant moral heroism, confirmed not only by the boy's fondness for Marlowe but by its effect on Nulty's moral rejuvenation. Furthermore, nearly everyone in the film, even Brunette, respects Marlowe. He is not friendless and contemptuously dismissed as is the Marlowe of *The Long Goodbye.* Instead, he is a man to contend with.

Like all of the post-1960 Marlowe films, and unlike all of the 1940s ones, Marlowe has no significant romantic involvement, and the plot is not structured around a developing romance. In the novel and in both of the earlier films based upon it, Ann provides a romantic interest for Marlowe. The film has no analogue to her, and the place she structurally supplies in the novel's plot is partially filled by the punchy news vendor, Georgie.

Most women in the film are unappealing or evil. Marlowe's flashback begins as he searches for a runaway high school girl in a dance hall. He has to get rid of a fat, middle-aged woman who aggressively approaches him, saying he reminds her of her "Harry." He finds the girl, and, as he delivers her to her parents, she hits him powerfully in his groin, and he doubles up in pain. The rest of his experiences with women in the film are comparable.

He is not presented as a celibate and is obviously attracted to Mrs. Grayle. When he leaves after her husband has discovered them kissing, she says, "You're old-fashioned, aren't you?" and he replies, "From the waist up." Later in the film, he invites her to "my place," and she says, "What for? You've got everything we need with you." Richards then cuts to a long shot of Marlowe's car parked at the beach, and, although we only see them necking, we suspect they have made love. Marlowe later tells Nulty, "She was incredibly beautiful. And she was something, Nulty, really something."

Mrs. Grayle is the film's center of desire and is destructive or deadly to all of her lovers or consorts—her husband, Moose, Marriott, Brunette—except Marlowe. The film presents most sexual activity as destructive, and it is much more explicit about sexuality and sexual deviation than the earlier films based upon the novel. Lindsey Marriott is explicitly established as a homosexual, and jokes are made about his sexual preference. There is also a lesbian, Florence Amthor (Kate Murtagh), the madam of a whorehouse in which Mrs. Grayle once worked. She is presented as repulsively fat and mannish in her behavior, and the film contrives one of Marlowe's triumphs at her expense. Marlowe is restrained by thugs, and she repeatedly provokes him, slapping him a number of times. Suddenly he explodes and punches her directly in the face, drawing blood.

Normally, the sight of a man punching a woman is encoded as "bad" in Hollywood films, but here it is presented as a moment of triumph. Amthor's lesbianism, her repulsive appearance, and her behavior allow the audience to sympathize with her punishment.

Like the other post-1960 Marlowe films, Marlowe finds himself surrounded by sexual excess and deviation. Censorship codes allowed many things to be shown and discussed that could only be hinted at in the 1940s, but a curious pattern in the post-1960 Marlowe films is that, permitted a freedom of sexual display unthinkable in the 1940s, they tend to display attitudes about sexuality that would have been conservative in the 1940s. The sexuality that is shown is often degenerate and punished severely, and a sign of the detective's integrity is the relative absence of sexuality from his life. In the 1940s, the "badness" of sexual excess and manipulation was counterbalanced by the "goodness" of the hero's salvation of, and sexual involvement with, the heroine. The only way for Marlowe to deal with the world of "bad" sex in the post-1960 world seems to be either minimal involvement or abstinence. In this film, Marlowe does not wind up a lover, with a young woman of his own, as in the earlier ones based upon the novel, but as a kind of asexual uncle to the one traditional family unit in the film: that of Tommy Ray. Although Tommy Ray's wife is now a widow, the film never allows the slightest hint of sexual attraction between her and Marlowe; his generosity will be without recompense, and avuncular. Their relationship remains "pure."

And the family is black. Like sex, race was a touchy topic for films of the 1940s, and neither of the earlier films uses any of the racial material developed in the novel. *Farewell, My Lovely* gives that motif central importance. Marlowe warns Malloy as they approach Florian's, "Hey, this is a colored neighborhood." When they enter the bar, a bouncer tells them, "No white folks in here, just for the colored." The atmosphere, as in the novel, is racially antagonistic, and the film also develops institutionalized racism as a cultural fact. Nulty tells Marlowe that Moose's killing of the black bar owner is irrelevant to the police but that they have to go through the motions of an investigation to avoid trouble from Eleanor Roosevelt.

Marlowe is aware of racial antagonism, but he himself shows no racial contempt and, furthermore, he becomes the champion of what in a racist society is a supreme sin: a "mixed" marriage. In the 1940s, miscegenation was explicitly forbidden as screen material by the Production Code. In this film, mixed marriage is presented as an act of courage: the white Tommy Ray lost his show business career because of his marriage to a black woman.

"No white folks in here, just for the colored." Moose Malloy (Jack O'Halloran) and Marlowe (Robert Mitchum) in the racially antagonistic atmosphere of Florian's bar in *Farewell, My Lovely* (Avco Embassy). *(Photo courtesy of Cinemabilia.)*

He and his family become the ultimate cultural underdog, and the film, made at the time of civil rights consciousness in the early 1970s, makes Marlowe, that glorious defender of lost causes, their enlightened champion.

Much of the generally favorable commentary upon the film made particular mention of Robert Mitchum's performance. Although Mitchum was nearly sixty when he played the role, making him the oldest of screen Marlowes, many critics felt that his world-weary, anarchic, self-contained, and powerful screen presence was ideal for their notion of Marlowe. Earlier, Peter Bogdanovich had wanted to star Mitchum in a version of *The Long Goodbye* that was never made.

The producers of *Farewell, My Lovely*, Elliott Kastner and Jerry Bick (who had also produced *The Long Goodbye*), soon became involved in their third Chandler-based film, *The Big Sleep* (1978), also starring Mitchum. Michael Winner directed, coproduced, and wrote the screenplay for the film, which not only differs from *Farewell, My Lovely* in its approach to Chandler's fiction, but is also unlike Howard Hawks's 1946 *The Big Sleep*. Winner set his film in London of the late 1970s, and made Marlowe an American who came over during World War II and remained. Little is made of the cultural differences, however, and Marlowe seems to fit into polite society readily. He is also more well-off financially than earlier screen Marlowes. Although Winner uses a voice-over retrospective narration for Marlowe, he avoids nostalgic associations of the part or of past genres—the film is set in and is about the present. Curiously, and regardless of these major differences in approach, this film follows the plotline of Chandler's novel much more closely than did the 1946 film.

It is daring to attempt another version of a well-respected film, because comparisons will inevitably be made, and, in most cases, the dice are sentimentally loaded against the newer film. Winner seems to have been careful to make his film as different in approach as possible from the earlier one, and his use of color and *mise-en-scène* provides one example.

One might say that Winner dragged Chandler's story line out of Hawks's black-and-white shadows and carefully placed it on a lush, green lawn. His settings are neither sleazy nor sinister. Furthermore, the film has none of the glossy surfaces or vinyl

seediness of "son of noir" films. Rather, the sets are luxurious,
spacious, almost untouched. The colors tend to rich blues and
greens. Mitchum is generally attired in elegantly tailored, pre-
dominantly blue outfits. The Hawks film develops images of
tight, cramped interior spaces, and of rain; the Winner film
emphasizes open, richly furnished spaces, and sunlight on lush
lawns. Hawks's Marlowe drives a cramped coupé; Winner's
Marlowe drives a Mercedes.

As soon as Hawks's Marlowe enters General Sternwood's
greenhouse at the beginning of the film, he begins to sweat. He
soon removes his jacket and sweats through his shirt. The
atmosphere is stifling. Winner's Marlowe simply lounges back
in the rich green environment. Although General Sternwood
(James Stewart) at one point mentions that the room is hot,
Marlowe never appears to be affected by it. One almost suspects
that Winner thought Mitchum looked so good in his dark blue
suit that he wouldn't let him remove his jacket.

And Mitchum does look good. As Marlowe in *Farewell, My
Lovely*, he is sagging, ill-dressed, and clammy—a tired, aging

General Sternwood (James Stewart) and a dapper Marlowe (Robert
Mitchum) in Sternwood's greenhouse in *The Big Sleep* (United Artists).
(Photo courtesy of Cinemabilia.)

man still holding it together, mostly by force of will. In *The Big Sleep*, he is elegantly dressed and socially facile, seems at least ten years younger, and is neither concerned with nor debilitated by age.

The greenhouse scenes provide a useful point of contrast between the two *Big Sleep* films. Hawks's junglelike greenhouse has a visible effect on Bogart's Marlowe: he sweats profusely. The greenhouse also appears claustrophobic, like a steaming jungle. The scene sets an appropriately oppressive atmosphere in which the case begins, and the atmosphere is important to the film's effect. Winner's greenhouse, on the other hand, is neither particularly hot nor claustrophobic; it is simply there, little more than an elegant backdrop. The scene could have as easily taken place in the parlor, and it points to a major difference in approach between the two films. Hawks's film is much more concerned with the environment in which its events occur than with the events themselves; Winner's film is more concerned with the events and less with their context.

Hawks's film confused many people. It concerned itself much more with atmospheric insinuation than with narrative clarity. Winner's film does the opposite. He seems to have gone out of his way to clarify potential narrative confusions. His plot is complex, but the loose ends are ultimately tied up. In fact, Winner clutters the film with flashbacks—which Hawks considered anathema—that often provide visual parallels to verbal narrative descriptions, in certain ways duplicating significant narrative information to make everything perfectly clear.

This film leaves no doubt as to who killed the chauffeur. We see a flashback in which Joe Brody describes precisely how he got the pictures from the chauffeur after he left Geiger's house. Then, a summary scene at the police station states that the chauffeur was not murdered but committed suicide.

Other plot events whose counterparts in Hawks's film caused confusion are similarly clarified, particularly in instances where censorship codes would not allow Hawks to present material from the novel. When in Winner's film, Marlowe enters Geiger's house after Geiger's murder, there is no ambiguity as to what has been going on. Camilla (Candy Clark) is not clothed in an Oriental-looking gown but is stark naked; the camera is not concealed in a Buddha-like head, but is mounted upon a tripod;

Camilla's spaced-out condition is not vaguely accounted for by Marlowe's sniffing at a glass, but explicitly by a hypodermic needle near her. There is no doubt in this film, as there is in Hawks's, that she has taken narcotics and that she is posing for pornographic pictures. In fact, we later see those pictures. In addition, Geiger and Lundgren's homosexual relationship is explicitly established, as are the reasons for the disappearance and reappearance of Geiger's body.

Such correspondences between films using the same source are frequently useless or even counterproductive critically. It generally makes little sense to take a preexistent plot and talk of a film in terms of what was "left in" and what was "taken out," because such discourse presumes that the preexistent plot is the most important aspect of the work. Such a notion of plot obviously does not hold for Hawks's film, in which a number of motifs are more important than narrative clarity. Hawks established different priorities. Winner's priorities seem to have been avoidance of the narrative confusions of the Hawks film, at which Winner succeeds, and "fidelity" to Chandler's novel, which is a more complex issue.

A popular assumption holds that films based upon fiction derive their value from their fictional source and should include as much of the source as possible. Generally, the term "fidelity" is used to indicate that the film follows the narrative line of the source, but it has sometimes been used to mean "fidelity" to the "spirit" of the source.

The term "faithful" is generally useless, its use often ignoring the enormous formal differences between literature and film. The term frequently obscures more than it clarifies. The two films based upon Chandler's *The Big Sleep* provide an almost ideal test case.

Hawk's film is infinitely more "unfaithful." The basic romantic plot structure, the inflation of the roles of Vivian and Eddie Mars and the diminution of that of Carmen force the narrative line to take a very different direction from that of the novel. The entire closing sequence has no parallel in the novel but is original to Hawks's film. Hawks's film, as was noted in chapter 7, has its own very carefully worked out formal and thematic coherences. It is as different from its source as Verdi's *Otello* is from Shakespeare's *Othello*.

Winner's *The Big Sleep* is much more "faithful" to its source.
It includes much more of Chandler's plotline, and the opening
and closing voice-over narrations are adapted from the opening
and closing sections of the novel. Things unclear in the novel,
such as the chauffeur's death, are made clear in the film. The
film does not give Marlowe a romantic interest as does the earlier
film but keeps him romantically alone, as in Chandler's novel.

The film is much more "faithful," then, and according to
popular notions of fidelity, should be a better film than the
Hawks one. But critics dismissed it roundly, it generated very
little popular interest, and it has been virtually forgotten since
its opening.

A basic problem with the film may emanate from the very
notion of "fidelity." A number of things in the film seem
curiously out of place. One concerns Geiger's store. In Chandler's
novel, it is a cover for expensive pornographic books. In Hawks's
film, its actual activities are suspicious but unclear. In Winner's
film, it is also a cover for expensive pornographic books. When
Marlowe sees one of these books, he is revolted and describes
it as "indescribably filthy." We see the book briefly, and it
contains nude photographs of women in provocative positions.

The problem arises because Winner sets his film in London
of the 1970s, not in Los Angeles of the mid-1930s. In the 1930s,
explicit pornography was an undercover business. In London of
the 1970s, however, one need only walk to Leicester Square and
openly purchase material that would have made Mae West blush.
Cultural attitudes toward the depiction of nudity and sexual
activity have changed, and one is not today surprised to see a
copy of *Playboy* on the coffee table of a banker. What we see of
the book Marlowe inspects is no more extreme than material
Playboy often prints.

Consequently, Marlowe's reaction to the dirty book, as well
as the intensely furtive nature of Geiger's store and the abject
terror of the man who throws the book away and flees because
he fears Marlowe may be a policeman, seems ridiculous. The
secretiveness and shame surrounding Geiger's store make us
suspect he may be dealing in opium, illegal organ transplants,
or nuclear warheads. When we learn that all this to-do is about
a book that can be openly purchased anywhere in London, it
seems much ado about little.

Winner seems to have worked at cross-purposes with himself. He uses many of the narrative events from the novel, but in "updating" the novel's setting, he does not seem to have taken into account the fact that different cultural environments might give the same action a very different dramatic impact. He seems to have been too "faithful" for his own good.

But the issue does not relate only to the time gap between the settings of novel and film. When Marlowe enters Geiger's store, he puts on a pair of glasses. Later he returns to the store and again puts on the glasses to identify himself. Why? There seems to be no real need to disguise himself, and the glasses do not do a particularly effective job.

In Chandler's novel, Marlowe tells us that, upon entering Geiger's store, "I had my horn-rimmed glasses on. I put my voice high and let a bird twitter in it."[4] He acts in an effeminate way, implicitly associating Geiger's store with effeteness and homosexuality. The glasses are part of a disguise. Hawks's film does the same thing. Bogart places glasses on, pushes his hat brim up, and enters the store in an agitated, effeminate manner— once more, acting in a way appropriate to the store and Geiger's sexuality. Mitchum just puts his glasses on. There is no need to hint at pornography or at Geiger's homosexuality, since they are explicitly identified.

One suspects that the only reason for the glasses is that they appear in the novel. But the use of the glasses without the affectation makes it a gesture without any context, a meaningless bit of business meant to enhance the film's "fidelity" to its source.

Like most of the other post-1960 Marlowe films, *The Big Sleep* has a strong dose of misogyny to it. Inspector Carson (John Mills) tells Marlowe at one point that "in real life, the good guy never gets the girl." Judging from the women in the film, that is very lucky for the good guy.

All of the women are unsympathetic. Charlotte Sternwood, who parallels the Vivian of the novel, is a sex-starved, embittered woman. She is constantly making lewd gestures, and, in playing her, Sarah Miles seems to act more with her tongue than with anything else. Her sister Camilla is a psychotic, sex-starved, drug-using murderess, who literally foams at the mouth when Marlowe thwarts her at the end. And Agnes Lozelle (Joan Collins), whom Marlowe describes as having enough sex appeal

to stampede a businessman's lunch, is unaffected by her involvement in the deaths of three men. Marlowe bitterly says, "Three
men dead . . . and she went walking off between the waters
with my two hundred in her bag and not a mark on her."

The atmosphere of the film is homoerotic. When Charlotte
suggests that she and Marlowe go to his apartment to have sex,
he turns her off with no real hint of regret. He tells her it would
be professionally unethical but gives no sense that declining her
offer requires much effort. When he finds Camilla in his bed,
he is disgusted and throws her out. Unlike the Marlowe in
Farewell, My Lovely, he never seems even faintly in danger of
succumbing to heterosexual lust.

His interest in the case comes from his affection for the dying
General Sternwood. The general, in turn, is motivated by his
deep affection for his daughter's husband, Rusty Regan. Charlotte
even tells Marlowe, "You're like my husband, Rusty. Oh, Rusty
was a lot of fun for dad, more fun for dad than for me."

At one point, Marlowe speaks of Charlotte with Inspector
Gregory (James Donald) and says that she would make a jazzy
weekend, but he wouldn't want her for a steady diet. Gregory
sadly responds that his own wife wouldn't even make a jazzy
weekend. Marlowe says "I never married," and the visible
difference between the handsome, healthy, elegant Marlowe and
the diminuative, browbeaten Gregory indicates that Marlowe
has made the right choice.

Unlike Hawks's film, in which the major confrontation is
between Marlowe and Eddie Mars, the major confrontation in
Winner's film is between Marlowe and the savage Lash Canino
(Richard Boone). Eddie Mars (Oliver Reed) goes off scot-free, or
does he? We last see him as he leaves the police station with
his wife, at which point Inspector Carson announces that the
good guy never gets the girl. In Chandler's novel, Marlowe
represses a strong attraction to Eddie Mars's wife. Here, Marlowe
is indifferent to her, but as she leaves with Eddie, she looks
back with interest at Marlowe, and Eddie pulls her towards the
door. We know that she was also interested in Rusty Regan. In
a later sequence, Marlowe tells us that Camilla killed Regan for
refusing her sexual advances, and we see her try to do the same
with Marlowe.

In the novel, the implication is that Eddie Mars goes off with a very desirable and loyal woman; in Winner's film, one senses that Eddie will receive his punishment, not from Marlowe, but from his wife. She has already embarrassed him with her involvement with Regan, and one suspects that Marlowe will not be the last man she will look at with interest. Given the film's sexual structure, long-term involvement with a woman is the punishment Eddie deserves.

It is also what the general gets. Since Rusty's death, the General has slowly rotted in the house with his two daughters. Marlowe tells Charlotte in his final speech that he has done what he has done "to protect what little pride a sick and broken man has in his family, so that he can believe his blood is not poisoned, that his little girls, though they may be a trifle wild, are not killers and perverts." But they are, and one suspects that an indication of the fact that the old man's blood is poisoned comes simply from the fact that he has two daughters rather than two sons. Marlowe closes by saying that soon the general will be out of the "nastiness" of life, that "he too, like Rusty Regan, would be sleeping the big sleep."

Raymond Chandler expressed little interest in the notion of a film's "fidelity" to his novels. He was aware of the many formal, cultural, and industry conditions that make such a notion untenable, and he did not complain about things being put in or left out. He looked rather for a film's own internal logic, and his affection for Hawks's *The Big Sleep* and contempt for Brahm's *The Brasher Doubloon* were on issues different from those of "fidelity."

The films based upon Chandler's fiction reflect much more than that fiction. They reflect cultural codes, film and literary traditions, and styles, as well as changing attitudes toward those codes, traditions, and styles. Very different filmmakers with very different preoccupations and styles have been drawn to Chandler's fiction over the past four decades. The fact that Chandler's novels continue to sell well and spawn imitators, such as Ross MacDonald and Robert P. Parker, that an increasing scholarly industry has grown up around Chandler's work, and that it continues to inspire popular films gives gathering testimony not only to the value of that work but to its genuine cultural resonance.

NOTES

PREFACE

1 *Selected Letters of Raymond Chandler,* ed., Frank MacShane (New York: Columbia University Press, 1981), p. 432. Future references to this edition in the text will be designated *Selected Letters.*

CHAPTER 1

1 Maurice Zolotow, *Billy Wilder in Hollywood* (New York: G. P. Putnam's, 1977), p. 114.

2 Raymond Chandler, "Writers in Hollywood," *Atlantic Monthly* 176 (November 1945): 52. Future references in the text will be designated "Writers in Hollywood".

3 Frank MacShane, *The Life of Raymond Chandler* (New York: Penguin Books, 1978), p. 42. Future references in the text will be designated MacShane, *The Life of Raymond Chandler.*

4 Raymond Chandler, "A Qualified Farewell," in *The Notebooks of Raymond Chandler and English Summer: A Gothic Romance,* ed., Frank MacShane (New York: Ecco Press, 1976), p. 69.

5 Tino Balio, "Retrenchment, Reappraisal, and Reorganization: 1948," in *The American Film Industry,* ed., Tino Balio (Madison: University of Wisconsin Press, 1976), p. 315.

6 Letter to James Sandoe, September 14, 1947. This letter, and subsequent ones, unless specified differently, is in the Raymond Chandler Collection in the Department of Special Collections at UCLA. Future references to letters in this collection will be designated, Letter to Sandoe (with date). Many have been printed in Frank MacShane's edition of *Selected Letters of Raymond Chandler.*

7 W. H. Auden, "The Guilty Vicarage: Notes on the Detective Story, by an Addict," *Harper's Magazine* 196, no. 1176 (May 1948): 406–12.

8 Stephen Pendo, *Raymond Chandler On Screen: His Novels into Film* (Metuchen, N.J.: Scarecrow Press, 1976), p. 18.

9 Quoted in Ivan Moffat, "On The Fourth Floor of Paramount: Interview With Billy Wilder," *The World of Raymond Chandler,* ed., Miriam Gross (New York: A and W Publishers, 1978), pp. 47–48. Future references in the text will be designated Wilder interview.

10 Richard T. Jameson, "Son of Noir," *Film Comment* 10, no. 6 (November–December 1974): 30–33.

CHAPTER 2

¹ Leo Braudy, *Jean Renoir: The World of His Films* (New York: Anchor Books, 1972), p. 59.

² Ernest Hemingway, *A Farewell to Arms* (New York: Scribner's, 1969), p. 249.

³ Edmund Wilson, *Classics and Commercials: A Literary Chronicle of the Forties* (New York: Vintage Books, 1962), p. 21.

⁴ Joyce Carol Oates, "Man under Sentence of Death: The Novels of James M. Cain," in *Tough Guy Writers of the Thirties,* ed., Donald Madden (Carbondale and Edwardsville: Southern Illinois University Press, 1968), pp. 112–113.

⁵ James M. Cain, *Double Indemnity* (New York: Vintage Books, 1978), p. 7. Future references in the text will be designated Cain, *Double Indemnity.*

⁶ James M. Cain, *The Postman Always Rings Twice* (New York: Vintage Books, 1978), pp. 7, 9.

⁷ Peter Forster, "Gentle Tough Guy," *John O'London's Weekly* 62 (6 March 1953): 189.

CHAPTER 3

¹ John Houseman, *Front and Center* (New York: Simon & Schuster, 1979), p. 135. Future references in the text will be designated Houseman.

² Unpublished screenplay for *And Now Tomorrow,* by Frank Partos and Raymond Chandler. © Paramount Pictures. Dated December 3, 1943, p. 5. In the Special Collection Branch of the Research Library at UCLA. Future references in the text will be designated *And Now Tomorrow.*

³ Press book for *And Now Tomorrow.* On file at the Motion Picture Division of the Library of Congress, Washington, D.C.

⁴ Press book for *The Unseen.* On file at the Motion Picture Division of the Library of Congress, Washington, D.C.

CHAPTER 4

¹ This quotation, and much of the preceding factual information, appears in MacShane, *The Life of Raymond Chandler,* p. 114.

² Raymond Chandler, *The Blue Dahlia: A Screenplay* (Carbondale and Edwardsville: Southern Illinois University Press, 1976), p. 127. Future references in the text will be designated *The Blue Dahlia.*

³ Maurice Zolotow, "Through a Shot Glass Darkly: How Raymond Chandler Screwed Hollywood," *Action* (January–February 1978): 57.

⁴ The dialogue quoted from *The Blue Dahlia*, unless otherwise designated, is from the film itself, rather than from the published screenplay. There are a great many differences between the two works, and since Chandler worked closely with Houseman during production and even claimed to have spent a good deal of time on the sets, I am assuming that the dialogue in the film is Chandler's, or at least had his approval, and is the ultimate text.

⁵ Raymond Chandler, *The Long Goodbye* (New York: Ballantine Books, 1971), p. 252.

CHAPTER 5

¹ *Raymond Chandler Speaking*, ed., Dorothy Gardiner and Kathrine Sorley Walker (Boston: Houghton Mifflin, 1977), p. 127. Future references in the text will be designated *Raymond Chandler Speaking*.

² Raymond Chandler, "Review of *The Hollywood Bowl*," *Atlantic Monthly* 179 (January 1947): 109.

³ This material is covered in MacShane, *The Life of Raymond Chandler*, p. 120.

⁴ *The Notebooks of Raymond Chandler*, p. 41.

⁵ Letter of March 26, 1957, to "Mr. Howard," in the UCLA Chandler archive.

⁶ Raymond Chandler, "Oscar Night in Hollywood," *Atlantic Monthly*, 181 (March 1948): 24–27.

⁷ MacShane, *The Life of Raymond Chandler*, pp. 162–65.

⁸ Ibid., pp. 145–48.

⁹ Eric Partridge, Letter to the *Listener*, 11 October 1951.

¹⁰ Raymond Chandler, *The Little Sister*, in *The Midnight Raymond Chandler* (Boston: Houghton Mifflin, 1971), p. 269. Future references in the text will be designated *The Little Sister*.

¹¹ Harry Wilson, "The Dark Mirror," *Sequence* no. 7 (Spring 1949): 21–22.

¹² MacShane, *The Life of Raymond Chandler*, p. 171.

¹³ François Truffaut, *Hitchcock* (New York: Simon & Schuster, 1967), p. 142.

¹⁴ *Raymond Chandler Speaking*, p. 138. The scene to which he refers is probably that in *The Blue Dahlia* in which Buzz meets Johnny's wife in a bar.

¹⁵ Raymond Chandler, "Ten Per Cent of Your Life," *Atlantic Monthly* 189 (February 1952): 51.

¹⁶ Zolotow, "Through a Shot Glass Darkly," p. 57.

¹⁷ Chandler, "A Qualified Farewell," p. 71. Future references in the text will be designated "A Qualified Farewell."

CHAPTER 6

¹ Raymond Chandler, *The High Window* (New York: Ballantine Books, 1971), p. 184. Future references in the text will be designated *The High Window*.

² Raymond Chandler, *Farewell, My Lovely* (New York: Ballantine Books, 1971), p. 78.

³ Edward Dmytryk, *It's a Hell of a Life but Not a Bad Living* (New York: Times Books, 1978), pp. 58–62.

CHAPTER 7

¹ Peter Bogdanovich, *The Cinema of Howard Hawks* (New York: Museum of Modern Art Film Library, 1962), p. 26.

² Raymond Chandler, *The Lady in the Lake* (New York: Vintage Books, 1976), p. 45. Future references in the text will be designated *The Lady in the Lake*.

CHAPTER 8

¹ Jameson, "Son of Noir," pp. 30–33.

² Jon Tuska, *The Detective in Hollywood* (Garden City, N.Y.: Doubleday, 1978), p. 328.

³ Raymond Chandler, *The Long Goodbye* (New York: Ballantine Books, 1971), pp. 229–30. Future references in the text will be designated *The Long Goodbye*.

⁴ Raymond Chandler, *The Big Sleep* (New York: Vintage Books, 1976), p. 20.

ADDRESSES OF 16-MM DISTRIBUTORS

Film-Makers' Cooperative
175 Lexington Avenue
New York, N.Y. 10016
Telephone: (212) 889-3820

Films Incorporated
440 Park Avenue South
New York, N.Y. 10016
Telephone: (212) 889-7910

Swank Motion Pictures
201 South Jefferson Avenue
St. Louis, Mo. 63166
Telephone: (314) 534-6300

United Artists 16 (UA/16)
729 Seventh Avenue
New York, N.Y. 10019
Telephone: (212) 575-3000

Universal 16
445 Park Avenue
New York, N.Y. 10022
Telephone: (212) 759-7500

FILMOGRAPHY
Chandler's Screen Credits

1. *DOUBLE INDEMNITY* (1944)

   Distribution Company: Paramount. *Director:* Billy Wilder. *Producer:* Joseph Sistrom. *Screenplay:* Raymond Chandler and Billy Wilder; based upon the novel by James M. Cain. *Cinematographer:* John F. Seitz (black and white). *Editor:* Doane Harrison. *Music:* Miklos Rozsa (original music and arrangements), and the D Minor Symphony by César Franck. *Set Direction:* Bertram Granger. *Art Decoration:* Hal Pereira. *Running Time:* 106 minutes. *16-mm Distributor:* Universal 16. *Cast:* Fred MacMurray (*Walter Neff*), Barbara Stanwyck (*Phyllis Dietrickson*), Edward G. Robinson (*Barton Keyes*), Porter Hall (*Mr. Jackson*), Jean Heather (*Lola Dietrichson*), Tom Powers (*Mr. Dietrichson*), Byron Barr (*Nino Zachette*), Richard Gaines (*Mr. Norton*), Fortunio Bonanova (*Sam Gorlopis*), John Philliber (*Joe Pete*).

2. *AND NOW TOMORROW* (1944)

   Distribution Company: Paramount. *Director:* Irving Pichel. *Producer:* Fred Kohlmar. *Screenplay:* Frank Partos and Raymond Chandler; based upon the novel by Rachel Field. *Cinematographer:* Daniel L. Fapp (black and white). *Editor:* Duncan Mansfield. *Music:* Victor Young. *Set Direction:* Ted von Hemert. *Art Decoration:* Hans Dreier and Hal Pereira. *Running Time:* 85 minutes. *16-mm Distributor:* Universal 16. *Cast:* Alan Ladd (*Dr. Merek Vance*), Loretta Young (*Emily Blair*), Susan Hayward (*Janice Blair*), Barry Sullivan (*Jeff Stoddard*), Beulah Bondi (*Aunt Em*), Cecil Kellaway (*Dr. Weeks*), Grant Mitchell (*Uncle Wallace*), Helen Mack (*Angeletta Gallo*), Anthony Caruso (*Peter Gallo*), Jonathan Hale (*Dr. Sloane*), George Carleton (*Meeker*), Connie Leon (*Hester*).

3. *THE UNSEEN* (1945)

Distribution Company: Paramount. *Director:* Lewis Allen. *Producer:* John Houseman. *Screenplay:* Hagar Wilde and Raymond Chandler; adapted by Miss Wilde and Ken Englund; based upon the novel *Her Heart in Her Throat* by Ethel Lina White. *Cinematographer:* John F. Seitz (black and white). *Editor:* Doane Harrison. *Music:* Ernest Toch. *Art Decoration:* Hans Dreier and Earl Hedwick. *Running Time:* 81 minutes. *16-mm Distributor:* Universal 16. *Cast:* Joel McCrea (*David Fleming*), Gail Russell (*Elizabeth Howard*), Herbert Marshall (*Dr. Charles Evans*), Richard Lyon (*Barnaby Fielding*), Nona Griffith (*Ellen Fielding*), Phyllis Brooks (*Maxine*), Isobel Elsom (*Marian Tygarth*), Norman Lloyd (*Jaspar Goodwin*), Mikhail Rasumny (*Chester*), Elisabeth Risdon (*Mrs. Norris*), Tom Tully (*Sullivan*), Mary Field (*Miss Budge*), Victoria Horne (*Lily*).

4. *THE BLUE DAHLIA* (1946)

Distribution Company: Paramount. *Director:* George Marshall. *Producer:* John Houseman. *Screenplay:* Raymond Chandler. *Cinematographer:* Lionel Lindon (black and white). *Editor:* Arthur Schmidt. *Music:* Victor Young. *Set Direction:* Sam Comer and Jimmy Walters. *Art Decoration:* Hans Dreier and Walter Tyler. *Running Time:* 98 minutes. *16-mm Distributor:* Universal 16. *Cast:* Alan Ladd (*Johnny Morrison*), Veronica Lake (*Joyce Harwood*), William Bendix (*Buzz Wanchek*), Howard DaSilva (*Eddie Harwood*), Doris Dowling (*Helen Morrison*), Tom Powers (*Captain Hendrickson*), Hugh Beaumont (*George Copeland*), Will Wright (*Dad Newell*), Don Costello (*Leo*), Howard Freeman (*Corelli*), Frank Faylen (*man*), Mae Busch (*maid*).

5. *STRANGERS ON A TRAIN* (1951)

Distribution Company: Warner Brothers. *Director/Producer:* Alfred Hitchcock. *Screenplay:* Raymond Chandler and Czenzi Ormonde; adapted by Whitfield Cook; based upon the novel *Strangers on a Train* by Patricia Highsmith. *Cinematographer:* Robert Burks (black and white). *Editor:* William H. Ziegler. *Music:* Dimitri Tiomkin. *Set Direction:* George James Hopkins. *Art Decoration:* Ted Haworth. *Running Time:* 101 minutes. *16-mm Distributor:* Swank Motion Pictures. *Cast:* Farley Granger (*Guy Haines*), Ruth Roman (*Anne Morton*), Robert Walker (*Bruno Antony*), Leo G. Carroll (*Senator Morton*), Patricia Hitchcock (*Barbara Morton*), Laura Elliott (*Miriam*), Marion Lorne (*Mrs. Antony*), Jonathan Hale (*Mr. Antony*), Howard St. John (*Capt. Turley*), John Brown (*Professor Collins*), Norma Varden (*Mrs. Cunningham*), Robert Gist (*Hennessey*), John Doucette (*Hammond*).

Films Based Upon Chandler's Fiction

1. *THE FALCON TAKES OVER* (1942)

   Distribution Company: RKO-Radio Pictures. *Director:* Irving Reis. *Producer:* Howard Benedict. *Screenplay:* Lynn Root and Frank Fenton; based upon the character created by Michael Arlen, and the novel *Farewell, My Lovely* by Raymond Chandler. *Cinematographer:* George Robinson (black and white). *Editor:* Harry Marker. *Music:* C. Bakaleinikoff. *Art Decoration:* Albert S. D'Agostino and Feild M. Gray. *Running Time:* 63 minutes. *16-mm Distributor:* Films Incorporated. *Cast:* George Sanders (*Gay Lawrence, the "Falcon"*), Lynn Bari (*Ann*), James Gleason (*Detective Mike O'Hara*), Allen Jenkins (*Goldy*), Helen Gilbert (*Diana*), Ward Bond (*Moose*).

2. *TIME TO KILL* (1942)

   Distribution Company: Twentieth Century-Fox. *Director:* Herbert I. Leeds. *Producer:* Sol M. Wurtzel. *Screenplay:* Clarence Upson Young; based upon the novel *The High Window* by Raymond Chandler, and the character "Michael Shayne" created by Brett Halliday. *Cinematographer:* Charles Clarke (black and white). *Editor:* Alfred Day. *Music:* Emil Newman. *Set Direction:* Thomas Little and Frank E. Hughes. *Art Decoration:* Richard Day and Chester Gore. *Running Time:* 5 reels. *16-mm Distributor:* Film-Makers' Cooperative. *Cast:* Lloyd Nolan (*Michael Shayne*), Heather Angel (*Merle*), Doris Merrick (*Linda Conquest*), Ralph Byrd (*Louis Venter*), Richard Lane (*Lieutenant Breeze*), Sheila Bromley (*Lois Morny*), Morris Ankrum (*Alex Morny*), Ethel Grieffies (*Mrs. Murdock*), James Seay (*Leslie Murdock*), Ted Hecht (*Phillips*), William Pawley (*Hench*), Syd Saylor (*postman*), Lester Sharpe (*Washburn*), Paul Guilfoyle (*manager*).

3. *MURDER, MY SWEET* (1944)

   Distribution Company: RKO-Radio Pictures. *Director:* Edward Dmytryk. *Producer:* Adrian Scott. *Screenplay:* John Paxton; based upon the novel *Farewell, My Lovely* by Raymond Chandler. *Cinematographer:* Harry J. Wild (black and white). *Editor:* Joseph Noreiga. *Music:* Roy Webb. *Set Direction:* Darrell Silvera and Michael Ohrenbach. *Art Decoration:* Albert S. D'Agostino and Carroll Clark. *Running Time:* 95 minutes. *16-mm Distributor:* Films Incorporated. *Cast:* Dick Powell (*Philip Marlowe*), Claire Trevor (*Velma/Mrs. Grayle*), Anne Shirley (*Ann*), Otto Kruger (*Amthor*), Mike Mazurki (*Moose Malloy*), Miles Mander (*Mr. Grayle*), Douglas Walton (*Marriott*), Don Douglas (*Lieutenant Randall*), Ralf Harolde (*Dr. Sonderborg*), Esther Howard (*Mrs. Florian*), Paul Phillips (*Detective Nulty*).

4. *THE BIG SLEEP* (1946)

    Distribution Company: Warner Brothers. *Director/Producer:*
    Howard Hawks. *Screenplay:* William Faulkner, Leigh Brackett,
    and Jules Furthman; based upon the novel *The Big Sleep* by
    Raymond Chandler. *Cinematographer:* Sidney Hickox (black and
    white). *Editor:* Christian Nyby. *Music:* Max Steiner. *Set Direction:*
    Fred M. MacLean. *Art Decoration:* Carl Jules Weyl. *Running
    Time:* 118 minutes. *16-mm Distributor:* UA/16. *Cast:* Humphrey
    Bogart (*Philip Marlowe*), Lauren Bacall (*Vivian Rutledge*), John
    Ridgley (*Eddie Mars*), Martha Vickers (*Carmen Sternwood*), Dor-
    othy Malone (*bookstore manager*), Peggy Knudsen (*Mona Mars*),
    Regis Toomey (*Bernie Ohls*), Charles Waldron (*General Stern-
    wood*), Charles D. Brown (*Norris*), Bob Steele (*Canino*), Elisha
    Cook, Jr. (*Harry Jones*), Louis Jean Heydt (*Joe Brody*), Sonia
    Darrin (*Agnes*), Tom Rafferty (*Carol Lundgren*).

5. *LADY IN THE LAKE* (1947)

    Distribution Company: Metro-Goldwyn-Mayer. *Director:* Robert
    Montgomery. *Producer:* George Haight. *Screenplay:* Steve Fisher
    and, uncredited, Raymond Chandler; based upon the novel *The
    Lady in the Lake* by Raymond Chandler. *Cinematographer:* Paul
    C. Vogel (black and white). *Editor:* Gene Ruggiero. *Music:* David
    Snell. *Set Direction:* Edwin B. Willis and Thomas Theuerkauf.
    Art Decoration: Cedric Gibbons and Preston Ames. *Running Time:*
    105 minutes. *16-mm Distributor:* Films Incorported. *Cast:* Robert
    Montgomery (*Phillip Marlowe*), Lloyd Nolan (*Lièutenant De-
    Garmot*), Audrey Totter (*Adrienne Fromsett*), Tom Tully (*Captain
    Kane*), Leon Ames (*Derace Kingsby*), Jayne Meadows (*Mildred
    Haveland*), Morris Ankrum (*Eugene Grayson*), Lila Leeds (*recep-
    tionist*), Richard Simmons (*Chris Lavery*), Kathleen Lockhart (*Mrs.
    Grayson*).

6. *THE BRASHER DOUBLOON* (1947)

    Distribution Company: Twentieth Century-Fox. *Director:* John
    Brahm. *Producer:* Robert Bassler. *Screenplay:* Dorothy Hannah;
    adapted by Dorothy Bennett and Leonard Praskins; based upon
    the novel *The High Window* by Raymond Chandler. *Cinematog-
    rapher:* Lloyd Ahern (black and white). *Editor:* Harry Reynolds.
    Music: David Buttolph and Alfred Newman. *Set Direction:* Thomas
    Little and Frank E. Hughes. *Art Decoration:* James Baseri and
    Richard Irvine. *Running Time:* 72 minutes. *16-mm Distributor:*
    Films Incorporated. *Cast:* George Montgomery (*Philip Marlowe*),
    Nancy Guild (*Merle Davis*), Conard Janis (*Leslie Murdock*), Roy
    Roberts (*Lieutenant Breeze*), Fritz Kortner (*Vannier*), Florence
    Bates (*Mrs. Murdock*), Marvin Miller (*Blair*), Houseley Stevenson
    (*Morningstar*), Bob Adler (*Sergeant Spangler*), Jack Conrad (*George
    Anson*), Alfred Linder (*Eddie Prue*), Jack Overman (*manager*),

Jack Stoney (*Mike*), Ray Spiker (*Figaro*), Paul Maxey (*coroner*), Reed Hadley (*Dr. Moss*).

7. *MARLOWE* (1969)

    Distribution Company: Metro-Goldwyn-Mayer. *Director:* Paul Bogart. *Producers:* Gabriel Katzka and Sidney Beckerman. *Screenplay:* Stirling Silliphant; based upon the novel *The Little Sister* by Raymond Chandler. *Cinematographer:* William H. Daniels (Metrocolor). *Editor:* Gene Ruggiero. *Music:* Peter Matz. *Set Direction:* Henry Grace and Hugh Hunt. *Art Decoration:* George W. Davis and Addison Hehr. *Running Time:* 95 minutes. *16-mm Distributor:* Films Incorporated. *Cast:* James Garner (*Philip Marlowe*), Gayle Hunnicutt (*Mavis Wald*), Carroll O'Connor (*Lieutenant Christy French*), Rita Moreno (*Dolores Gonzales*), Sharon Farrell (*Orfamay Quest*), William Daniels (*Mr. Crowell*), H. M. Wynant (*Sonny Steelgrave*), Jackie Coogan (*Grant W. Hicks*), Kenneth Tobey (*Sergeant Fred Beifus*), Bruce Lee (*Winslow Wong*), Corinne Comacho (*Julie*), Paul Stevens (*Dr. Vincent Lagardie*), Christopher Cary (*Chuck*), George Tyne (*Oliver Hady*), Roger Newman (*Orrin Quest*).

8. *THE LONG GOODBYE* (1973)

    Distribution Company: United Artists. *Director:* Robert Altman. *Producers:* Elliott Kastner and Jerry Bick. *Screenplay:* Leigh Brackett; based upon the novel *The Long Goodbye* by Raymond Chandler. *Cinematographer:* Vilmos Zsigmond (*Technicolor and Panavision*), *Editor:* Lou Lombardo. *Music:* John Williams. *Running Time:* 112 minutes. *16-mm Distributor:* UA/16. *Cast:* Elliott Gould (*Philip Marlowe*), Nina Van Pallandt (*Eileen Wade*), Sterling Hayden (*Roger Wade*), Mark Rydell (*Marty Augustine*), Henry Gibson (*Dr. Verringer*), David Arkin (*Harry*), Jim Bouton (*Terry Lennox*), Warren Berlinger (*Morgan*), Jo Ann Brody (*Jo Ann Eggenweiler*), Jack Knight (*hood*), Pepe Callahan (*Pepe*), Ken Sanson (*colony guard*), Vince Palmieri (*hood*), Arnold Strong (*hood*), Jack Riley (*piano player*), Arnold Schwarzenegger (*muscle man*), Kate Murtagh (*nurse*).

9. *FAREWELL, MY LOVELY* (1975)

    Distribution Company: Avco Embassy. *Director:* Dick Richards. *Executive Producers:* Elliott Kastner and Jerry Bick. *Producers:* George Pappas and Jerry Bruckheimer. *Screenplay:* David Zelag Goodman; based upon the novel *Farewell, My Lovely* by Raymond Chandler. *Cinematographer:* John A. Alonzo (Fujicolor, Panavision). *Editors:* Walter Thompson and Joel Cox. *Music:* David Shire. *Set Direction:* Bob Nelson. *Art Decoration:* Angelo Graham. *Running Time:* 97 minutes. *16-mm Distributor:* Swank Motion

Pictures. *Cast:* Robert Mitchum *(Philip Marlowe)*, Charlotte Rampling *(Mrs. Grayle/Velma)*, John Ireland *(Nulty)*, Sylvia Miles *(Mrs. Florian)*, Anthony Zerbe *(Laird Brunette)*, Harry Dean Stanton *(Billy Rolfe)*, Jack O'Halloran *(Moose Malloy)*, Joe Spinell *(Nick)*, Sylvester Stallone *(Jonnie)*, Kate Murtagh *(Frances Amthor)*, John O'Leary *(Marriott)*, Walter McGinn *(Tommy Ray)*, Burton Gilliam *(cowboy)*, Jim Thompson *(Mr. Grayle)*, Jimmie Archer *(Georgie)*, Ted Gehring *(Roy)*.

10.   *THE BIG SLEEP* (1978)

Distribution Company: United Artists. *Director:* Michael Winner. *Producer:* Elliott Kastner and Michael Winner. *Screenplay:* Michael Winner; based upon the novel *The Big Sleep* by Raymond Chandler. *Cinematographer:* Robert Paynter (Technicolor and Panavision). *Editor:* Freddie Wilson. *Music:* Jerry Fielding. *Set Direction:* Harry Pottle. *Art Decoration:* John Graysmark. *Running Time:* 100 minutes. *16-mm Distributor:* UA/16. *Cast:* Robert Mitchum *(Philip Marlowe)*, Sarah Miles *(Charlotte Sternwood)*, Richard Boone *(Lash Canino)*, Candy Clark *(Camilla Sternwood)*, Joan Collins *(Agnes Lozelle)*, Edward Fox *(Joe Brody)*, John Mills *(Inspector Carson)*, James Stewart *(General Sternwood)*, Oliver Reed *(Eddie Mars)*, Harry Andrews *(Norris)*, Colin Blakely *(Harry Jones)*, Richard Todd *(Commissioner Barker)*, Diana Quick *(Mona Grant)*, James Donald *(Inspector Gregory)*.

SELECTED BIBLIOGRAPHY

I. Material by Chandler

Novels:

(In chronological order of original American publication. Later editions consulted are found in the text and Notes.)

The Big Sleep. New York: Alfred A. Knopf, 1939.
Farewell, My Lovely. New York: Alfred A. Knopf, 1940.
The High Window. New York: Alfred A. Knopf, 1942.
The Lady in the Lake. New York: Alfred A. Knopf, 1943.
The Little Sister. Boston: Houghton Mifflin, 1949.
The Long Goodbye. Boston: Houghton Mifflin, 1954.
Playback. Boston: Houghton Mifflin, 1958.

Relevant Published Articles:

"Writers in Hollywood." *Atlantic Monthly* 176 (November 1945): 50–54.
"Review of *The Hollywood Bowl*." *Atlantic Monthly* 179 (January 1947): 108–9.
"Critical Notes." *Screenwriter* (July 1947): 31–32.
"Oscar Night in Hollywood." *Atlantic Monthly* 181 (March 1948): 24–27.
"Ten Per Cent of Your Life." *Atlantic Monthly* 189 (February 1952): pp. 48–51.

Published Screenplays:

Double Indemnity (with Billy Wilder). In *Best Film Plays of 1945.* Edited by John Gassner and Dudley Nichols. New York: Crown Publishers, 1946. Pp. 115–74.
The Blue Dahlia: A Screenplay. Carbondale and Edwardsville: Southern Illinois University Press, 1976.

Unproduced Screenplays:

The Lady in the Lake. M-G-M, 1945. Based upon Chandler's novel. This screenplay provided the basis for Steve Fisher's final screenplay for the 1947 film *Lady in the Lake.*
The Innocent Mrs. Duff. Paramount, 1946. Based upon the novel by Elisabeth Sanxay Holding.
Playback. Universal-International, 1947–1948. An original screenplay that became the basis for Chandler's last novel, *Playback.*

198

Related Material:

Chandler before Marlowe: Raymond Chandler's Early Prose and Poetry, 1908–1912. Edited by Matthew J. Bruccoli. Columbia: University of South Carolina Press, 1973.

The Notebooks of Raymond Chandler and English Summer: A Gothic Romance. Edited by Frank MacShane. New York: Ecco Press, 1976.

Raymond Chandler Speaking. Edited by Dorothy Gardiner and Kathrine Sorley Walker. Boston: Houghton Mifflin, 1977.

Selected Letters of Raymond Chandler. Edited by Frank MacShane. New York: Columbia University Press, 1981.

II. Secondary Material

Auden, W. H. "The Guilty Vicarage: Notes on the Detective Story, by an Addict." *Harper's Magazine* 196, no. 1176 (May 1948): 406–12.

Bellour, Raymond. "The Obvious and the Code." *Screen* 15, no. 4 (Winter 1974/75): 7–17.

Blades, John. *"The Big Sleep." Film Heritage* (Summer 1970): 7–15.

Bishop, Paul. "The Longest Goodbye, or the Search for Chandler's Los Angeles." *Mystery* 1, no. 2 (March–April 1980): 33–36.

Bogdanovich, Peter. *The Cinema of Howard Hawks.* New York: Museum of Modern Art Film Library, 1962.

Bonitzer, Pascal. "Partial Vision: Film and the Labyrinth." *Cahiers du Cinéma,* no. 301 (June 1979): 35–41, translated by Fabrice Ziolkowski and reprinted in *Wide Angle,* 4, no. 4: 56–63.

Borde, Raymond and Etienne Chaumeton. "The Sources of Film Noir," *Film Reader 3* (February 1978), 58–66.

Brackett, Leigh. "From *The Big Sleep* to *The Long Goodbye* and More or Less How We Got There." *Take One,* 23 January 1974, pp. 26–28.

Bruccoli, Matthew J. *Raymond Chandler: A Descriptive Bibliography.* Pittsburgh: University of Pittsburgh Press, 1979.

Cain, James M. *Double Indemnity.* New York: Vintage Books, 1978.

Cain, James M. *The Postman Always Rings Twice.* New York: Vintage Books, 1978.

Cawelti, John G. *Adventure, Mystery, and Romance: Formula Stories as Art and Popular Culture.* Chicago: University of Chicago Press, 1976.

Clarens, Carlos. *Crime Movies: An Illustrated History.* New York: W. W. Norton, 1980.

Damico, James, "Film Noir: A Modest Proposal," *Film Reader 3* (February 1978) 48–57.

Davis, Brian. *The Thriller: The Suspense Film from 1946.* London: Studio Vista, 1973.

Dmytryk, Edward. *It's a Hell of a Life but Not a Bad Living.* New York: Times Books, 1978.

Durham, Philip. *Down These Mean Streets a Man Must Go: Raymond Chandler's Knight*. Chapel Hill: University of North Carolina Press, 1963.

Everson, William K. *The Detective in Film*. Secaucus, N.J.: Citadel Press, 1972.

Film Comment 10, no. 6 (November–December 1974). Issue devoted to *film noir*. Particularly useful articles are Paul Jensen, "The Writer: Raymond Chandler and the World You Live In," pp. 18–26; and Richard T. Jameson, "Son of Noir," pp. 30–35.

Film Noir: An Encyclopedic Reference to the American Style. Edited by Alain Silver and Elizabeth Ward. Woodstock, N.Y.: Overlook Press, 1979.

Film Scripts One. Edited by George P. Garrett, O. B. Hardison, Jr., and Jane R. Gelfman. New York: Appleton-Century-Crofts, 1971. Pp. 137–329. Contains the script for Hawks's *The Big Sleep* by William Faulkner, Leigh Brackett, and Jules Furthman.

Gabree, John. *Gangsters: From Little Caesar to the Godfather*. New York: Pyramid Publications, 1973.

Gregory, Charles. "Knight without Meaning?" *Sight and Sound* 42, no. 3 (Summer 1973): 155–59.

Guérif, François. *Le Film noir Américain*. Paris: Editions Henri Veyrier, 1979.

Highsmith, Patricia. *Strangers on a Train*. New York: Penguin Books, 1974.

Holding, Elisabeth Sanxay. *The Innocent Mrs. Duff*. New York: Simon & Schuster, 1946.

Houseman, John. *Front and Center*. New York: Simon & Schuster, 1979.

Kass, Judith M. *Robert Altman: American Innovator*. New York: Popular Library, 1978.

Kerr, Paul. "Out of What Past? Notes on the 'B' Film Noir." *Screen Education*, Nos. 32–33 (Autumn/Winter 1979/80). 45–65.

Kings of the B's. Edited by Todd McCarthy and Charles Flynn. New York: E. P. Dutton, 1975.

Kuhn, Annette. "*The Big Sleep:* A Disturbance in the Sphere of Sexuality." *Wide Angle* 4, no. 3: 4–11.

McArthur, Colin. *Underworld U.S.A.* New York: Viking Press, 1972.

MacShane, Frank. *The Life of Raymond Chandler*. New York: Penguin Books, 1978.

MacShane, Frank. "Raymond Chandler and Hollywood." Part 1 in *American Film* 1, no. 6 (April 1976): 62–69. Part 2 in *American Film* 1, no. 7 (May 1976): 54–60.

Madsen, Axel. *Billy Wilder*. Bloomington: Indiana University Press, 1969.

Monaco, James. "Notes on *The Big Sleep*, Thirty Years After." *Sight and Sound* (Winter 1974/75): 34–38.

Orr, Christopher. "The Trouble with Harry: A Reading of Hawks's *The Big Sleep*. Paper delivered at the Ohio University Film Conference, 1981.

Pendo, Stephen. *Raymond Chandler On Screen: His Novels into Film.* Metuchen, N.J.: Scarecrow Press, 1976.

Place, J. A. and Peterson, L. S. "Some Visual Motifs of Film Noir." *Film Comment* 10, no. 1 (January–February 1974): 30–35.

Porter, Dennis. *The Pursuit of Crime: Art and Ideology in Detective Fiction.* New Haven and London: Yale University Press, 1981.

Speir, Jerry. *Raymond Chandler.* New York: Frederick Ungar, 1981.

Steinbrunner, Chris and Penzler Otto. *Encyclopedia of Mystery and Detection.* New York: McGraw-Hill, 1976.

Symonds, Julian. "The Case of Raymond Chandler." *New York Times Magazine,* 23 December 1973, pp. 13–27.

Tarantino, Michael. "Movement as Metaphor: *The Long Goodbye." Sight and Sound* (Spring 1975): 98–102.

Tough Guy Writers of the Thirties. Edited by Donald Madden. Carbondale and Edwardsville: Southern Illinois University Press, 1968.

Truffaut, François. *Hitchcock.* New York: Simon & Schuster, 1967.

Tuska, Jon. *The Detective in Hollywood.* Garden City, N.Y.: Doubleday, 1978.

Wilson, Harry. "The Dark Mirror." *Sequence,* no. 7 (Spring 1949): 19–22.

Women in Film Noir. Edited by E. Ann Kaplan. London: British Film Institute, 1979.

Wood, Robin. *Hitchcock's Films.* New York: Castle Books, 1969.

Wood, Robin. *Howard Hawks.* Garden City, N.Y.: Doubleday, 1968.

The World of Raymond Chandler. Edited by Miriam Gross. New York: A and W Publishers, 1978.

Zolotow, Maurice. *Billy Wilder in Hollywood.* New York: G. P. Putnam's, 1977.

Zolotow, Maurice. "Through a Shot Glass Darkly: How Raymond Chandler Screwed Hollywood." *Action* (January-February 1978): 52–57.

INDEX